Kanaka ʻŌiwi Methodologies

Published by University of Hawai'i Press
in Association with

Hawai'inuiākea School of Hawaiian Knowledge
University of Hawai'i at Mānoa
Dean Maenette K. P. Ah Nee-Benham

Volume Editors: Katrina-Ann R. Kapā'anaokalāokeola Nākoa Oliveira
and Erin Kahunawaika'ala Wright
Managing Editor: Lilinoe Andrews

Hawai'inuiākea is available online through
Project MUSE (http://muse.jhu.edu).

Hawaiʻinuiākea No. 4

Kanaka ʻŌiwi Methodologies
Moʻolelo and Metaphor

Edited by
Katrina-Ann R. Kapāʻanaokalāokeola Nākoa Oliveira
and Erin Kahunawaikaʻala Wright

Hawaiʻinuiākea School of Hawaiian Knowledge

University of Hawaiʻi Press

Honolulu

21 20 19 18   6 5 4 3

Library of Congress Cataloging-in-Publication Data

Kanaka 'ōiwi methodologies : mo'olelo and metaphor / edited by Katrina-Ann R. Kapā'anaokalāokeola Nākoa Oliveira and Erin Kahunawaika'ala Wright.
    pages cm — (Hawai'inuiākea ; no. 4)
    Includes bibliographical references.
    ISBN 978-0-8248-5585-7 (pbk. : alk. paper)
  1. Hawaii—Study and teaching (Higher) 2. Research—Hawaii—Methodology.
    3. Research—Hawaii—Philosophy. I. Oliveira, Katrina-Ann R.
Kapā'anaokalāokeola Nākoa, editor.   II. Wright, Erin Kahunawaika'ala, editor.   III. Series: Hawai'inuiākea monograph ; 4.
    DU624.5.K34 2016
    996.9—dc23
    2015021072

Cover image: *Uncovering the Layers Within Us*
by Haley Kailiehu

Contents

From the Dean

Welina Mai!

In the summer of 1997, at the edge of the twenty-first century, I gathered a group of indigenous educators from Aotearoa, Australia, Hawai'i, Alaska, and North America to share ancestral knowledge and best practices for the education of indigenous children and youth. We met together at Sol y Sombra Ranch in Santa Fe, New Mexico. Dr. Valorie Johnson, our program director from the W. K. Kellogg Foundation, which funded this forum, described this event as follows: "No team of individuals could have fully planned the sacred, natural events that occurred, nor could any foundation, even with every resource in the world, have purchased the outcomes. In numerous and magical ways, we were reminded of an attribute that has sustained indigenous peoples for years—a deep sense of spirituality. We thank the Creator for that gentle reminder. *Nyah weh.*" These educational leaders generated the first volume of *Indigenous Educational Models for Contemporary Practice: In Our Mother's Voice* (edited by M. Ah Nee-Benham and J. Cooper [New York: Routledge/Erlbaum, 2000], Johnson's quote appears on p. xvii). A second volume was published in 2008 as a result of a similar gathering of indigenous educators. It presented the intergenerational voices of teachers and students weaving together their stories of nā pua, nā lei, and nā mamo (past-present-future) into a "critical movement that opens a gracious space to live-into the *Contemporary is Native* truth" (Ah Nee-Benham 2008, p. 11).

I open this fourth volume of the Hawai'inuiākea Series with the *In Our Mother's Voice* story to emphasize the value of generative processes that come from the sharing of ancestral and contemporary knowledge in its many storied texts (e.g., visual arts, song, oral story, dance, nature, and so on). Our first three volumes compelled us to engage and learn from the life stories of beloved kumu, explore deeply the life lessons and stories of our 'āina, and study and appreciate the artistry and functionality of what we create with our hands. In this fourth volume, we are asked to make sense of the diverse ways that we use story to tangle with capacious questions; that is, how to express our kanaka frameworks and methodologies that we, as kanaka researchers, work with in our contemporary and disciplined fields of study. Conveying this thinking is important not only to kanaka but also to everyone working with 'ike Hawai'i.

Just as did the educational leaders who contributed to the two-volume *In Our Mother's Voice*, the authors contributing to this book have intentionally engaged in learning, exploring, and teaching through stories. This very courageous act of framing and articulating knowledge regenerates ritual (knowledge and wisdom of ceremony), responsibility (role and obligation), and reciprocity (the vibrant action of indigenous education that sustains legacy). Some contributions introduce the genesis of an idea, whereas other pieces present more mature frameworks, but collectively the chapters add value to our work as scholars.

In Our Mother's Voice spoke to us at the turn of the century; this volume, *Kanaka 'Ōiwi Methodologies: Mo'olelo and Metaphor*, similarly speaks to the importance of mo'okū'auhau as the grounding force of our ontological pathways, to the power of mo'olelo as the source of spiritual wisdom, and to the leo of our kūpuna that calls us to action, "Ho'i hou i ke kumu!"

Na'u me ka ha'aha'a!
Dr. Maenette K. P. Ah Nee-Benham, Dean
Hawai'inuiākea School of Hawaiian Knowledge
University of Hawai'i at Mānoa

Editors' Note

Into our light
I will go forever.

Into the wa'a of
Kanaloa, voyaging
moana nui.

Into our sovereign suns,
drunk on the mana
of Hawai'i.

—Haunani-Kay Trask (2002), from her poem,
"Into Our Light I Will Go Forever"

To capture the 'ano (character, condition) of *Kanaka 'Ōiwi Methodologies: Mo'olelo and Metaphor,* we begin this volume on Kanaka 'Ōiwi research methodologies[1] with verses from Trask's poem, "Into Our Light I Will Go Forever." Her seemingly somber words evoke the grounded yet hopeful and adventurous knowledge-seeking spirit of our seafaring kūpuna (ancestors) that is also found echoed in the voices of our contributors as they share their journeys across Moana Nui through research. Her words also speak to the na'au (intestines, of heart or mind) of our (kākou) work in engaging in research; that is, to illuminate 'ike (knowledge, insight, understanding) that guides, (re)builds, strengthens, and sustains our ea (life, breath).

For our purposes, we use the term "Kanaka 'Ōiwi methodologies" much like Denzin, Lincoln, and Smith (2008) use Evans, Hole, Berg, Hutchinson, and Sookraj's[2] definition of "Indigenous methodologies" as "research by and for Indigenous peoples, using techniques and methods drawing from the traditions and knowledges of those peoples" (p. 6), with a particular focus on Kanaka 'Ōiwi epistemologies. As indicated by the volume's title, the chapters in this collection feature two prominent and interrelated concepts: mo'olelo (stories, narratives, histories) and metaphors. Of course, these concepts are not unique to Kanaka 'Ōiwi epistemologies, but the specific ways in which our contributors discuss, use (as methodologies and methods), and express these knowledge structures to connect to their research are unique, thereby adding to the rich, diverse, localized, and growing body of knowledge on Indigenous methodologies and methods (Chilisa 2011; Denzin et al. 2008; Kovach 2010; Meyer 2004; Smith 2012; Wilson 2009).

The timeliness and significance of this collection cannot be overstated. Although scholarship has always been part of our rich tradition as Kanaka ʻŌiwi, its representation in the academy has not. In the last decade, however, there has been tremendous growth in the number of Kanaka ʻŌiwi scholars and the volume of scholarship, especially at the University of Hawaiʻi at Mānoa (UHM). For example, if we look to the academy's traditional sources of knowledge production we find increases in the numbers of both Native Hawaiian PhDs and faculty. Since 1995, UHM has awarded seventy-one PhDs to Native Hawaiians, forty-nine of those in the last eight years.[3] Likewise, there has been a slight increase in Native Hawaiian faculty in diverse disciplines as well.[4] From an outsider perspective, many may attribute this success to UHM's ability to create supportive environments for Kanaka ʻŌiwi. From an insider perspective, Kanaka ʻŌiwi and their allies have charted a strategic course since the 1986 publication of the Kaʻū Report, an influential document mapping the path for Native Hawaiian students, faculty, and programs in the University of Hawaiʻi system, while also creating new ones for students coming to study at UHM.[5] This growth reminds us of the ʻōlelo noʻeau (wise saying, proverb), "E kolo nō ka ēwe i ka ʻiewe," literally translated as "the umbilical cord/navel string follows the placenta." Metaphorically, it speaks to Kanaka ʻŌiwi seeking out one another. With increasing numbers of Kanaka ʻŌiwi scholars and emerging scholars in the academy who have research interests focused on Kanaka ʻŌiwi people and knowledge structures, there is an equally growing need to understand, develop, and determine Kanaka ʻŌiwi research methodologies and appropriate methods. Furthermore, we also view this growth as essential to the perpetuation of Kanaka ʻŌiwi knowledge. Like Kovach (2008), we assert that for "cultural knowledge to thrive, it must live in many sites including Western education and research" (Location 207).

Kanaka ʻŌiwi Methodologies: Moʻolelo and Metaphor has two aims. The first aim is to generate dialogue around Kanaka ʻŌiwi research methodologies and to explore the different ways in which Kanaka ʻŌiwi scholars engage in the research process. Even with the diversity of individuals contributing to this collection, consistent themes emerge, especially related to research protocol, positionality, and the importance of ʻike kūpuna (ancestral knowledge), ʻāina (land, that which feeds), and kuleana (responsibility, authority, privilege, burden). In addition, the collection illustrates the inherent duality of Kanaka ʻŌiwi research methodologies that seek to simultaneously dismantle old paradigms and build new ones shaped by Kanaka 'Ōiwi epistemologies. Likewise, this collection should also generate deep questions about the meaning(s) of Kanaka 'Ōiwi research methodologies. How shall we define and delineate Kanaka 'Ōiwi research methodologies? Should we even be thinking about demarcating these areas? Who should be included in the discussion?

This volume's second aim is to advance the myriad ways in which Kanaka 'Ōiwi scholars think about, approach, practice, and articulate research. How do these scholars identify and decide which research pathways to pursue? What are the ways in which inquiry is developed, pursued, and analyzed? How are Kanaka 'Ōiwi knowledge structures articulated in western contexts? How are these processes different from other kinds of research? Together, these chapters take us on a journey through the different ways in which Kanaka 'Ōiwi scholars engage in research.

We have gathered diverse contributors to participate in this conversation. They come from a variety of disciplines, research areas, theoretical frameworks, and practices reflective of different kinds of training, positionalities, and experiences. Honoring this diversity is paramount. For example, our decision not to standardize the formal writing style was one way to recognize the importance of the multiple and multilayered 'ike that our contributors bring to bear in these pages. It honors their 'ike and the 'ike of their kumu (teachers) and kūpuna as 'ōlapa (dancers), artists, kumu 'ōlelo Hawai'i (Hawaiian language teachers), environmental scientists, mahi'ai kalo (taro farmers), activists, geographers, kumu hula (hula teachers), assessment specialists, and educators. Additionally, rather than following western notions of neutrality in research, our contributors deliberately engage these multiple identities and demonstrate the ways in which this multiplicity and consequent complexity uniquely enlighten our understanding of the world.

Stylistically, our use of our 'ōlelo makuahine (mother tongue) is also nonstandard. Although we offered suggestions on usage, we left the kuleana to our contributors, given the intimate knowledge we felt each author had with his or her contribution. Each of our contributors chose the name he or she would use for our people: Kanaka, Kanaka 'Ōiwi, Kanaka Maoli, or Native Hawaiian. And, as with naming, we also left the kuleana to our contributors to decide to include (or not) diacritical markings and English translations.[6] Yet even with this diversity, you will find consistencies, for example, in using 'āina-based metaphors (e.g., lei making, 'auwai, kīpuka) and terms denoting certain feelings or values relating to the practice of research (e.g., kuleana). For us, this volume is a very powerful first pass at discussing Kanaka 'Ōiwi methodologies in a collective, collaborative way.

This journey "into our light" begins with Haley Kailiehu's cover art titled "Uncovering the Layers Within Us," a multilayered reflection on the artist's journey to the summit of Mauna a Wakea and to Waiau, the lake at the summit of the mountain; her brief essay about that journey follows. In "Reproducing the Ropes of Resistance: Hawaiian Studies Methodologies," Noelani Goodyear-Kaʻōpua interweaves the life of her dynamic kupuna, Tūtū Ana Kaʻauwai, with her own journey as a Kanaka ʻŌiwi scholar navigating the emerging discipline of Hawaiian studies. She illustrates the need to use a Hawaiian studies methodology when conducting research by identifying four aho (cords, lashings) that when braided together form a strong rope connecting the scholar to the scholarship. We glean more ʻike from the Kaʻōpua ʻohana about the kuleana of research with "He Lei Aloha ʻĀina," written by another one of Tūtū Ana's moʻopuna kualua (great-great-grandchild), Mehana Blaich Vaughan. She recounts the lessons of her tūtū, wili-style lei maker[7] Amelia Ana Kaʻōpua Bailey (Tūtū Ana's moʻopuna and namesake), in gathering and fashioning lei and likens these lessons in mindfulness, reciprocity, respect, and accountability to the way she approaches her research and how she understands the relationships between particular ʻāina and people.

In Kapā Oliveira's chapter, "Ka Wai Ola: The Life-Sustaining Water of Kanaka Knowledge," she challenges us to consider the complexities of using ʻōlelo Hawaiʻi-based methodologies in Kanaka ʻŌiwi research. Using her own experience as a geographer and kumu ʻōlelo Hawaiʻi, she shares her insight into how she has used collaborative approaches to adequately balance the ʻike emerging from ʻōlelo Hawaiʻi with expressing that ʻike in a non-Hawaiian context (until such time as a critical mass of scholars versed in ʻōlelo Hawaiʻi is built, she reminds us). Her piece also offers very valuable practical advice regarding the use of ʻōlelo Hawaiʻi, especially for researchers interested in publishing their work.

Kahunawai Wright and Nālani Balutski put forth their first iteration of an emerging theoretical piece, "Ka ʻIkena a ka Hawaiʻi: Toward a Kanaka ʻŌiwi Critical Race Theory"; it explores approaches to understanding and expressing the higher educational moʻolelo of Kanaka ʻŌiwi based in critical race theory and shaped by interviews with Kanaka ʻŌiwi graduates of higher education.

The next three chapters all draw inspiration from mele (songs, poems) and oli (chants) in forming their methodological frameworks. In "Moʻolelo for Transformative Leadership: Lessons from Engaged Practice," Kaiwipunikauikawēkiu Lipe shares her experiences in navigating her doctoral research in building places of Hawaiian learning through her interviews with eight wahine (female) educators at the University of Hawaiʻi at Mānoa. She highlights her own struggle with the cultural dissonance of being a Native Hawaiian scholar grounded in Hawaiian culture pursuing a Hawaiian-focused research topic in a predominantly non–Native Hawaiian institution. More importantly, however, she discusses her process as she develops a framework around moʻolelo and the metaphor of the ʻaʻaliʻi (*Dodonaea*, a native shrub) to understand and analyze her informants' leadership experiences through 'ōlelo no'eau, mele, and oli. Drawing similar inspiration from mele, R. Keawe Lopes Jr. uses "Ua Noho Au A Kupa I Ke Alo" composed by King Kalākaua to explain the ways this beautiful mele ended up providing the infrastructure for his approach to conducting research with Indigenous peoples. Maya L. Kawailanaokeawaiki Saffery's chapter, "He Ala Nihinihi Ia A Hiki I Ka Mole: A Precarious Yet Worthwhile Path to Kuleana Through Hawaiian Place-Based Education," reflects her journey to uncovering the ways in which this mele by Queen Emma, acting as her "epistemological repository," served as a significant theoretical framework for her doctoral research on Hawaiian place-based education. Saffery's choice of mele also reflects the journey of this collection, which at times can feel precarious in its uncertainty and discomfort, especially for those readers moored in positivist approaches to research. Ultimately, however, the journey is valuable because it reveals new and deepened perspectives, insight, and approaches to the Kanaka research landscape. Similarly, Brandy Nālani McDougall's piece, "Nā 'Ili'ili," tells a story reminding us of the strength and sanctity of our 'ike kūpuna (ancestral knowledge) and the important ways it guides us in both apparent and unconscious ways. Her use of the mo'o (lizard) also offers a powerful metaphor for the regenerative power of our 'ike kūpuna and all the (re)connections that "mo'o" have in our cultural epistemologies, such as mo'olelo, mo'okū'auhau (genealogy, ancestry), and kuamo'o (backbone, spine, trail, path).

Summer Puanani Maunakea ends our collection with her chapter, "Arriving at an 'Āina Aloha Research Framework: What Is Our Kuleana as the Next Generation of 'Ōiwi Scholars?" It contains interviews from two seasoned Kanaka 'Ōiwi scholar-activists, professors Jonathan Kamakawiwo'ole Osorio and Davianna Pōmaika'i McGregor. She reflects on the ways their wisdom interweaves with her own journey as an emerging scholar of education in the process of developing her Aloha 'Āina research methodology derived from her work at Ka Papa Lo'i 'o Kānewai, the Native Hawaiian cultural garden at the University of Hawai'i at Mānoa.

Me ke aloha, Kahunawai & Kapā'anaokalāokeola

NOTES

1. Our operational definition for methodologies is the ways in which research is conducted; methodologies are not to be confused with methods, which are particular tools or techniques.

2. This article was in press when Denzin et al. included it in their book. It was published in 2009.

3. University of Hawai'i, Operational Data Store, 2013.

4. Native Hawaiian Advancement Task Force Final Report, 2012.

5. Noelani Goodyear-Kaʻōpuaʻs chapter in this collection does an excellent job of providing much of the historical context to the rise of Kanaka-focused programs at UHM.

6. These issues around using ʻōlelo Hawaiʻi in non–ʻōlelo Hawaiʻi contexts are discussed in Kapāʻanaokalāokeola Oliveiraʻs chapter.

7. A style of lei that winds and twists the materials together.

BIBLIOGRAPHY

Chilisa, B. (2011). *Indigenous research methodologies*. Thousand Oaks, CA: Sage.

Denzin, N. K., Y. S. Lincoln, and L. T. Smith (2008). *Handbook of critical and Indigenous methodologies*. Thousand Oaks, CA: Sage.

Evans, M., R. Hole, L. Berg, P. Hutchinson, D. Sookraj, and Okanagan Urban Aboriginal Health Research Collective (2009). Common insights, differing methodologies: Towards a fusion of indigenous methodologies, participatory action research, and white studies in an urban Aboriginal research agenda. *Qualitative Inquiry, 15*(5), 893–910.

Kovach, M. (2010). *Indigenous methodologies: Characteristics, conversations, and contexts* [Kindle version]. Retrieved from Amazon.com.

Meyer, M. A. (2004). *Hoʻoulu: Our time of becoming: Early collected writings of Manulani Aluli Meyer*. Honolulu: ʻAi Pōhaku Press.

Smith, L. T. (2012). *Decolonising methodologies: Research and indigenous peoples* (2nd ed.). London: Zed.

Trask, H. K. (2002). *Night is a sharkskin drum*. Honolulu: University of Hawaiʻi Press.

Wilson, S. (2009). *Research is ceremony: Indigenous research methods*. Winnipeg: Fernwood.

A Note on the Cover Art

"Uncovering the Layers Within Us" is a piece I painted to reflect on and forever remember a special experience I shared with my kāne, No'eau, and two friends as we journeyed to Waiau on the summit of Mauna a Wākea. Consciously and subconsciously, we were all there seeking something: clarification, knowledge, a deeper understanding of ourselves, our kupuna, the 'āina.

As we slowly made our way up the mauna along an old dirt road, popularly known as Mānā Road, which stems from Waimea and winds around the northeastern side of the summit, we were forced to view the 'āina at a very slow yet intimate pace. As No'eau drove us through acres of pastureland and eventually into old koa forests, he shared with us a stream of stories passed on to him from his grandfather. In the areas that were still being grazed by cattle, the 'āina was desolate and barren. All that seemed to remain were a few koa trees and, of course, the cattle. Next to the koa, the cattle seemed so invasive and intrusive, having spent many years on our 'āina consuming all the native vegetation while preventing any new growth. Once we passed through pastures, gaining altitude in our ascent, we entered areas where fences had been erected to keep out the cattle. In these areas the koa flourished. There were thousands of newly sprouting keiki layered beneath larger koa that were standing ten to fifteen feet high. The same trend continued as we drove beyond the koa and into the 'ōhi'a lehua forest. In the areas where cattle roamed freely the land was barren, but in the areas where they were kept out, the Native plants flourished and the 'āina was healthy. Given the proper space and conditions, the Native seed bank just below the surface has the potential and ability to grow.

In thinking metaphorically about what I was viewing outside the cabin of our truck, I thought of the many "cattle" in my life. These cattle take different forms, and they continuously graze through our lives, suppressing the seeds of potential growth within us. While I was growing up, these cattle prevented me from seeing, understanding, and experiencing the layers that lay just beneath the surface of our 'āina and within me. I thought of how I spent all of my young life, from preschool until I graduated from high school, in a private Catholic school where I was taught to be ashamed of being Kanaka Maoli. The lessons I received were not only taught solely in the language of the colonizer, American English, but they were also lessons that reflected the colonizer worldview. My teachers instilled in me a sense that I was not a quality student or person if I did not conform to their standards. I gave up a part of myself, my home language, the value of what I experienced and learned at home and outside of school because I started to think that this was the only way to succeed. I see now that I gave up many of the unique aspects of my being that derived directly from my experiences with ʻohana and ʻāina. The cattle had entered my forest, and they were grazing on the passions and beliefs that grew there.

Now that I see the consequences that these decisions have on our ʻāina and ourselves, I am reminded of the importance of what our kūpuna taught us. Like the result of the cattle grazing, I believe that my pre-college education served to distance me from my moʻokūauahau and thus distance me from my kuleana as a Kanaka Maoli. I think of how the process of decolonization on a personal level is similar to what I observed on our journey. Like the fences put in place to prevent further intrusive grazing and erosion, I think it is important that we find ways to (re)establish spaces and conditions for our people to grow and fulfill our potential, so the seeds beneath the surface can sprout.

In this artistic composition, I focused on our journey to the summit of Mauna a Wākea and to Waiau. Mauna a Wākea is represented as the central triangle with three different dominant layers of colors—red, green, and yellow; these colors symbolize the dominant Native Hawaiian trees of the mauna's forests—ʻōhiʻa lehua, koa, and māmane—arranged according to the different wao in which they grow. The summit is covered with the white snows of Poliahu. Within each horizontal level are patterns that represent those resilient seed layers, the layers within us, where we find the essence of who we are. The moon and sun are painted at the top to remind us of the constant cycles that continue every day, every month, every year. They symbolize our traditions that continue to guide us and remind us of phases that occur over and over and will continue to happen on and on, forever. The moon, the sun, as well as the whales, are a constant reminder of the continuum of genealogy that connects us to who we are. These elements are always around and within us and will always serve as a pathway to uncovering layers and liberation.

Haley Kailiehu

Reproducing the Ropes of Resistance: Hawaiian Studies Methodologies

Noelani Goodyear-Ka'ōpua

I am slyly
reproductive: ideas
books, history
politics, reproducing
the rope of resistance
for unborn generations.
Haunani-Kay Trask, from her poem "Sons"

Engaging in academic research and writing can mean spending a lot of time alone in archives, in labs, in libraries, in "the field," and often in front of computers. But as the great physician, health researcher, and Hawaiian independence advocate, Kekuni Akana Blaisdell, once said, "Our ancestors are always with us as long as we think of them, talk to them, engage them in our thinking and planning and beliefs and actions."[1] Similarly, Trask poetically reassures us that, before we were born, those Kanaka who came before us have been twining stores of intellectual rope for us to use. Thus, we who consider ourselves to be Hawaiian studies practitioners are never really alone. Our kūpuna join us in our work, whether we recognize them or not.

When I use the phrase "Hawaiian studies" here, I mean it in a broad sense. I am not simply referring to scholarship produced by those who are directly connected to Hawaiian studies departments as students, faculty, or alumni; rather I am motioning toward a dynamic, interdisciplinary field that is constituted by practitioners in a range of diverse locations but who maintain some shared commitments and driving questions. Yet what makes this field cohere? What makes Hawaiian studies different from other studies of Hawai'i or of Kanaka Hawai'i?[2] What makes various works *Hawaiian* studies, as distinct from geography, or history, or botany projects that, for instance, investigate Hawaiian content?

The conversation about what constitutes Hawaiian studies—its theories and methods, its pasts and its futures, its potentials and its limitations—is one that merits volumes and volumes. This chapter is just one modest attempt to map some of the methodological foundations that have been laid by late twentieth- and early twenty-first-century scholars who birthed contemporary Hawaiian

LĀHUI
Does this research help Kanaka Maoli assert who we are as a people on our own terms?
Does it help us assess and understand our collective status?
Does it propose ways to improve our collective well-being as a people?
Does it critically examine what is at stake when defining "Hawaiianness"?

EA
How can the lived experiences of Kanaka on the 'āina inform this research?
How does this research support the ability of Kanaka to exercise ea?
How does it support the revitalization of vessels (material, ideological, spiritual, linguistic) that promote a healthy and robust flow of ea?

What is at stake in this research?
How can I nurture reciprocal relationships?
How can I share any benefits that may come to me because of this research?
How can I use the momentum from this research to catalyze positive social change?

KULEANA

How are the benefits of this research accruing? To whom? To what end?
What emergent lines of research may effectively challenge structural relations of power and wealth that hinder Hawaiian survivance?
Is research regenerating the ways of life that allow us to be in balance with this 'āina?

PONO

Methodological Ropes for Research and Resurgence. This figure represents four 'aho that form the methodological rope of Hawaiian studies research. These concepts—lāhui (collective identity and self-definition), ea (sovereignty and leadership), kuleana (positionality and obligations), and pono (harmonious relationships, justice, and healing)—are central commitments and lines of inquiry in contemporary Hawaiian studies research. Image by Lianne Charlie.

studies.[3] I discuss four concepts that might be seen as niho stones in a kahua that has been laid before us. We can think about *lāhui* (collective identity and self-definition), *ea* (sovereignty and leadership), *kuleana* (positionality and obligations), and *pono* (harmonious relationships, justice, and healing) as central commitments and lines of inquiry that are hallmarks of Hawaiian studies research.

Each of these four principles could also be seen as 'aho, single cords, that when braided together form what political scholar and poet, Haunani-Kay Trask, describes as a "rope of resistance."[4] It is a rope that holds this wide and growing field together. It provides a means of connection for our people.[5] My goal is to draw out these particular 'aho of Hawaiian studies intellectual production. I humbly offer my reflections on how these principles or lines of inquiry have been useful for my own practice as just one scholar among a growing wave of Hawaiian academic practitioners. This chapter should also be seen as an invitation for new generations of practitioners to consider and extend what it means to "do" Hawaiian studies.[6] What other 'aho exist that we may take up and reproduce for future generations? New waves of Hawaiian studies scholarship will address this question over time and in relation to new contexts.

I enter and participate in the field of Hawaiian studies as someone who examines, engages in, and writes about contemporary Hawaiian politics. My research, writing, and teaching generally focus on current relations of power. Not a day goes by when I do not think about how our kūpuna ʻŌiwi of both the remote and recent past remain relevant to issues of land, identity, education, sustainability, and governance today and into our futures. In this reflective chapter, my exploration of Hawaiian studies methodologies is guided by my tūtū kualua, my maternal great-great-grandmother, Ana Kaʻauwai. She was not a writer or a scholar, but her ʻano and her stories represent what I aspire to be and how I hope to inhabit my role as a Kanaka academic. Thus I begin with her story and weave reflections of her throughout this chapter. After all, Hawaiian studies research enabled me to reconnect with her. In many ways Hawaiian studies research is deeply personal and can be healing on individual, familial, and lāhui levels. It is a rope that allows us to pull toward one another against powerful forces that attempt to fragment and obliterate us as a Lāhui Kanaka ʻŌiwi.

E ana i ka ʻauwai: Look to the Routes of Ancestral Knowledge

Ana Kaʻauwai was born and raised in Kohala. She passed into the ao ʻaumakua long before I was born. Growing up, I did not know anything about her—not even her name. My grandfather had passed into the ao ʻaumakua very young, at age thirty-one, and his mother died early as well, at only forty-one. Like the many ways our people have been cut off from the waiwai of our ancestors by the deaths that imperialism demands, my branch of the family became disconnected from stories of my great-great-grandmother, Tūtū Ana.

Ana was still alive in the memories of some of my elder relatives, but it was not until I was a Hawaiian studies major in college and doing genealogy research that I learned about her. The research required two types of methods: interviewing kūpuna and searching for genealogy documents in various government- and church-maintained archives. Each of these two paths produced important insights about my tūtū kualua that inform my understanding of what it means to be a Hawaiian studies researcher.

Tūtū Ana first came alive for me through the stories of her granddaughter, Auntie Amelia Ana Bailey, who is my grandfather's older sister. Through her recollections I learned that Tūtū Ana had a distinctively strong voice. In her parlor, fragranced with the many flowers of a lei maker, Auntie Amelia generously shared her most vivid memory of her grandmother and namesake: the arrival of Tūtū Ana at their Kalihi home for her daughter's wake. Kamila (Ana's daughter and Amelia's mama) had passed unexpectedly at the young age of forty-one after having a stroke. So Tūtū Ana traveled from Kohala to Oʻahu to honor her child and to hānai one of the young babies Kamila had left behind. She stood at the doorway chanting. The smell of lei pikake draped over Kamila. The small plantation-style home reverberated with Tūtū Ana's oli and uē as she approached the quiet body of her daughter. Auntie Amelia's story taught me that, above all, Ana had a voice, a powerful voice that she used to remind us of who we are and how we are connected.

As a student and young academic, I never felt confident in my own voice. My kumu in Hawaiian studies—Haunani-Kay Trask, Lilikalā Kameʻeleihiwa, Jon Osorio, and Kanalu Young—were powerful orators. I could never imagine being as eloquent as them or having anything to say that would be as valuable as their words. When I went on to graduate school in Santa Cruz, California, I felt like I was literally the dumbest person in every classroom. And yet the times when I felt certain enough to speak and to write were those when I was not speaking as an individual, but as someone with ancestors and a community who needed to be heard.

As ʻŌiwi researchers, finding our voices is such an important element of the scholarly path, and nurturing our connections to those ancestors and communities can be a valuable part of that process. Too many of our people have been silenced. Yet, so many have also spoken or (more appropriately for this chapter) have published. One of the duties of a Hawaiian studies scholar then is to know and critically engage with the body of published work by Kānaka, lest we unwittingly participate in their silencing and marginalization.

Ana i ka ʻikena a ka Lāhui Hawaiʻi: Surveying the Terrain of Contemporary Hawaiian Studies

In Hawaiʻi, Hawaiian culture continues to be commercially exploited and degraded, the Hawaiian language ignored or abused, Hawaiian history neglected and distorted, and Native Hawaiians dispossessed in their own Native land. On the ten campuses of the University of Hawaiʻi system, this plight is reflected in the menial status of Hawaiian Studies and of Hawaiian persons in academic matters. Hawaiian Studies Task Force Report, 1986

If the 1970s were considered to be a Hawaiian cultural and political renaissance, the publication in 1986 of the *Kaʻū: University of Hawaiʻi Hawaiian Studies Task Force Report* (hereafter called the *"Kaʻū Report"*) signified an emergent ʻŌiwi academic renaissance. The task force, made up of Hawaiian educators from across the University of Hawaiʻi (UH) system,[7] argued that a strong commitment to Hawaiian studies and Hawaiian people on UH campuses would begin to address some of the dire "social, economic, and political obstacles confronting Native Hawaiians."[8] At the time, there were no facilities devoted to Hawaiian studies, nor was there a coordinated Hawaiian studies undergraduate or graduate curriculum on any of the UH campuses. On the UH Mānoa (UHM) campus, where the resources for Hawaiian studies were greatest, the program was given only a small room with four desks in the Department of Geography, two faculty positions (not designated solely to Hawaiian studies), and a budget of only $66,000. Approximately 1 percent of tenure-track positions at UHM were held by Kānaka Maoli when the report was released.[9]

In the mid-1980s a collection of writing by Kānaka Maoli seemed difficult to imagine. A year before the *Ka'ū Report* was issued, a volume of poetry and creative writing, titled *Mālama, Hawaiian Land and Water*, was published as a special issue of *Bamboo Ridge: Hawai'i Writers' Quarterly*. Editor and poet, Dana Naone Hall, illustrated in her introduction to the special issue just how little publication attention and energy had been given to 'Ōiwi intellectual production in the twentieth century up to that point:

> When the idea for editing a special issue on Hawaiian writing was brought up a year ago, no one knew what it would look like, what kinds of writing it would include, or how it would sound once it was put together. The issue had been proposed on faith and the belief that a new body of writing was developing in the islands, writing about Hawai'i by Hawaiians.[10]

In the nearly three decades since publication of *Mālama, Hawaiian Land and Water* and the *Ka'ū Report*, Hawaiian writing about Hawai'i has flourished in ways that the first generation of the Hawaiian academic renaissance may not have imagined.

In our 'ōlelo makuahine the word "ana" has several meanings that are appropriate for thinking about research: to measure, to survey, to evaluate, or to fathom. It implies both taking stock and thus coming to understand something. In the next section I survey some of the existing and diverse literature in Hawaiian studies with particular attention to the ways these works are all concerned with issues of lāhui-hood, the first strand of the aho: asserting who Kānaka Maoli are as a people, assessing and understanding our status as a people, proposing ways to improve our collective well-being as a people, and/ or stepping back to critically examine what is at stake when defining "Hawaiianness." The studies described in this section represent a small fraction of the Hawaiian studies scholarship written by Kānaka Maoli. It is not meant to be comprehensive, but rather to give the reader a glimpse of the breadth and depth of recent Hawaiian scholarship by Kānaka.

Although there are certainly non-'Ōiwi who have influenced and made important research contributions to Hawaiian studies, I highlight the intellectual work of 'Ōiwi scholars for two reasons.[11] First, Kanaka have historically been cast as students, not teachers; as informants, not analysts or scientists; as characters in, rather than the authors of, history and literature. Second, there exists a politics of citation, whether or not we are conscious of it. Too often people who write about and do research in Hawai'i participate in a politics of citation that perpetuates the primacy of non-Native scholarship over scholarship by Kanaka 'Ōiwi. However, the burgeoning of Hawaiian academic writing over the last three decades has brought us to a historical moment in which we can clearly assert that it is intellectually irresponsible and untenable to do Hawai'i-focused research without seriously engaging Hawaiian studies scholarship.

One of the hallmarks of Hawaiian studies research is a commitment to ensuring the survivance of Kanaka Maoli as a lāhui, a people.[12] Contemporary Hawaiian studies research holds at its core a "who we are/who are we" dialectic. Kanaka author and benefactor to the Hawaiian academic and cultural renaissance, John Dominis Holt, heralded the concern with asserting who we are as Native people in his 1964 essay, *On Being Hawaiian*. Tired of others trying to define Hawaiians and of being "pummeled into accepting the stranger's view of ourselves as being cute, all-abiding, friendly nincompoops," Holt described Hawaiians instead as a "people with a history . . . the native connective tissue to forebears who used these islands superbly for the production of goods and the enjoyment of life."[13]

Kanaka Maoli are defined by our ancestry. This is *who we are*. Hawaiian studies research fleshes out this assertion. At the same time, the confident articulation of who we are is held in productive tension with the question, Who are we? As historian and musician Jonathan Kamakawiwo'ole Osorio puts it, "'O ia ka nīnau maoli (That is the real question). Who the hell are we? If our own activism and scholarship does [sic] not continually seek the answers to that question, then it is activism and scholarship for someone else."[14] Like our 'āina we are a dynamic and changing people, and thus Hawaiian studies practitioners continue to explore what it means to be 'Ōiwi because the answers are never complete. This tension—between powerfully asserting who we are against forces that work toward our extinction and holding open space to acknowledge that who we are is not a closed question—animates Hawaiian studies scholarship.

For instance, in his article " 'What Kine Hawaiian Are You?': A Mo'olelo About Nationhood, Race, History, and the Contemporary Sovereignty Movement in Hawai'i," Osorio describes ways in which the category of race (intertwined with class) became embedded in nineteenth-century laws that stripped Kanaka Maoli of land and political enfranchisement. His mo'olelo, focused on the 1887 "Bayonet Constitution," highlights the ways that questions of Hawaiian identity, over who and what counts as Hawaiian, reflect larger contestations that have material effects on lands, bodies, and minds. His mo'olelo is also a warning to Kanaka Maoli against becoming too focused on devising responses to settler laws, particularly when those laws try to define us as a people. Such preoccupations with law, he argues, fragment the lāhui. Laws alone can never adequately answer the question of who we are.[15]

In the context of the ongoing U.S. occupation of Hawai'i, one of the central challenges for Hawaiian studies practitioners is the need to strategically assert and nurture our collective identity in the face of American discourses of assimilation and citizenship, without getting stuck in idealized and ossified notions of exactly *who we are* as 'Ōiwi. Scholars from a variety of fields have tackled this challenge. Health researchers have documented physical and mental health disparities among Native Hawaiians and investigated ways to address those disparities through various culturally grounded approaches.[16] Educationalists have critiqued historical and contemporary policies, practices, and curriculum materials that alienate Kanaka Maoli youth, looked at effective pedagogical practices for Hawaiian culture- and language-based schools, and offered organizational and epistemological models for transforming relationships between schools and communities.[17] Hawaiian language scholars have worked to translate, analyze, and make accessible the massive body of Hawaiian language printed material from the nineteenth century, arguing for the importance of language in maintaining collective identity. They have also been instrumental in revitalizing 'Ōlelo Hawai'i as a living language by supporting Hawaiian immersion schools throughout the islands, publishing in 'Ōlelo Hawai'i, and creating various other forms of Hawaiian language media.[18]

Contemporary Kanaka Maoli scholars coming from a range of academic disciplines have written mo'olelo (histories/stories of past and present experiences) of our people. For instance, historians have reminded us that Kanaka of the eighteenth and nineteenth centuries were active agents, negotiating turbulent periods of cultural and political change, fighting to assert our humanity, our distinctiveness, and our independence.[19] Political analysts have documented various ways that Kanaka Maoli resisted American imperialism and occupation.[20] And writers from various fields have published mo'olelo asserting the continued central importance of the relationship between Kanaka and 'āina, which provides the bedrock of who we are as 'Ōiwi.[21]

In addition to such mo'olelo composed in prose, scholars of Hawaiian mele and hula have provided a foundation showing that Kanaka 'Ōiwi have since time immemorial used mele to express and explore who we are. Many of these mele and hula scholars are practitioners in the double sense of being both researchers-writers and composers-performers, and even kumu hula.[22] Some have published books and academic journal articles, whereas others have directed their research efforts toward enriching the experiences of hālau hula and other forms of community education.[23]

Mele and moʻolelo not only explain but also reproduce the lāhui; they provide insights as to how to live as ʻŌiwi. In considering Hawaiian studies scholarship, we cannot overlook the collected artistry of ʻŌiwi poets such as Dana Naone Hall, ʻĪmaikalani Kalahele, Mahealani Wendt, Wayne Kaumualiʻi Westlake, and Haunani-Kay Trask, as well as members of a newer generation such as Brandy Nālani McDougall, Noʻu Revilla, and Sage Takehiro. Together with spoken word performers such as Travis Thompson, Jamaica Osorio, Alakaʻi Kotrys, and Kealiʻi McKenzie, these lyricists express the range of experiences of Kanaka who celebrate the power of our ancestral lineages and ʻāina while also wrestling with the lived realities of dispossession, racism, militarization, and urbanization.[24]

Supporting affirmation with critique, scholars employing critical approaches to Hawaiian studies have interrogated the ways that Hawaiian subjectivities (our senses of who we are, as shaped within larger relations of power) are affected and inhabited through introduced notions or categories of race, class, and gender.[25] They point toward the importance of Hawaiian studies methodologies that give us the ability to negotiate discrepant relations of power and authority embedded within different ways of defining and mobilizing Hawaiian identity. They also suggest a more complex picture than seeing Kanaka as either victims or agents, either authentic or assimilated; they call us instead to consider the political stakes—such as the material effects on Hawaiian lands and bodies—of different ways of understanding and living our Hawaiianness. To that end, Hawaiian studies scholars have also helped us think about Kanaka Maoli collective political status and claims. Whereas some who focus on law have helped elucidate Native Hawaiian rights to lands, waters, and cultural practices within existing state frameworks, others have directly challenged the current relationship between the lāhui Hawaiʻi and the United States.[26]

By using a "who we are/who are we" dialectical approach to inquiries of Hawaiian lāhui-hood, Hawaiian studies remains a practice of ʻŌiwi survivance. As Anishinaabe author and cultural critic, Gerald Vizenor writes, "Survivance is the continuance of stories, not a mere reaction, however pertinent."[27] Survivance is about our lāhui's "renewal and continuity into the future . . . through welcoming unpredictable cultural reorientations."[28]

E ana mau i ka ʻauwai

While Tūtū Ana came alive for me in my auntie's moʻolelo, I also learned about her by tracking her name through birth, death, and marriage records. Just as for so many Kanaka who research family genealogies, following Tūtū Ana was not an easy or linear process. Sometimes her name had an unusual spelling or even appeared altogether different from one document to another. I would see the name "Anna Kalama," for instance, and wonder whether this was referring to the same person. Taking detailed notes, cross-referencing documents with family stories, and keeping track of my steps were all helpful in drawing closer to her.

As I tried to chart important milestones in Tūtū Ana's life and the lives of her children, I realized that she had taken three "husbands" at different points in her life. I set "husbands" off with quotation marks because she did not marry any of these men. Rather, they were three kāne with whom she had consecutive, committed relationships that produced children. My immediate cousins and I descend from the relationship with her second kāne, a Chinese man named Amina.

Tūtū Ana was what I like to call *selectively promiscuous.* In this regard, her approach to survivance and to reproducing the lāhui provides inspiration and guidance to my own thinking about how to engage in Hawaiian studies practice and how to be an 'Ōiwi intellectual. I see the kind of selective promiscuity that many of our kūpuna practiced as a valuable way to approach our scholarship. As producers and reproducers of knowledge, we first draw heavily on our 'Ōiwi lineage, but we also selectively bring in other lineages or thinkers who provide us with traction to move the lāhui forward. And of course, we experience pleasure in partaking of the mana and beauty of diverse intellectual traditions. In this chapter, I try to demonstrate examples of selective promiscuity in articulating and practicing Hawaiian studies methodologies.

Ke ea o ka 'āina: Ke ea i ke ana

Hawaiian studies methodologies require that research practitioners be conscious of the political stakes of our research. We realize that our research does not take place in a vacuum. We incorporate the lived experiences of our people on our 'āina into the way we frame, conduct, and present our research. What distinguishes *Hawaiian studies* from *studies of* Hawaiian topics is a commitment to revitalizing the collective ability of Kanaka Hawai'i to exercise our ea in healthy, respectful, and productive ways. Hawaiian studies methodologies support the revitalization of vessels that promote a robust flow of ea.

The word "ea" has several meanings. As Hawaiian language and political scholar Leilani Basham argues, each utterance of the word carries all these meanings at once, even when one meaning may be emphasized. Ea refers to political independence and is often translated as "sovereignty." It also carries the meanings "life," "breath," and "emergence," among other things. A shared characteristic in each of these translations is that ea is an active state of being. Like breathing, ea cannot be achieved or possessed; it requires constant action day after day, generation after generation.

Ea, in fact, extends back to the birth of the land itself. Basham writes, "'O ke ea nō hoʻi ka hua ʻōlelo no ka puka ʻana mai o kekahi mea mai loko mai o ka moana, e laʻa me ka mokupuni."[29] Indeed, ea is a word that describes the act of rising up, such as volcanic islands emerging from the depths of the ocean. In looking to mele Hawaiʻi—Hawaiian songs and poetry—Basham points out that the term "ea" is foregrounded within a prominent mele koʻihonua, or creation and genealogical chant for Hawaiʻi: "*Ea* mai Hawaiinuiakea / *Ea* mai loko mai o ka po."[30] The islands emerge from the depths, from the darkness that precedes their birth. Basham argues that, similarly, political autonomy is a beginning of the collective life of a people.

Although "ea" has long referred to political independence as well as to life itself, the term first became associated with state-based forms of sovereignty in the 1840s following the promulgation of the first constitution of the Hawaiian Kingdom. After a rogue British captain claimed the islands for Great Britain in 1843, Hawaiian emissaries secured the restoration of sovereign government. King Kamehameha III famously proclaimed, "Ua mau ke ea o ka ʻāina i ka pono." Hawaiian language and politics scholars such as Basham and Kaleikoa Kaʻeo have called our attention to the fact that the king did not reaffirm the sovereignty of the government (ke ea o ke aupuni), but rather the sovereignty and life of the land itself (ke ea o ka ʻāina) to which Kanaka are inextricably connected.[31] Ea can be seen as both a concept and a diverse set of practices that make land primary over government, while not dismissing the importance of autonomous governing structures to a people's health and well-being.

Unlike Euro-American philosophical notions of sovereignty, ea is based on the experiences of people on the land, on relationships forged through the process of remembering and caring for wahi pana, storied places.[32] In our practice as Hawaiian studies researchers, we should take cues from personal and collective experiences on the ʻāina. We should strive to allow those embodied practices of ea to inform our theoretical frames, methods of gathering and analyzing information, and the styles through which we present our work.

In my own work, I have tried to document and understand how ʻŌiwi communities live and practice ea through educational and social movement initiatives. Throughout my research career thus far, the educators and activists I have had the privilege of interviewing and working alongside have talked about how the health/breath of the people is directly linked to the health/breath of the land.

For example, mālama ʻāina in Hālau Kū Māna public charter school's project-based curriculum has helped kumu and haumāna live the connections between personal and collective self-determination. These students understand mālama ʻāina as the "actual hana" of caring for the land on a regular and long-term basis. Reflecting on the relevance of ʻāina and ea to his practice as a teacher of Hawaiian and American history, Hawaiian and English languages, and kalo cultivation since 2004, Kumu ʻĪmaikalani Winchester spoke to me of lessons learned by restoring loʻi kalo:

> Learning at the loʻi is about producing food and being self-sustainable. . . . It is the idea of taking care of the entire system instead of just your own parcel. The idea of being accountable to more than just one person—oneself. I think these are all values that are critical in the pursuit of ea or independence, not only within the political context but also as a personal statement to oneself. When we develop an understanding that Hawaiʻi and its people can live . . . without the support or constant intervention by outside forces, Hawaiians can be out there saying: "We have the ability to take care of ourselves. We are not wards of the state. Our traditions have meaning, and they have purpose. They have power, and they have wealth."

He went on to further explain the ways an ʻŌiwi Hawaiʻi notion of *ke ea o ka ʻāina* has as much to do with proliferating and nurturing relationships in balanced interdependence as it does with asserting autonomy and being self-sufficient:

> Ea, I think, is the full realization that our purpose here is greater than owning material wealth, that our purpose needs to be aligned with aloha, with pono, with mālama ʻāina, with finding some sort of balance in our interactions between ourselves and nature, between ourselves and one another. . . . The push toward sovereignty and independence is as much about **interdependence** and the realization of it. The emphasis that we place on individual success is going to start to become overshadowed by the need for interdependent cooperation. And we see interdependence in action every time we are working ʻāina. . . . For a sixteen-year-old kid who knows nothing else other than living downtown some place, if they can get out and experience some different things, return to their past, they can actually **breathe** that life—that ea—into our culture and traditions again. So it's not relics of the past but rather a living and breathing function of who we are as people. Then [they see] why we need to be connected to this place, why we need to take care of our water, why we need to take care of our lands, why we need to take care of our beaches and reefs, why we need to take care of one another. . . . Hawaiian education is carrying the heavy kuleana of introducing collectivist ideas into a very individualist world, where private

property, capitalism, and the free market runs or guides most decision making and policies.[33]

In a separate interview, Pōmaikaʻi Freed (Winchester's former student) relayed to me some of the lessons she had learned from developing a relationship with the ʻāina. She talked about how the work of hoʻokahe wai (to cause the waters to flow) was one of her favorite regular tasks at the loʻi because it was an embodied and metaphorical healing practice. "The thought behind hoʻokahe wai is to prepare," she explained as she talked about cleaning the leaves, rocks, and branches that inevitably collect within a flowing, natural waterway. She continued,

> Even before you do the work to open up loʻi, you have to make sure the water that will feed you has a steady flow. I believe in that process is where you make those sacrifices, so that one day you may reap the benefits. Every day you walk up that stream to go clean a little bit further, a little bit further, so that one day you can build the ʻauwai and watch water flow into your work. To hoʻōla. To bring that mana into it.

She explained that moving upstream to clear the waterway paralleled the process of journeying deeper and deeper into oneself to deal with the emotional and physical blockages caused by old wounds, unresolved tensions, and just the everyday sediment of life:

> Hoʻokahe wai is also to do that within yourself so that your own mana can flow better, in a more pono way. To have your own mana flowing better, you have to face some things within yourself, so you can clear the blockages that we slowly set up. It's definitely a process, but we come out stronger for it.[34]

When water, or mana, or knowledge can flow properly, healthy growth can occur. And this process must be repeated again and again over time for balanced and healthy functioning of the system.

Just as Freed emphasized the importance and priority of maintaining the vessels or channels that support growth and well-being, in this case the streams and ʻauwai, Hawaiian studies practitioners engage in research that restores and strengthens structures that allow for a robust flow of ea. Hawaiian studies methodologies support the revitalization of vessels—material structures, ways of thinking, speaking, and behaving—that foster healthy ea. These vessels could include a variety of elements—from educational pathways to waʻa, from imu to ʻŌiwi governing structures, from central linguistic or ideological concepts to ancestral rituals and ceremonies. The ana might also be considered as one such vessel.

The word "ana" refers to the larynx or what we commonly call the "voice box." It is within the larynx—the ana—that we produce pitch and regulate the volume of our voices. We simply would not have humanly intelligible or aesthetically beautiful voices if it were not for our ana. Similarly, research can give us collective voice as Kanaka ʻŌiwi. It is not the ultimate source of our voice; the ultimate source of our voices is our ea—our breath, our life, our sovereignty. But research shapes and can give power to our ea. It can collect and help us make sense of otherwise unnoticed pieces of our collective experience. Meaningful Hawaiian studies research can project our ea in directions that affect our shared futures. Just as the larynx is the conduit of our breath, ke ana o ke ea, the ʻāina is the conduit of our sovereignty. It is the landscape that gives our life and our existence meaning, ke ea o ka ʻāina.

Thus, our research becomes richer when we bring our lived experiences and those of our people on the ʻāina into our work. Such experiences allow Kanaka ʻŌiwi to reflexively engage in continuous processes of becoming who we are meant to be. Hawaiian studies practitioners have an ethical responsibility to support such processes for our lāhui.

This is similar to what Osage scholar Robert Allen Warrior has called a "process-oriented intellectual sovereignty." In his context, Warrior calls on American Indian intellectuals committed to the political freedom and well-being of their people to live the struggle through their own intellectual production and to make that work more inclusive of contemporary Indian experience. Such critical work assumes that sovereignty does not mean insularity or state-based governing apparatuses alone. Instead, it allows for the articulation or practice of sovereignty to emerge as we critically reflect on the struggles and experiences of our people.[35] Discussing Standing Rock Sioux author Vine Deloria Jr.'s book, *We Talk, You Listen,* Warrior writes that Deloria has taught us that freedom cannot be "immediately defined. . . . Rather the challenge is to articulate what sort of freedom as it 'emerge[s]' through the experience of the group to exercise the sovereignty which they recognize in themselves."[36]

Pointing out the colonial baggage of the term "sovereignty" and instead bringing to the fore the central importance of restoring Indigenous concepts and the land-based relationships that allow us to be who we are, Indigenous writers such as Taiaiake Alfred (Kanienʻkehaka/Mohawk) and Leanne Simpson (Michi Saagiig Nishnaabeg) have urged us to think and act in terms of "Indigenous resurgence."[37] There is no single definition of this term, because its meanings emerge with the collective action of diverse Indigenous nations and peoples. However, *resurgence* signifies building ourselves up from within. As Simpson writes, such resurgences mean

> significantly re-investing in our own ways of being: regenerating our political and intellectual traditions; articulating and living our legal systems; language learning; ceremonial and spiritual pursuits; creating and using our artistic and performance-based traditions. All of these require us—as individuals and collectives—to diagnose, interrogate, and eviscerate the insidious nature of conquest, empire and imperial thought in every aspect of our lives.[38]

This work is never done. Living as 'Ōiwi is a continual process of becoming. Like breathing, resurgence and ea must be continuous to sustain healthy life. Hawaiian studies methodologies require its practitioners to strive to support such processes.

Ko kākou kuleana: Ethical Hawaiian Studies Research

As individual researchers, finding our personal/professional voice is an important part of our methodological path. Learning to use our literal and figurative ana to shape the tone and rhythm of our voice, depending on the audience, the content, and our purpose, is an essential part of what it means to be a Hawaiian studies scholar. What we can and cannot say is deeply influenced by kuleana, and Hawaiian studies methodologies take kuleana with the utmost seriousness. As practitioners who assert our own voices, we must always consider our positionality and our obligations.

What is at stake in my methods of research and writing? To whom am I accountable? Who is at risk and how? Who might benefit and how? What obligations to specific communities, families, individuals, stories, and places do I have in this project? How can I mālama the relationships that precede and extend beyond this particular research project? These are all ethical questions that those of us who engage in Hawaiian studies research should ask ourselves. And we should ask these questions again and again throughout the process of our research and beyond.

The protocols of accountability for those doing research in jobs or degree programs are usually weighted toward the ways one is accountable to the institution. For example, master's degree and doctoral students are required to submit drafts for review by an academic committee. They are required to follow existing protocols for citing the work of other scholars. These protocols of accountability are important and useful, and they are built into the process of writing a thesis or dissertation. However, the kuleana of a Hawaiian studies scholar goes far beyond these basic forms of academic obligation.

Eddie Kaanana and Ilei Beniamina, respected Hawaiian educators, both emphasize the ways kuleana is tied to the well-being of the 'ohana or learning community. Becoming a contributing member of the extended family and community is an essential part of processes of learning and research.[39] In her master's thesis, Mehana Blaich wrote that when she interviewed 'Anakala Eddie about the meaning of kuleana, he talked immediately about "feeding one's family, caring for one's children, and all other kuleana [that] depended on one's ability to mālama that primary kuleana, to care for that piece of land and to make it productive."[40] Based on 'Anakala Eddie's description, Blaich argues that "rights are earned only by first fulfilling responsibilities and every right or privilege comes with increased levels of responsibility. . . . All rights and responsibilities, are inextricably rooted in the land itself and in how well we care for it."[41] Learning and knowledge are forms of privilege that come with attendant responsibilities to a larger collective and to the 'āina on which we depend for life. As a learner masters new skills, he or she takes on more complex responsibilities. In turn, it is through the fulfillment of more challenging duties in caring for the land and the community that one learns.

To be an academic researcher is to occupy a position of privilege. With more knowledge comes more kuleana. Any research project requires that we take the time to establish or nurture the appropriate relationships and to be affirmed that "yes, indeed, I am the one who is supposed to undertake this inquiry."

My own research has relied heavily on ethnographic methods. That is, I work with living people, and I think and write about cultural and political dynamics. As people share their knowledge and build relationships of trust in a researcher as someone who will be writing about them, they make themselves vulnerable.

As part of my first major project I wrote about the process of creating a Hawaiian-culture–based charter school, Hālau Kū Māna (HKM).[42] Because of my position as an "insider"—someone who was part of the group that founded the school and was also working there—I had wide access to what people were thinking, feeling, and doing on a day-to-day basis. Thus, it was important to be vigilantly sensitive about the boundaries of where my research started and ended, or about what should or should not be written. My priority needed to be concern for the well-being of the community.

In this regard, one interview I conducted during my dissertation research on HKM sticks out in my mind. I was scheduled to talk with one of the parents who had been involved in the school's founding, and we had planned to meet before the school board meeting that we were both attending later one evening. With her permission, we began the recorded interview in a private room. I proceeded to ask a few warm-up questions. It soon became apparent that she was troubled and preoccupied with another issue, which she began to share in the course of our conversation.

Anger and frustration brewed within her. There was an important decision related to her child to be made at that meeting that night. Because we had established a level of trust and comfort, she allowed me to hear and see things that would not have ordinarily been part of a typical research interview. As tears, memories, and criticisms gushed forth, I knew I needed to shift gears and put aside my research agenda. She did not need an interview; she needed to process her emotions with someone before this emotionally charged board meeting. Although she had not asked me to, I turned off the recorder. I just listened and tried to aloha her without judgment or analysis, without wearing my researcher hat. It was a moment where I first understood the limits of my kuleana as a writer and prioritized my kuleana as a member of the HKM community.

Establishing, and maintaining, long-term kuleana after completion of a research project is important. From our mea hana noʻeau, such as our master canoe or rock-formation builders, we know that the kuleana to a place, a being, or a community begins before and extends after the actual building process. One does not just build an ahu or restore a loʻi kalo and then abandon it. Similarly, after finishing a paper, completing a research grant, or publishing books and articles, ethical Hawaiian studies practitioners continue to ask ourselves these questions: What is at stake in the dissemination of the knowledge that came out of my research and writing? How can I continue to nurture the reciprocal relationships I built in this process? How can I share any benefits that may come to me because of this research (such as professional advancement, public recognition, or renumeration)? How can I use the momentum from this research to catalyze positive social change for this community?

Various scholars in Indigenous studies provide other useful frameworks for thinking about research ethics. In her classic, *Decolonizing Methodologies*, Linda Tuhiwai Smith writes about "sharing knowledge" in ways that are reciprocal, so that the conventional relationship of authority between the "researcher" and the "researched" is disrupted. When sharing knowledge, the entire process enriches the community that participates in the inquiry.[43]

Taiaiake Alfred urges us to think about practicing "warrior scholarship" by recognizing that the institutions (such as universities) in which we work and study are "grounds of contention," where our responsibility is to challenge forces that work to destroy our peoplehood and to nurture "visionaries of a dignified alternative to the indignity of cultural assimilation and political surrender."[44]

Similarly, Jeff Corntassel proposes a framework of "sustainable self-determination" that resonates with the difference between ʻŌiwi notions of kuleana and Western notions of rights. He argues that Indigenous people focus on our individual, family, and community responsibilities; regenerate

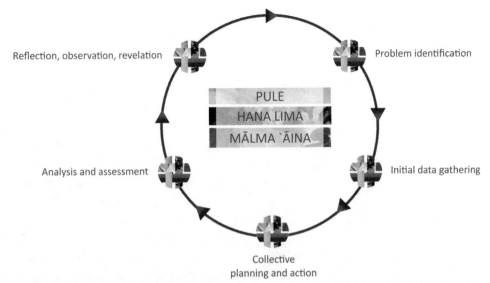

Reflection, observation, revelation

Problem identification

PULE
HANA LIMA
MĀLMA ʻĀINA

Analysis and assessment

Initial data gathering

Collective
planning and action

A Sample Process of Ethically Conscious Hawaiian Research. This figure graphically represents one Hawaiian studies practitioner's approach to striving for an ethical practice of
research. The perimeter of the circle indicates progressive stages or phases in the process. The items in the middle represent practices that ground the researcher throughout
the process. Image by Lianne Charlie.

local and regional Indigenous economies; and recognize the interconnection
of social, spiritual, environmental, and political aspects of self-determination.[45]

What does the process of research look like when one takes seriously questions of kuleana? Recognizing that each researcher will operationalize ethics
in his or her own ways through the course of the research process, I offer an
outline of my own process as just one example.

As someone who engages in community-engaged, participatory, qualitative
research, I see research as a recursive process.[46] In every phase, it is important
to stay in conversation with partners/participants who do not necessarily occupy academic institutional spaces. Additionally, practices that would typically
be seen as "nonacademic" within the conventional Western academy are central
to the process: pule (prayer on my own and sometimes with other participants);
connecting with the ʻāina (keeping my hands to the ground); and working
alongside research partners in activities that are not necessarily directly related to my own research agenda.

Pehea lā e pono ai?: Research for Healing and Justice

In this chapter, I have suggested *lāhui, ea,* and *kuleana* as central commitments
and questions that are hallmarks of Hawaiian studies research. I conclude
with one final ʻaho—*pono*—which I understand as signifying the search for

and maintenance of harmonious relationships, justice, and healing. Lilikalā Kameʻeleihiwa's question is as applicable for Hawaiian studies scholars today as when she posed it more than twenty years ago in the title of her landmark book, *Native Lands and Foreign Desires: Pehea lā e pono ai?* How do we restore balance, bring about healing, and assure that justice is realized? These are still persistent questions. Indeed, pehea lā e pono ai?

Since the early 1980s Hawaiian academic renaissance that sparked what we know as Hawaiian studies today, the lāhui Hawaiʻi has made important gains, but there is still such a long distance to go. For instance, studies completed in the early 1980s—such as the Native Hawaiian Educational Assessment project and the Native Hawaiian Study Commission report, both completed in 1983— showed that Kanaka Maoli had the highest rates of family poverty, incarceration, academic underachievement (including dropout and absentee rates), and various negative health indicators, including behavioral health outcomes such as suicide and depression. For our people as a whole, data from the first decade of the 2000s show that these statistics remain largely unchanged thirty years later. Despite the academic renaissance, the larger social trends remain unchanged. There have been significant personal and familiar gains that we should not minimize. And yet, we cannot stop asking, "Pehea lā e pono ai?" We still face rapacious foreign desires for our native lands, and the legacies of dispossession still plague our people. Political philosopher Kaleikoa Kaʻeo suggests that, as a lāhui, "we don't have an economic problem, we have a political problem."[47] In my own work, I have argued that we will never see a significant change in the historically rooted educational inequities observable in Hawaiʻi's school systems until we address the unresolved issues of land and sovereignty.

As Hawaiian studies researchers, we should consciously think about how our individual projects contribute to collective discussion and action around pono. At a micro level, we might consider questions such as the following: How are the benefits of this research accruing? To whom? To what end? And at a macro level, we should continuously assess how Hawaiian studies as a field is contributing to changing the intolerable conditions our people and lands continue to face. We might ask questions like: How are benefits of predominant lines of Hawaiian studies inquiry accruing differently across different segments of the lāhui? Where do research funds tend to be channeled? How can we support emergent lines of research that may more effectively challenge the structural relations of power and wealth that hinder Hawaiian survivance? Are we making a significant reinvestment in regenerating the ways of life that sustained our lāhui for hundreds of generations and are in balance with this ʻāina?

In the end, perhaps the fundamental question for academic practitioners is similar to what Hawaiian practitioners of various hana noʻeau consider: How do I live my life with integrity to my craft, to my kūpuna, to my family, to my community? How do I live pono? In that regard, Kaumakaiwa Kanaka'ole recently offered a beautiful interpretation of pono: "The greatest definition of pono, to me, is not being righteous, but being the most authentic . . . neither right nor wrong, both are acknowledged and both are valuable."[48]

If there is one thing that I take away from the story of Tūtū Ana coming to Honolulu to bury her daughter and mālama her mo'opuna, it is that, even in the wake of the darkest tragedies, we carry on. The extended family that is our lāhui has suffered huge losses between the time of Tūtū Ana's life and my own. Like her entry into what was a moment of heartbreaking family loss, we must care for the young ones and bring them to their 'āina kulāiwi. We must surround them with oli, mele, and the profound voices of their kūpuna. We must find selectively promiscuous ways to reproduce the ropes of resistance and of survivance. We must train new generations in how these ropes have historically been used and also allow them to practice finding innovative uses of their own. In these ways, Hawaiian studies research can continue to be a practice of 'Ōiwi resurgence and of ea.

NOTES

1. Harden, *Voices of Wisdom*, 11.
2. In my usage of Kanaka/Kānaka, "Kānaka" is a countable plural form. It is not used for an indefinite plural, but only when the actual number can be estimated. "Kanaka," the singular-generic form, refers to an individual person or to the whole class of people. It is also the form that is used when the word is used as an adjective. My usage in this text is guided by kumu 'ōlelo Hawai'i No'eau Warner and Noenoe K. Silva, but I take full responsibility for any mistakes.
3. To be clear, "methodological" refers to the philosophical assumptions and rationale underlying lines of research and selection of methods; the theories, ethics, values, and principles that determine how methods are deployed; or how research is carried out. In short, methodologies deal with "why" we do what we do as researchers. "Methods" refers to the specific approaches, tools, and techniques for gathering and interpreting data.
4. Trask, *Light in the Crevice Never Seen*, 55–56.
5. In the documentary film *A Mau A Mau*, kumu hula John Ka'imikaua talks about the 'aho/'aha metaphor as it informs traditional governance practices. His description has informed my thinking here. See John Ka'imikaua, Nālani Minton, and Nā Maka o ka 'Āina, *A Mau A Mau: To Continue Forever*.
6. I specifically use the term "practitioners" because it is a category that is often reserved for certain kinds of cultural practices within the Hawaiian community. Research has been a cultural practice since time immemorial for Kanaka, and writing/publishing became an important means of cultural production and transmission from the moment that Kanaka first grasped these technologies. Thus, just as Hawaiian musicians who play ukulele or guitar are considered cultural practitioners, so too should we Hawaiian studies scholars see ourselves as cultural practitioners.

7. The task force included the following members: Isabella Abbott, Jean Ilei Benia-mina, Kekuni Blaisdell, Lilikalā Dorton (now Kameʻeleihiwa), Lucy Gay, Alberta Pua Hopkins, Kauanoe Kamanā, Edward Kanahele, Pualani Kanahele, Larry Kimura, Davianna Pōmaikaʻi McGregor, Edith McKinzie, Richard "Dutch" Mossman, Midge Oler, Abraham Piʻianāiʻa, David Sing, Haunani-Kay Trask, and Ilima Williams.

8. Hawaiian Studies Task Force, University of Hawaiʻi, *Kaʻū Report*, ix.

9. Ibid., 5.

10. Hall, *Mālama: Hawaiian Land and Water*, p. 6.

11. The issue of whether Hawaiian studies should be produced primarily by Kanaka Maoli is one that warrants further discussion by scholars in the field and is beyond the scope of this chapter.

12. The term "survivance" comes from the work of author and literary theorist Gerald Vizenor (Anishinaabe). It speaks to the dynamic presence, rather than the mere survival, of Native peoples. See, for example, Vizenor, *Survivance: Narratives of Native Presence*.

13. Holt, *On Being Hawaiian*, 9–10.

14. Osorio, " 'What Kine Hawaiian Are You?': A Moʻolelo About Nationhood, Race, History, and the Contemporary Sovereignty Movement in Hawaiʻi," 375.

15. Although published in 2001, Osorio's intervention remains particularly salient at the time of this writing (February 2014) as Kanaka Maoli reckon with a state roll, a list of Native Hawaiians eligible to participate in the creation of a new governing entity under settler state laws.

16. Native Hawaiian Health Research Consortium Mental Health Task Force, *E Ola Mau*; Nahulu et al., "Psychosocial Risk and Protective Influences in Hawaiian Adolescent Psychopathology"; Makini et al., "Risk and Protective Factors Related to Native Hawaiian Adolescent Alcohol Use"; Andrade et al., "The National Center on Indigenous Hawaiian Behavioral Health Study of Prevalence of Psychiatric Disorders in Native Hawaiian Adolescents"; Crabbe, "Initial Psychometric Validation of He ʻAna Manaʻo O Nā Moʻomeheu Hawaiʻi: A Hawaiian Ethnocultural Inventory (HEI) of Cultural Practices"; Kaʻōpua and Mueller, "Treatment Adherence Among Native Hawaiians Living with HIV"; Kaʻōpua, "Developing a Culturally Responsive Breast Cancer Screening Promotion with Native Hawaiian Women in Churches"; Kaʻōpua et al., "Why Are Native Hawaiians Underrepresented in Hawaiʻi's Older Adult Population?"; Kaʻōpua et al., "The Lived Experience of Native Hawaiians Exiting Prison and Reentering the Community"; Kaholokula, Iwane, and Nacapoy, "Effects of Perceived Racism and Acculturation on Hypertension in Native Hawaiians"; Kaholokula et al., "Sociodemographic, Behavioral, and Biological Variables Related to Weight Loss in Native Hawaiians and Other Pacific Islanders"; Mokuau, "Culturally Based Solutions to Preserve the Health of Native Hawaiians"; Carpenter, Kamaka, and Kaulukukui, "An Innovative Approach to Developing a Cultural Competency Curriculum: Efforts at the John A. Burns School of Medicine, Department of Native Hawaiian Health"; Niheu, Turbin, and Yamada, "The Impact of the Military Presence in Hawaiʻi on the Health of Nā Kānaka Maoli."

17. Benham and Heck, *Culture and Educational Policy in Hawaiʻi*; Warner, "Kuleana"; Kaomea, "A Curriculum of Aloha?"; Kaomea, "Indigenous Studies in the Elementary Curriculum"; Kahakalau, "Kanu O Ka ʻĀina—Natives of the Land from Generations Back: A Pedagogy of Hawaiian Liberation"; Meyer, *Hoʻoulu*; Blaich, "Mai Uka a i Kai: From the Mountains to the Sea, ʻĀina-Based Education in the Ahupuaʻa of Waipā";

Beyer, "Female Seminaries in America and Hawai'i During the 19th Century"; Beyer, "Manual and Industrial Education During Hawaiian Sovereignty"; Beyer, "The Connection of Samuel Chapman Armstrong as Both Borrower and Architect of Education in Hawai'i"; Cashman, "Still Looking in the Hole with My Three-Prong Cocked: Fire the Pōhaku Cannon"; Iokepa-Guerrero, "E Nānā i ke Kumu. A Look at the Teacher"; Wright, "Education for the Nation"; Goodyear-Ka'ōpua et al., "Teaching amid U.S. Occupation: Sovereignty, Survival and Social Studies in a Native Hawaiian Charter School"; Goodyear-Ka'ōpua, *The Seeds We Planted*.

18. Warner, "The Movement to Revitalize Hawaiian Language and Culture"; Kawai'ae'a, Housman, and Alencastre, "Pūā I Ka 'Ōlelo, Ola Ka 'Ohana: Three Generations of Hawaiian Language Revitalization"; Wilson and Kamanā, "'Mai Loko Mai O Ka 'I'ini: Proceeding from a Dream': The 'Aha Pūnana Leo Connection in Hawaiian Language Revitalization"; ibid.; Wong, "He Hāwa'e Kai Nui a Kau Ma Kula"; Ho'oulumāhiehie, *Ka Mo'olelo Hiwahiwa o Kawelo*; Silva and Badis, "Early Hawaiian Newspapers and Kanaka Maoli Intellectual History, 1834–1855"; Basham, "I Mau ke Ea o ka 'Āina i ka Pono: He Puke Mele Lāhui no ka Lāhui Hawai'i"; Wong, "Kuhi Aku, Kuhi Mai, Kuhi Hewa Ē: He Mau Loina Kuhikuhi 'Ākena no ka 'Ōlelo Hawai'i"; Kamanā, "Mo'oki'ina Ho'oponopono"; Kimura, "He Kālailaina i ka Panina 'Ōlelo a ka Mānaleo Hawai'i."

19. Kame'eleihiwa, *Native Land and Foreign Desires*; Osorio, *Dismembering Lāhui: A History of the Hawaiian Nation to 1887*; Young, "Kuleana: Toward a Historiography of Hawaiian National Consciousness, 1780–2001"; Arista, "Listening to Leoiki"; Arista, "Captive Women in Paradise 1796–1826"; Cook, "Kahiki"; Beamer, "Na Wai Ka Mana?: 'Ōiwi Agency and European Imperialism in the Hawaiian Kingdom"; Iaukea, *The Queen and I*.

20. Trask, "The Birth of the Modern Hawaiian Movement: Kalama Valley, O'ahu"; Trask, *From a Native Daughter: Colonialism and Sovereignty in Hawai'i*; Silva, *Aloha Betrayed: Native Hawaiian Resistance to American Colonialism*; Kamahele, "'Īlio'ulaokalani: Defending Native Hawaiian Culture"; McGregor, *Nā Kua'āina*; Basham, "I Mau ke Ea o ka 'Āina i ka Pono: He Puke Mele Lāhui no ka Lāhui Hawai'i"; Walker, *Waves of Resistance*.

21. Andrade, *Hā'ena*; Kikiloi, "Rebirth of an Archipelago: Sustaining a Hawaiian Cultural Identity for People and Homeland"; Perkins, "Kuleana: A Genealogy of Native Tenant Rights"; Peralto, "Mauna a Wākea: Hānau Ka Mauna, the Piko of Our Ea"; Oliveira, *Ancestral Places: Understanding Kanaka Geographies*.

22. Stillman, "No ka Po'e i Aloha i ka 'Āina"; Stillman, "Of the People Who Love the Land"; Basham, "Mele Lāhui: The Importance of Pono in Hawaiian Poetry"; Basham, "Ka Lāhui Hawai'i: He Mo'olelo, He 'Āina, He Loina, a He Ea Kākou"; Lopes, "Ka Waihona A Ke Aloha"; Kanahele, *Ka Honua Ola*; ho'omanawanui, *Voices of Fire: Reweaving the Lei of Pele and Hi'iaka Literature*.

23. For instance, the scholarship and exhaustive mele research conducted by Kīhei de Silva stand out in this regard. Although his work remains largely unpublished in conventional academic outlets, a small slice of his vast intellectual production on mele Hawai'i can be found at http://www.halaumohalailima.com/HMI/Waihona_Mele .html, which includes essays on more than sixty different mele. The Papakū Makawalu researcher-practitioner team has also produced numerous resources that are available at http://www.edithkanakaolefoundation.org/shop/.

24. Kalahele, *Kalahele*; Perez-Wendt, *Uluhaimalama*; Westlake, *Westlake: Poems by Wayne Kaumuali'i Westlake (1947–1984)*; Trask, *Light in the Crevice Never Seen*; Trask, *Night Is a Sharkskin Drum*; McDougall, *The Salt-Wind: Ka Makani Pa'akai*; Revilla, *Say Throne*; Takehiro, *Honua*.

25. Kauanui, *Hawaiian Blood: Colonialism and the Politics of Sovereignty and Indigeneity*; Tengan, *Native Men Remade: Gender and Nation in Contemporary Hawai'i*; Aikau, *A Chosen People, A Promised Land: Mormonism and Race in Hawai'i*; Teves, "We're All Hawaiians Now: Kanaka Maoli Performance and the Politics of Aloha"; Arvin, "Pacifically Possessed."

26. MacKenzie, *Native Hawaiian Rights Handbook*; Mililani Trask, "Hawai'i and the United Nations"; Kanehe, "The Akaka Bill"; Kauanui, "Precarious Positions: Native Hawaiians and U.S. Federal Recognition"; Sproat and Moriwake, "Ke Kalo Pa'a O Waiāhole: Public Trust as a Tool for Environmental Advocacy"; Sai, "The American Occupation of the Hawaiian Kingdom: Beginning the Transition from Occupied to Restored State"; Vogeler, " 'For Your Freedom and Ours': The Prolonged Occupations of Hawai'i and the Baltic States"; Perkins, "Kuleana."

27. Vizenor, *Survivance*, 1.

28. Kroeber, "Why It's a Good Thing Gerald Vizenor Is Not an Indian," 25.

29. Basham, "Ka Lāhui Hawai'i," 50.

30. Ibid., 51, emphasis added.

31. Ibid., 54.

32. For further reading in Hawaiian and Indigenous studies on the relationships between place, power, and Indigenous conceptions of sovereignty, see Basso, *Wisdom Sits in Places*; Deloria, *The World We Used to Live In*; Barker, *Sovereignty Matters*; Andrade, *Hā'ena*; Beamer and Duarte, "I Palapala No Ia Aina"; Basham, "Ka Lāhui Hawai'i"; Kikiloi, "Rebirth of an Archipelago"; Bacchilega, *Legendary Hawai'i and the Politics of Place*; Moreton-Robinson, "I Still Call Australia Home"; Moreton-Robinson, *Sovereign Subjects*; Somerville, *Once Were Pacific*.

33. 'Īmaikalani Winchester, interviewed October 8, 2008, in Pahala, Hawai'i.

34. Pōmaika'i Freed, interviewed May 1, 2011, in Waimānalo, Hawai'i.

35. Warrior, *Tribal Secrets*, 98.

36. Ibid., 91.

37. Alfred, *Wasáse*; Simpson, *Dancing on Our Turtle's Back*.

38. Simpson, *Dancing on Our Turtle's Back*, 17–18.

39. Beniamina, "Tēnā: A Learning Lifestyle," 16.

40. Blaich, "Mai Uka a i Kai," 64.

41. Ibid., 63–64.

42. Goodyear-Ka'ōpua et al., "Teaching amid U.S. Occupation"; "Rebuilding the 'Auwai: Connecting Ecology, Economy and Education in Hawaiian Schools"; *The Seeds We Planted*.

43. Smith, *Decolonizing Methodologies: Research and Indigenous Peoples*.

44. Alfred, "Warrior Scholarship: Seeing the University as a Ground of Contention," 95.

45. Corntassel, "Toward Sustainable Self-Determination: Rethinking the Contemporary Indigenous-Rights Discourse."

46. Russell Bishop proposes a Kaupapa Māori approach to operationalizing similar ethics, outlining a reciprocal process that considers the following aspects or stages of

research: initiation, benefits, representation, legitimation, and accountability. See Bishop, "Freeing Ourselves from Neocolonial Domination in Research: A Kaupapa Māori Approach to Creating Knowledge."

47. Ka'eo offered this analysis during a debate with Kana'iolowalu Native Hawaiian Roll Commissioner, Māhealani Wendt, at the University of Hawai'i, Maui College, on January 17, 2014.

48. Snow, "Beyond the Binary," 29.

BIBLIOGRAPHY

Aikau, Hokulani. *A Chosen People, A Promised Land: Mormonism and Race in Hawai'i.* Minneapolis: University of Minnesota Press, 2012.

Alfred, Taiaiake. "Warrior Scholarship: Seeing the University as a Ground of Contention." In *Indigenizing the Academy: Transforming Scholarship and Empowering Communities,* 88–99. Lincoln: Bison Books, 2004.

———. *Wasáse: Indigenous Pathways of Action and Freedom.* Toronto: Broadview Press, 2005.

Andrade, Carlos. *Hā'ena: Through the Eyes of the Ancestors.* Honolulu: University of Hawai'i Press, 2008.

Andrade, Naleen N., Earl S. Hishinuma, John F. McDermott, Ronald C. Johnson, Deborah A. Goebert, George K. Makini, Linda B. Nahulu, et al. "The National Center on Indigenous Hawaiian Behavioral Health Study of Prevalence of Psychiatric Disorders in Native Hawaiian Adolescents." *Journal of the American Academy of Child and Adolescent Psychiatry* 45, no. 1 (2007): 26–36.

Arista, Noelani. "Captive Women in Paradise 1796–1826: The 'Kapu' on Prostitution in Hawaiian Historical Legal Context." *American Indian Culture and Research Journal* 35, no. 4 (2012): 39–55.

———. "Listening to Leoiki: Engaging Sources in Hawaiian History." *Biography* 32, no. 1 (2009): 66–73.

Arvin, Maile Renee. "Pacifically Possessed: Scientific Production and Native Hawaiian Critique of the 'Almost White' Polynesian Race." PhD diss., University of California at San Diego, 2013.

Bacchilega, Cristina. *Legendary Hawai'i and the Politics of Place: Tradition, Translation, and Tourism.* Philadelphia: University of Pennsylvania Press, 2007.

Barker, Joanne, ed. *Sovereignty Matters: Locations of Contestation and Possibility in Indigenous Struggles for Self-Determination.* Lincoln: University of Nebraska Press, 2005.

Basham, Leilani. "I Mau ke Ea o ka 'Āina i ka Pono: He Puke Mele Lāhui no ka Lāhui Hawai'i." PhD diss., University of Hawai'i at Mānoa, 2007.

———. "Ka Lāhui Hawai'i: He Mo'olelo, He 'Āina, He Loina, a He Ea Kākou." *Hūlili: Multidisciplinary Research on Hawaiian Well-Being* 6 (2010): 37–72.

———. "Mele Lāhui: The Importance of Pono in Hawaiian Poetry." *Te Kaharoa* 1 (2008): 152–164.

Basso, Keith H. *Wisdom Sits in Places: Landscape and Language Among the Western Apache.* Albuquerque: University of New Mexico Press, 1996.

Beamer, B. Kamanamaikalani. "Na Wai Ka Mana? 'Ōiwi Agency and European Imperialism in the Hawaiian Kingdom." PhD diss., University of Hawai'i, 2008.

Beamer, B. Kamanamaikalani, and T. Kaeo Duarte. "I Palapala No Ia Aina—Documenting the Hawaiian Kingdom, A Colonial Venture?" *Journal of Historical Geography* 35 (2009): 66–86.

Benham, Maenette K. P., and Ronald H. Heck. *Culture and Educational Policy in Hawai'i: The Silencing of Native Voices.* Sociocultural, Political, and Historical Studies in Education. Mahwah, NJ: Lawrence Erlbaum Associates, 1998.

Beniamina, Jean Ilei Keale. "Tēnā: A Learning Lifestyle." *Hūlili: Multidisciplinary Research on Hawaiian Well-Being* 6 (2010): 9–23.

Beyer, Carl Kalani. "The Connection of Samuel Chapman Armstrong as Both Borrower and Architect of Education in Hawai'i." *History of Education Quarterly* 47, no. 1 (2007): 23–48.

———. "Female Seminaries in America and Hawaii During the 19th Century." *Hawaiian Journal of History* 37 (2003): 91–118.

———. "Manual and Industrial Education During Hawaiian Sovereignty: Curriculum in the Transculturation of Hawai'i." PhD diss., University of Illinois at Chicago, 2004.

Bishop, Russell. "Freeing Ourselves from Neocolonial Domination in Research: A Kaupapa Māori Approach to Creating Knowledge." In *The Landscape of Qualitative Research,* 3rd edition, 109–138. Thousand Oaks, CA: Sage, 2008.

Blaich, Mehana. "Mai Uka a i Kai: From the Mountains to the Sea, 'Āina-Based Education in the Ahupua'a of Waipā." Master's thesis in education, University of Hawai'i at Mānoa, 2003.

Carpenter, Dee-Ann L., Martina L. Kamaka, and C. Malina Kaulukukui. "An Innovative Approach to Developing a Cultural Competency Curriculum: Efforts at the John A. Burns School of Medicine, Department of Native Hawaiian Health." *Hawaii Medical Journal* 70, no. 11 Suppl. 2 (2011): 15–19.

Cashman, Kimo. "Still Looking in the Hole with My Three-Prong Cocked: Fire the Pōhaku Cannon." *AlterNative: An International Journal of Indigenous Peoples* 5, no. 2 (2009): 28–45.

Cook, Kealani R. "Kahiki: Native Hawaiian Relationships with Other Pacific Islanders, 1850–1915." PhD diss., University of Michigan, 2011.

Corntassel, Jeff. "Toward Sustainable Self-Determination: Rethinking the Contemporary Indigenous-Rights Discourse." *Alternatives: Global, Local, Political* 33 (2008): 105–132.

Crabbe, Kamana'opono M. "Initial Psychometric Validation of He 'Ana Mana'o O Nā Mo'omeheu Hawai'i: A Hawaiian Ethnocultural Inventory (HEI) of Cultural Practices." PhD diss., University of Hawai'i at Mānoa, 2002.

Deloria, Vine, Jr. *The World We Used to Live In: Remembering the Powers of the Medicine Men.* Golden, CO: Fulcrum Publishing, 2006.

Goodyear-Ka'ōpua, Noelani. "Rebuilding the 'Auwai: Connecting Ecology, Economy and Education in Hawaiian Schools." *AlterNative: An International Journal of Indigenous Peoples* 5, no. 2 (2009): 46–77.

————. *The Seeds We Planted: Portraits of a Native Hawaiian Charter School*. Minneapolis: University of Minnesota Press, 2013.

Goodyear-Ka'ōpua, Noelani, Willy Kauai, Kaleilehua Maioho, and 'Īmaikalani Winchester. "Teaching amid U.S. Occupation: Sovereignty, Survival and Social Studies in a Native Hawaiian Charter School." *Hūlili: Multidisciplinary Research on Hawaiian Well-Being* 5 (2008): 155–201.

Hall, Dana Naone, ed. *Mālama: Hawaiian Land and Water*. Honolulu: Bamboo Ridge Press, 1985.

Harden, M. J. *Voices of Wisdom: Hawaiian Elders Speak*. Kula: Aka Press, 1999.

Hawaiian Studies Task Force, University of Hawai'i. *Ka'ū, University of Hawai'i Hawaiian Studies Task Force Report*. Honolulu: University of Hawai'i, 1986.

Holt, John Dominis. *On Being Hawaiian*. Honolulu: Ku Paa Publishing, 1995 (originally published in 1964).

ho'omanawanui, ku'ualoha. *Voices of Fire: Reweaving the Lei of Pele and Hi'iaka Literature*. Minneapolis: University of Minnesota Press, 2014.

Ho'oulumāhiehie. *Ka Mo'olelo Hiwahiwa o Kawelo*. Honolulu: Bishop Museum Press, 2008.

Iaukea, Sydney L. *The Queen and I: A Story of Dispossessions and Reconnections in Hawai'i*. Berkeley: University of California Press, 2011.

Iokepa-Guerrero, B. Noelani. "E Nānā i ke Kumu. A Look at the Teacher: A Study of the Essential Competencies of a Pūnana Leo Teacher." EdD diss., University of Southern California, 2004.

Kahakalau, Kū. "Kanu O Ka 'Āina—Natives of the Land from Generations Back: A Pedagogy of Hawaiian Liberation." PhD diss., Union Institute, 2003.

Kaholokula, Joseph Keawe'aimoku, Marcus K. Iwane, and Andrea H. Nacapoy. "Effects of Perceived Racism and Acculturation on Hypertension in Native Hawaiians." *Hawaii Medical Journal* 69, no. 5 Suppl. 2 (2010): 11–15.

Kaholokula, Joseph Keawe'aimoku, Claire K. M. Townsend, Arlene Ige, Ka'imi A. Sinclair, Marjorie K. Mau, Anne Leake, Donna-Marie Palakiko, Sheryl R. Yoshimura, Puni Kekauoha, and Claire Hughes. "Sociodemographic, Behavioral, and Biological Variables Related to Weight Loss in Native Hawaiians and Other Pacific Islanders." *Obesity* 21, no. 3 (2013): 196–203.

Ka'imikaua, John, Nālani Minton, and Nā Maka o ka 'Āina. *A Mau A Mau: To Continue Forever*. Honolulu: Nā Maka o ka 'Āina, 2000.

Kalahele, Imaikalani. *Kalahele: Poetry and Art*. Honolulu: Kalamaku Press, 2002.

Kamahele, Momiala. "'Īlio'ulaokalani: Defending Native Hawaiian Culture." In *Asian Settler Colonialism: From Local Governance to the Habits of Everyday Life in Hawai'i*, 76–98. Honolulu: University of Hawai'i Press, 2008.

Kamanā, Kauanoe P. W. "Mo'oki'ina Ho'oponopono: Ke Ō o ka 'Ike Ku'una Hawai'i ma ke Kula 'O Nāwahīokalani'ōpu'u." PhD diss., University of Hawai'i at Hilo, 2010.

Kame'eleihiwa, Lilikalā. *Native Land and Foreign Desires: Pehea La E Pono Ai?* Honolulu: Bishop Museum Press, 1992.

Kanahele, Pualani Kanaka'ole. *Ka Honua Ola: 'Eli'eli Kau Mai.* Honolulu: Kamehameha Publishing, 2011.

Kanehe, Le'a Malia. "The Akaka Bill: The Native Hawaiians' Race for Federal Recognition." *University of Hawai'i Law Review* 23, no. 2 (2001): 857–906.

Kaomea, Julie. "A Curriculum of Aloha? Colonialism and Tourism in Hawai'i's Elementary Textbooks." *Curriculum Inquiry* 30, no. 3 (Fall 2000): 319–344.

———. "Indigenous Studies in the Elementary Curriculum: A Cautionary Hawaiian Example." *Anthropology and Education Quarterly* 36, no. 1 (2005): 24–42, doi:10.1525/aeq.2005.36.1.024.

Ka'ōpua, Lana. "Developing a Culturally Responsive Breast Cancer Screening Promotion with Native Hawaiian Women in Churches." *Health and Social Work* 33, no. 3 (2008): 169–177.

Ka'ōpua, Lana Sue, Kathryn L. Braun, Colette V. Browne, Noreen Mokuau, and Chaibin Park. "Why Are Native Hawaiians Underrepresented in Hawai'i's Older Adult Population? Exploring Social and Behavioral Factors of Longevity." *Journal of Aging Research* (2011), doi:701232.

Ka'ōpua, Lana Sue I., and Charles W. Mueller. "Treatment Adherence Among Native Hawaiians Living with HIV." *Social Work* 49, no. 1 (2005): 55–63.

Kaōpua, Lana Sue I., Amanda Petteruti, R. Nalani Takushi, James H. Spencer, Soon H. Park, Tressa P. Diaz, Shalia K. Kamakele, and Kaipo C. Kukahiko. "The Lived Experience of Native Hawaiians Exiting Prison and Reentering the Community: How Do You Really Decriminalize Someone Who's Consistently Being Called a Criminal?" *Journal of Forensic Social Work* 2, no. 2–3 (2012): 141–161.

Kauanui, J. Kehaulani. *Hawaiian Blood: Colonialism and the Politics of Sovereignty and Indigeneity.* Durham: Duke University Press, 2008.

———. "Precarious Positions: Native Hawaiians and U.S. Federal Recognition." *Contemporary Pacific* 17, no. 1 (2005): 1–27.

Kawai'ae'a, Keiki K. C., Alohalani K. Housman, and Makalapua Alencastre. "Pūā I Ka 'Ōlelo, Ola Ka 'Ohana: Three Generations of Hawaiian Language Revitalization." *Hūlili: Multidisciplinary Research on Hawaiian Well-Being* 4, no. 1 (2007): 183–237.

Kikiloi, Kekuewa. "Rebirth of an Archipelago: Sustaining a Hawaiian Cultural Identity for People and Homeland." *Hūlili: Multidisciplinary Research on Hawaiian Well-Being* 6 (2010): 73–115.

Kimura, Larry Lindsey. "He Kālailaina i ka Panina 'Ōlelo a ka Mānaleo Hawai'i: Ka Ho'ohālikelike 'ana i ka 'Ōlelo Mānaleo a nā Hanauna 'Elua, 'o ka 'Ōlelo Kūmau a ka Makua a me ka 'Ōlelo Kūpaka a ke Keiki." PhD diss., University of Hawai'i at Hilo, 2012.

Kroeber, Karl. "Why It's a Good Thing Gerald Vizenor Is Not an Indian." In *Survivance: Narratives of Native Presence*, 25–38. Lincoln: University of Nebraska Press, 2008.

Lopes, Robert Keawe. "Ka Waihona A Ke Aloha: Ka Papahana Ho'oheno Mele: An Interactive Resource Center for the Promotion, Preservation and Perpetuation of Mele and Mele Practitioners." PhD diss., University of Hawai'i at Mānoa, 2010.

MacKenzie, Melody Kapilialoha. *Native Hawaiian Rights Handbook*. Honolulu: Native Hawaiian Legal Corporation, 1991.

Makini, George K., Earl S. Hishinuma, S. Peter Kim, Barry S. Carlton, Robin H. Miyamoto, Linda B. Nahulu, Ronald C. Johnson, Naleen N. Andrade, Stephanie T. Nishimura, and 'Iwalani R. N. Else. "Risk and Protective Factors Related to Native Hawaiian Adolescent Alcohol Use." *Alcohol and Alcoholism* 36, no. 3 (2001): 235–242.

McDougall, Brandy Nālani. *The Salt-Wind: Ka Makani Pa'akai*. Honolulu: Kuleana 'Ōiwi Press, 2008.

McGregor, Davianna. *Nā Kua'āina: Living Hawaiian Culture*. Honolulu: University of Hawai'i Press, 2007.

Meyer, Manulani Aluli. *Ho'oulu: Our Time of Becoming: Collected Early Writings of Manulani Meyer*. Honolulu: 'Ai Pōhaku Press, 2003.

Mokuau, Noreen. "Culturally Based Solutions to Preserve the Health of Native Hawaiians." *Journal of Ethnic and Cultural Diversity in Social Work* 20, no. 2 (2011): 98–113.

Moreton-Robinson, Aileen M. "I Still Call Australia Home: Indigenous Belonging and Place in a White Postcolonising Society." In *Uprootings/Regroundings: Questions of Home and Migration*, edited by Sarah Ahmed, 23–40. Berg Publishing, 2003.

———, ed. *Sovereign Subjects: Indigenous Sovereignty Matters*. Crows Nest, New South Wales: Allen & Unwin, 2008.

Nahulu, Linda B., Naleen N. Andrade, George K. Makini, Noelle Y. C. Yuen, John F. McDermott, George P. Danko, Ronald C. Johnson, and Jane A. Waldron. "Psychosocial Risk and Protective Influences in Hawaiian Adolescent Psychopathology." *Cultural Diversity and Mental Health* 2, no. 2 (1996): 107–114.

Native Hawaiian Health Research Consortium. Mental Health Task Force. *E Ola Mau: Native Hawaiian Health Needs Study*. Honolulu: Native Hawaiian Health Research Consortium, Alu Like, Inc., 1985.

Niheu, Kalamaoka'aina, Laurel Mei Turbin, and Seiji Yamada. "The Impact of the Military Presence in Hawai'i on the Health of Nā Kānaka Maoli." *Pacific Health Dialog* 14, no. 1 (2007): 205–212.

Oliveira, Katrina-Ann R. Kapā'anaokalāokeola Nākoa. *Ancestral Places: Understanding Kanaka Geographies*. Corvallis: Oregon State University Press, 2014.

Osorio, Jonathan Kamakawiwo'ole. *Dismembering Lāhui: A History of the Hawaiian Nation to 1887*. Honolulu: University of Hawai'i Press, 2002.

———. "'What Kine Hawaiian Are You?' A Mo'olelo About Nationhood, Race, History, and the Contemporary Sovereignty Movement in Hawai'i." *Contemporary Pacific* 13, no. 2 (2001): 359–379.

Peralto, Leon No'eau. "Mauna a Wākea: Hānau Ka Mauna, the Piko of Our Ea." In *A Nation Rising: Hawaiian Movements for Life, Land and Sovereignty*. Durham: Duke University Press, 2014.

Perez-Wendt, Māhealani. *Uluhaimalama*. Honolulu: Kuleana 'Ōiwi Press, 2007.

Perkins, 'Umi. "Kuleana: A Genealogy of Native Tenant Rights." PhD diss., University of Hawai'i at Mānoa, 2013.

Revilla, No'u. *Say Throne: Poems*. Kāne'ohe: Tinfish Press, 2011.

Sai, David Keanu. "The American Occupation of the Hawaiian Kingdom: Beginning the Transition from Occupied to Restored State." PhD diss., University of Hawai'i at Mānoa, 2008.

Silva, Noenoe K. *Aloha Betrayed: Native Hawaiian Resistance to American Colonialism*. Durham: Duke University Press, 2004.

Silva, Noenoe K., and Iokepa Badis. "Early Hawaiian Newspapers and Kanaka Maoli Intellectual History, 1834–1855." *Hawaiian Journal of History* 42 (2008): 105–134.

Simpson, Leanne. *Dancing on Our Turtle's Back: Stories of Nishnaabeg Re-creation, Resurgence and a New Emergence*. Winnipeg: Arbeiter Ring Publishing, 2011.

Smith, Linda Tuhiwai. *Decolonizing Methodologies: Research and Indigenous Peoples*. London: Zed Books, 1999.

Snow, Jad. "Beyond the Binary: Portraits of Gender and Sexual Identities in the Hawaiian Community." *Mana: The Hawaiian Magazine*, March 2014.

Somerville, Alice Te Punga. *Once Were Pacific: Maori Connections to Oceania*. Minneapolis: University of Minnesota Press, 2012.

Sproat, D. Kapua'ala, and Isaac Moriwake. "Ke Kalo Pa'a O Waiāhole: Public Trust as a Tool for Environmental Advocacy." In *Creative Common Law Strategies for Protecting the Environment*, 247–284. Washington, DC: Environmental Law Institute, 2007.

Stillman, Amy Kuuleialoha. "No ka Po'e i Aloha i ka 'Āina: Poetics of the Hula Ku'i." Honolulu: A. K. Stillman, 1994.

———. "Of the People Who Love the Land: Vernacular History in the Poetry of Modern Hawaiian Hula." *Amerasia Journal* 28, no. 3 (2002): 85–108.

Takehiro, Sage U'ilani. *Honua: A Collection of Poetry*. Honolulu: Kahuaomānoa Press, 2007.

Tengan, Ty P. Kawika. *Native Men Remade: Gender and Nation in Contemporary Hawai'i*. Durham: Duke University Press, 2008.

Teves, Stephanie Nohelani. "We're All Hawaiians Now: Kanaka Maoli Performance and the Politics of Aloha." PhD diss., University of Michigan, 2012.

Trask, Haunani-Kay. "The Birth of the Modern Hawaiian Movement: Kalama Valley, O'ahu." *Hawaiian Journal of History* 21 (1987): 126–153.

———. *From a Native Daughter: Colonialism and Sovereignty in Hawai'i*. Revised edition. Honolulu: University of Hawai'i Press, 1999.

———. *Light in the Crevice Never Seen*. Revised edition. Corvallis, OR: Calyx Books, 1999.

———. *Night Is a Sharkskin Drum*. Honolulu: University of Hawai'i Press, 2002.

Trask, Mililani. "Hawai'i and the United Nations." In *Asian Settler Colonialism: From Local Governance to the Habits of Everyday Life in Hawai'i*, 67–70. Honolulu: University of Hawai'i Press, 2008.

Vizenor, Gerald, ed. *Survivance: Narratives of Native Presence*. Lincoln: University of Nebraska Press, 2008.

Vogeler, Stephen Kuhio. "'For Your Freedom and Ours': The Prolonged Occupations of Hawai'i and the Baltic States." PhD diss., University of Hawai'i at Mānoa, 2009.

Walker, Isaiah Helekunihi. *Waves of Resistance: Surfing and History in Twentieth-Century Hawai'i.* Honolulu: University of Hawai'i Press, 2011.

Warner, Sam L. No'eau. "Kuleana: The Right, Responsibility, and Authority of Indigenous Peoples to Speak and Make Decisions for Themselves in Language and Cultural Revitalization." *Anthropology and Education Quarterly* 30, no. 1 (1999): 68–93, doi:10.1525/aeq.1999.30.1.68.

———. "The Movement to Revitalize Hawaiian Language and Culture." In *The Green Book of Language Revitalization in Practice*, 133–146. San Diego: Academic Press, 2001.

Warrior, Robert Allen. *Tribal Secrets: Recovering American Indian Intellectual Traditions.* Minneapolis: University of Minnesota Press, 1995.

Westlake, Wayne. *Westlake: Poems by Wayne Kaumuali'i Westlake (1947–1984).* Honolulu: University of Hawai'i Press, 2009.

Wilson, William H., and Kauanoe Kamanā. "'Mai Loko Mai O Ka 'I'ini: Proceeding from a Dream': The 'Aha Pūnana Leo Connection in Hawaiian Language Revitalization." In *The Green Book of Language Revitalization in Practice*, 147–176. San Diego: Academic Press, 2001.

Wong, K. Laiana. "He Hāwa'e Kai Nui a Kau Ma Kula." *Educational Perspectives* 37, no. 1 (2004): 31–39.

———. "Kuhi Aku, Kuhi Mai, Kuhi Hewa Ē: He Mau Loina Kuhikuhi 'Ākena no ka 'Ōlelo Hawai'i." PhD diss., University of Hawai'i at Mānoa, 2006.

Wright, Erin Kahunawaika'ala. "'Education for the Nation': Forging Indigenous Hawaiian Identity in Higher Education." PhD diss., University of California at Los Angeles, 2003.

Young, Kanalu. "Kuleana: Toward a Historiography of Hawaiian National Consciousness, 1780–2001." *Hawaiian Journal of Law and Politics* 2 (2006): 1–33.

Ua Noho Au A Kupa I Ke Alo

R. Keawe Lopes Jr.

Ua noho au a kupa i ke alo
A kama'āina lā i ka leo
Ka hi'ona a ka mana'o lā i laila
I 'ane'i ka waihona a ke aloha

"Kaniakapupu Song," more popularly known today as "Ua Noho Au A Kupa I Ke Alo," was composed by "Figg,"[1] a pseudonym for King David Kalākaua, who ruled the kingdom of Hawai'i from 1874 to 1891. Most credit the song's popularity to its beautiful melody line and to the unforgettable musicians who have recorded and thus preserved it throughout the years. The lyrics are a timeless depiction of the benefits one can receive through the experience of love. On a personal level, they detail the importance of investing in a relationship characterized by an allegiance to commitment, thereby obliging oneself to its ongoing success. The lyrics further lend themselves to interpretations that provide insight to a Hawaiian approach to conducting research while acquiring knowledge and information from kūpuna (elders), community participants, practitioners, and teachers. They describe attitudes that I consider essential to the methodology by which research in general should be conducted.

With the increase in the number of indigenous people conducting research in our native communities, many have taken on a more concerted effort to carefully consider our values and beliefs as relevant methodological approaches. Renowned indigenous Māori scholar Linda Tuhiwai Smith (1999), author of *Decolonizing Methodologies*, explains that the methodology and the methods by which data are collected are the most important part of any research study and that ultimately "processes are expected to be respectful, to enable people to heal and to educate" (p. 128). Smith recommends that we make a conscious effort to develop the tools that we need to conduct our own research. Smith further explains that we, as the indigenous, have the opportunity through research to present "our position in history . . . tell our own stories, write our own versions, in our own ways, for our own purposes" (p. 28).

Jelena Porsanger (2004), reflecting on Smith's book, explains that "the main aim of indigenous methodologies is to ensure that research on indigenous issues can be carried out in a more respectful, ethical, correct, sympathetic, useful and beneficial fashion, seen from the point of view of indigenous peoples" (p. 108). Porsanger informs us that it is not enough for research conducted about our people to be respectful and ethical, but that it should also improve, bring to light, and show the perspective of the indigenous, further supporting our people's efforts "to be independent; not only legally, politically or economically, but first and foremost intellectually" (p. 117).

Margaret Maaka (2003), in her contribution to *Educational Perspectives*,[2] offers a hopeful scenario for budding indigenous researchers like myself and provides the necessary encouragement for us to include our own beliefs in creating our methodologies. She writes, "Given the multitude of questions to which indigenous peoples are seeking answers, it is very clear that one single approach will not suffice. We need multiple methodologies that are grounded in our indigenous traditions" (p. 6).

In reflecting on my personal journey with research inquiry, I am aware that my beliefs as a Hawaiian father, researcher, educator, and mele (Hawaiian chant, song, music) and hula (Hawaiian traditional dance) practitioner are influenced by how I was raised by my 'ohana (family) and by the mele and hula communities. My upbringing has guided the decisions I have made and provided me valuable experiences to which I constantly refer for direction.

In this chapter, I highlight terms from King Kalākaua's mele that embody important mannerisms that I consider necessary to investing in lasting relationships with kūpuna, community participants, practitioners, and teachers when conducting research. I refer to them as "mentors," those who are generally more seasoned in age and responsible for providing counsel, encouragement, support, advice, and correction. I also share the ingenuity of King Kalākaua's mele in informing us that incorporating certain mannerisms into relationship building is the necessary protocol to recognizing "ka hi'ona a ka mana'o" (the physical manifestation of intentions) and experiencing what he refers to as "ka waihona a ke aloha" (the repository of aloha).

"Ua noho au a kupa i ke alo / A kama'āina lā i ka leo"

In conducting research within our communities, building relationships with mentors is vital to acquiring information. The quality of knowledge shared and gained is dependent on the depth of the relationship. The first two lines of the mele state "ua noho au a kupa i ke alo, a kama'āina lā i ka leo," which means, "I have sat, inhabited, and tarried here until I have become accustomed to you in your presence and familiar with your voice." The words *"noho," "kupa,"* and *"kama'āina"* highlight appropriate mannerisms one may consider when building relationships. The varied contexts within which these terms are used provide valuable information that further supports why these considerations are valid.

Noho: Commitment to Humility and Respect

Pukui and Elbert (1986) explain that the term "noho" means "to live, reside, inhabit, occupy (as land), dwell, stay, tarry, marry, sit" and has the connotation of establishing oneself in a certain place or with a particular person (p. 268). "Noho" then is reflective of one who has made a commitment to establish a relationship with a place or a person. Historically, to noho was to express humbleness and respect, and this behavior was seen even among the *aliʻi* (chiefs). King Kamehameha I needed to crawl to approach his most sacred of wives, Keōpūolani: "She possessed a kapu moe, which meant that those who were in her presence had to prostrate themselves, face down, for it was forbidden to look at her" (Moʻokini 1998, p. 7). John Papa ʻĪʻī, renowned Hawaiian historian of the nineteenth century, explains the importance of being familiar with the "kapu noho" when encountering an aliʻi while traveling. It was important to know the appropriate time to sit when the call to noho was heard, lest you lose your life (1963, p. 28):

> It was the only way for all to safeguard themselves while passing along the road. If a person was wearing a lei on neck or head, he must remove it and throw it away when the cry to squat down (*noho*) was heard, otherwise the penalty would be death.

Equally as important was the presentation of mele and lei to an aliʻi. As part of my mele and hula training with Kimo Alama Keaulana,[3] I learned that the presentation of mele and lei to those of the aliʻi class was done primarily as a noho. When I learned the mele lei[4] "Kaʻiulani," Uncle Kimo explained the following:

> When a lei was presented to an *aliʻi*, it was first shown. . . . If the *aliʻi* wished to wear it, the attendant would then place the lei around the *aliʻi* neck, careful that his or her hands never go over the head of the *aliʻi*. After the lei was presented, the mele lei then followed. If it was done with an accompanying hula, it was usually done as a *hula noho, a seated dance*, at the foot of the beloved chief or chiefess.

If we think of our mentors as aliʻi who oversee the well-being of our progress, then the explanation that Uncle Kimo provides informs us that there are protocols to observe in the care of this affiliation. The first is to noho. This requires us to commit to the establishment of the relationship and to maintain it with humility and respect. It encourages us to be always mindful of our mentors, so that we maintain the relationship with fortitude and devotion.

Kupa: Investment of Patience and Sacrifice

King Kalākaua's mele further informs us that it is important to invest in the relationship by committing to it until "kupa." To better understand the meaning of this term, Mrs. Sarah Keli'ilōlena Nākoa, one of Hawai'i's beloved kūpuna, provided us a wonderful example of its usage in the opening passage of the mo'olelo (historical account) titled *Honokawailani*. It is the first of seven personal mo'olelo that appear in her book, *Lei Momi O 'Ewa*. Mrs. Nākoa writes,

> He kupa kēia wahi mea kākau no kēlā 'āina 'o 'Ewa, i 'ōlelo 'ia, no laila mai kā Ka Maka 'Ewa'ewa. Akā hū a'ela ko'u aloha no nā maka-maka i hala i ho'ālo iki 'ole ko lākou mau maka i kahi 'ē ke hiki mai ka malihini, a i hō'ike i ke ākea o ko lākou mau pu'uwai hāmama i piha palena 'ole ho'i i ke aloha. (Nākoa, Wilson, Merritt, and 'Ahahui Olelo Hawaii 1979, p. 6)

> This dear author is a "kupa," a native belonging to this land known as 'Ewa, from where it has been said that this term regarding "indifferent eyes" or people with such characteristics derives. However, my love has overflowed for dear friends who have since passed, whose eyes never shunned the arrival of a stranger, who showed the vastness of their open hearts filled boundlessly with love. (Translation provided by the author)

In this opening passage, Mrs. Nākoa explains first and foremost that she is a kupa of the district of 'Ewa. She describes her familiarity with the elders of her hometown, who unselfishly showed their generosity to many, even those with whom they were not familiar. Mrs. Nākoa uses this opening passage to refute the refrain of Hi'iaka, the beloved younger sister of the fire goddess Pele, who described the people of O'ahu as "maka 'ewa'ewa" (indifferent eyes) for not coming to her aid in mending a canoe for her journey to Kaua'i (Pukui and Elbert 1986, p. 42). The mo'olelo suggests that Mrs. Nākoa was not only a longtime resident of 'Ewa and was familiar with the people who lived there but also that she was aware of this negative reference about her hometown, which came from a more ancient past. Therefore, when looking at Mrs. Nākoa's usage of the term "kupa" we can conclude that, to identify oneself as a kupa, one must be a longtime resident, possessing personal and lasting relationships with the people and the mo'olelo of that place, both ancient and modern.

The term "kupa" further implies that the commitment to our mentors is a lifelong investment. In my experience of learning mele and hula with Uncle Kimo, there were days when I would be with him for hours. I would leave

Halelani, his Mānoa home, sometimes at dawn with just enough time to return to my house, shower, and prepare for my first UH class at 7:30 a.m. Often the real in-depth learning of contextual information related to mele and hula began after our regular class sessions were done. Sometimes it continued for hours in the parking lot. In such moments exciting moʻolelo of mele and hula exponents of the past were shared. This experience taught me that, to persevere in a lasting relationship with our mentors, we must be truly passionate and extremely patient. These qualities will enable us to endure both good times—days of great epiphany and hours of captivating conversations—and bad. True patience considers the cost and makes the necessary sacrifices to always be ready and available for learning, no matter the time or place.

Kamaʻāina: Connection Bound by Allegiance

Similar to kupa, the term "kamaʻāina" reinforces the importance of investment; moreover, it implies the idea of being embraced genealogically. Kamaʻāina is made up of two words: "kama" and "ʻāina." The term "kama" means "descendant" or "child." It also means to be bound or tied to something. The term "ʻāina" means "land." "Kamaʻāina" therefore are genealogical descendants of the land, bound and secured to it and who benefit from a reciprocal relationship with her. As a result, kamaʻāina care for the well-being of the land while maintaining a mutual relationship with her.

This type of reciprocation is seen in student-mentor relationships as well. The relationship Uncle Kimo had with his kumu hula, the late Adeline Nani Maunupau Lee,[5] was established and maintained with humbleness and respect until her passing. I remember Uncle Kimo telling me a story of how the Kalihi-Pālama Culture and Arts Society asked him to be featured in a book titled *Nānā i Nā Loea Hula*, which documented the remaining hula masters living at the time. Uncle Kimo refused the invitation, deferring the opportunity to his kumu hula, who was not initially invited. Fortunately, Aunty Adeline was featured in the inaugural printing of this book; an account of her work with hula was included among many of the other great hula masters. What is important to note is that, in the opening sentence of Aunty Adeline's account, she wrote that she treasured her relationship with Uncle Kimo: "The best thing about my life today is that I am able to pass on my knowledge to an alakaʻi" (Uemoto et al. 1984, p. 117). The alakaʻi is the lead pupil in a hālau (hula school), and this particular alakaʻi was Uncle Kimo.

In my experience, many students are eager to leave the tutelage of their mentors for the spotlight. Uncle Kimo was not that kind of student. His character was reflective of one learned in older mannerisms. Humble, respectful, and possessing the disposition of a devoted kamaʻāina, he was committed to this relationship with Aunty Adeline until the very end. At Aunty Adeline's passing, which occurred eight years after that book was published, the feelings she expressed about Uncle Kimo were validated by her gift of her vast collection of mele and hula to his care. Many people since, including my 'ohana and my students at the university and in our hālau, have benefited from Uncle Kimo's faithful stewardship of what Aunty Adeline entrusted to him.

Alo: Trust and Entrusted Through Contact

Students who are patient and willing to make the sacrifices necessary to invest in a lasting relationship with a mentor are blessed with sharing a variety of memorable moments. However, I have taught students who were too preoccupied and missed out on great learning opportunities because they were unavailable. These types of students are preconditioned to think that learning only occurs within the scheduled class time, as is the case with most educational institutions. However, dedicated and serious mentors deem these types of students to be too distracted to make the needed commitment to acquire and retain knowledge.

Uncle Kimo would often say, "Our cultural knowledge is not a buffet." In other words, we cannot just take whatever we want, whenever, and then leave. The quality and length of time spent with a mentor reflect whether or not you have a vested interest in gaining that knowledge. Kalākaua's mele informs us that it is not enough to spend time with someone, but that quality investment requires keen attention to the "alo" and "leo."

The "alo" is the front, face, or presence of a person (Pukui 1983, p. 21). It tells us where our attention is directed and where our interests lie. It is my belief that if we turn our alo toward our mentors and keep our interest faced in their direction, they will know that we truly have a vested interest in gaining knowledge and value the relationship we have with them. When our mentors decide to turn their attention to us, it is then that we realize that we are just as important to them. It is when our alo and the alo of our mentors are attentive to each other that the most effective teaching and learning opportunities occur. This type of experience is known as "he alo a he alo" or "face to face" (Pukui 1983, p. 21).

He alo a he alo is the way in which relationships are built and the way knowledge is transmitted, communicated, and received. There is no clearer way to be in a relationship or in communion with another person than he alo a he alo. Pukui and Elbert (1986) provide several examples that help explain its significance. A favorite grandchild who is well cared for by his or her grandparents is referred to as "ka mo'opuna i ke alo," or the grandchild in the front (p. 21). A wife is referred to as a "pilialo" or one who is related to or connected with the front (p. 21). The "aloali'i" is a reference to the royal court, which comprised the retinue of nobles, primarily made up of the royal family, and who were considered the most trustworthy (p. 21).

Mrs. Kākaʻe Kaleiheana, a native speaker and featured guest on the Hawaiian language radio show "Ka Leo Hawaiʻi," provided a personal account of being in contact with our aliʻi; she noted that she was blessed to see and meet some of them, including Queen Liliʻuokalani, during her lifetime. She also shared that she was especially close to Prince Kūhiō. As a result, Kaleiheana was familiar with the mannerisms that were required to serve in the alo of an aliʻi. Kaleiheana explained that one must move with great caution and with the utmost reverence in the presence of the aliʻi. She referred to this behavior as being extremely ʻihiʻihi (reverent, holy):

> Auē! He ʻihiʻihi maoli nō . . . no ka mea, ke haki nō ʻoe i nā kānāwai, pilikia nō kou ma laila. Kūpono wale nō na ka poʻe maikaʻi ka noʻonoʻo, haʻahaʻa kou ʻano hiki ai iā ʻoe ke mālama i nā loina me nā lula o ke ʻano o ka noho ʻana i mua o ke aloaliʻi. ʻAʻole me ka haʻakei o kou naʻau, ʻaʻole me ka hoʻokiʻekiʻe akā me ka haʻahaʻa hiki ai iā ʻoe ke mālama i kēlā mau mea. I koʻu noʻonoʻo ʻana i ka hoʻomaopopo ʻana i ka moʻolelo o ke au o nā aliʻi, ua like nō ia me ko kākou aliʻi nui, ko kākou Akua i loko o ka lani, e mālama kākou i kona mau kapu, me ka haʻahaʻa me ke akahai me ke aloha. Pēlā nō e launa mai ai kona lokomaikaʻi me kākou. (Transcription provided by the author)

> Oh! It is extremely reverent . . . because if you break any of the laws, you will have trouble there. It is only appropriate for those who have good intentions . . . [if] you are humble you can observe the traditions and rules of that type of lifestyle in the presence of royalty, not with haughtiness or conceit but with humility you are able to observe those things. To me, in my recollection of the stories about the period of the aliʻi, it was like our king, our God in the heaven, we observe his sacredness with humility, patience and love. That is how we encounter his goodness. (Translation provided by the author)

Today, with unlimited access to mele and hula performances on the internet, many have substituted the alo of a mentor with a computer screen. I have had students who were unprepared for a performance because of their lack of commitment, which was demonstrated in their poor attendance at class. They then had the audacity to insist that they were ready to perform because they had learned the repertoire by imitating a previous performance of ours that was posted on the internet. I was appalled and did not allow these students to participate in the performance.

Kaleiheana teaches us that the alo is a very serious and sacred place and those who are ha'akei (haughty) and ho'oki'eki'e (conceited) are not allowed access to it. We are reminded to be ever reverent, mindful of the appropriate mannerisms required, and truly attentive. And even though "our cultural knowledge is not a buffet," the alo of a mentor is indeed a place where a feast of wisdom and knowledge can be acquired if one is granted access to it.

Leo: Engagement of the Voiced
In an oral-based society, the leo (voice) is an important tool of expert orators who keep our people connected to the past by reciting our ancient mele and mo'olelo. Our mentors today also provide the leo that celebrates our present and is responsible for our ongoing mentorship. They enlighten us with insight that becomes embedded in our memory. The leo is the eternal link between our people past and present. It transcends place and time and is audible even beyond the physical.

In my experience with Uncle Kimo, I have been encouraged knowing that, although the physical nature of our mentors passes, their leo continue to be with us and guide us long after they are physically gone. Such was the case at the 2006 summer mele program "Nā Mele No Kaua'i me Ni'ihau" organized by Ka Waihona A Ke Aloha[6]:

> It was a mid-summer afternoon, on the beautiful island of Kaua'i, as our mele class, enjoyed the singing of one final number, to bid a fond aloha to a wonderful week of learning mele that were composed specifically for places on the islands of Kaua'i and Ni'ihau. The unanimously selected mele to end Hawaiian 483, Ka Papa Mele Wahi Pana summer course, was the sweet Ka Ua Noe o Kōloa. As we were singing, I peered across the room closely observing our teacher and noticed the tears running down the sides of his cheeks. As we approached the ending of this wonderful rendition, we exclaimed in a crescendo climactic ending, "Nā dews kēhau o ke aumoe!" As we were leaving the classroom, Uncle Kimo softly said to me, "I could hear my teacher singing with us."

The powerful message of the opening line of our final song states "Nani Hā'upu kū kila i ka la'i" (Oh how beautiful is a recollection that stands vividly in the calm) and could not have been better expressed than by the tears Uncle Kimo shed as he reminisced about his Kumu Hula. Hearing his revered mentor's leo, as she sang with us fourteen years after her passing, must have been too beautiful of a thought to comprehend, validating his present as he sat in her place teaching another generation this lovely mele he once learned from her. Later, Uncle Kimo told me that Aunty Adeline was happy with his work and happy that a mele such as *Ka Ua Noe o Koloa* was being taught on the island of Kauaʻi where it was composed. This wonderful experience has remained with me ever since that day, and its lasting impression has nourished my memory with recollections that encourage me daily.

I too have shed many tears reminiscing about this beautiful experience of learning how significant mele are to the preservation and perpetuation of our cultural knowledge and to the continuation of our mentors' leo as it continues to instruct and inform our present. I was most touched when I realized that I was in the very presence of my teacher's teacher and that, with our children in attendance, there were four generations present.

"Ka Hiʻona A Ka Manaʻo Lā I Laila"

A committed relationship with our mentors keeps our alo in direct line with theirs, always ready and willing to be engaged with important discussions. A lack of this kind of privileged involvement could lead to assumptions and misconceptions that may hinder any type of progress; thus the saying, "Hili hewa kahi manaʻo ke ʻole ke kūkākūkā," which means that "ideas run wild without discussion" (Pukui 1983, p. 106). As Pukui explains, to learn and be aware of the specifics of any knowledge, it is necessary to be personally involved (p. 24).

This involvement is necessary for learning the manaʻo (thoughts, intentions, beliefs) of our mentors (Pukui and Elbert 1986, p. 236). Pukui explains that the manaʻo is not something that is readily seen: It is concealed in a number of layers of interpretations. As it is said, "He ana ka manaʻo o ke kanaka, ʻaʻole ʻoe e ʻike ia loko," which means that "the thoughts of man are like caves whose interiors one cannot see" (Pukui 1983, p. 64). The term "hiʻona" is "the general appearance, as of a person" (Pukui and Elbert 1986, p. 72), and therefore, when we are committed to both the alo and the leo of our mentors, Kalākaua's mele informs us that their manaʻo begin to take shape. I believe that this occurs when the manaʻo of our mentors become more real and alive, taking on a more physical nature and perhaps making it easier to see visually.

"I ʻAneʻi Ka Waihona A Ke Aloha"

As explained, by being in constant contact with our mentors' alo and leo we are able to experience their intentions, thoughts, and beliefs. This is when we are allowed access to the "waihona." A waihona, according to Pukui and Elbert, is a "depository, closet, cabinet, vault, file, receptacle, savings, or a place for laying up things in safe-keeping" (1986, p. 378). A waihona could also be a person, as expressed in the saying "Ka waihona o ka naʻauao," which is a reference to a person who is a repository of knowledge and is considered to be learned (Pukui 1983, p. 178).

The location of this waihona to which Kalākaua's mele refers is "i 'ane'i" (right here) within our reach. It is a waihona that contains aloha or that has been cared for by aloha or is in the possession of aloha. Aloha is commonly associated with hello and goodbye and the niceties of love. Today, some even think of the word "aloha" as a quality associated with passiveness, a disposition not callous or bold enough to represent an indigenous point of view. In contrast, I feel that it was aloha that fueled our kūpuna's desire to endure and, in the chaotic turmoil of our colonial past, courageously documented the wonderful mele and mo'olelo that exist today in Hawaiian language newspapers, books, wax cylinders, vinyl recordings, and manuscripts from which we benefit.

I have heard kūpuna share that the term "aloha" is made up of two words—alo (presence) and hā (breath)—and its meaning is so much more than a kind disposition. Aloha is that which births in all of us the patience to endure, the courage to hold fast to our traditions, and the strength to face any adversity. Pilahi Paki, a renowned kupuna, explained that each of the letters that make up the word "aloha" have meaning that comprises its overall significance:

Akahai, meaning kindness to be expressed with tenderness;
Lōkahi, meaning unity, to be expressed with harmony;
'Olu'olu, meaning agreeable, to be expressed with pleasantness;
Ha'aha'a, meaning humility, to be expressed with modesty;
Ahonui, meaning patience, to be expressed with perseverance.

Paki added, "These are traits of character, the spirit of a land known throughout the world in these words of wisdom, intelligence, knowledge, and understanding: what the world knows in the word aloha." Paki's description of aloha led the Hawai'i State Legislature to add the "Aloha Spirit Law" to the Hawai'i Revised Statutes in 1986 (State of Hawai'i, L 1986, c 202, § 1).

Paki encouraged us "to hear what is not said, to see what cannot be seen and to know the unknowable." I find this very true for those of us who invest in relationships and experience the alo and leo of our mentors, who know that even when things are not said there is something to listen for, when there is nothing to see there is something to notice, and when the unforeseen arises we rest assured of what we have already been taught.

Today, as a Hawaiian father, researcher, educator, and mele and hula practitioner, I often find myself repeating stories that Uncle Kimo shared with me. I realize that the investment made with Uncle Kimo's alo and leo has enriched my present practice with information not necessarily found in books, but with insight that has been voiced by this legacy of faithful stewardship.

There are many today who passively boast that they are "so and so's" student, so as to give status to their present practice of mele and hula. There are others who like to say this is "my style" and "this is how we do it where we come from." The truth, however, lies in what is produced. If their presentations include manifestations of their mentor's teaching, then this validates the lineal relationship they have to their mentor's knowledge.

Faithful students are invested in the continued survival of the knowledge entrusted to them; they are ever mindful of their place and role in the community. They do not boast of their conclusions as being definite or final. They first defer to the kūpuna of that particular knowledge to speak on its behalf. More importantly they defer to their mentors, their waihona, those responsible for sharing that knowledge with them, to represent it. They acknowledge first that these waihona, these repositories of aloha, are not only in the possession of their mentors but also that these repositories are, indeed, their mentors.

Mentors are the key component to research inquiry, and their cooperation is critical to its success. We must therefore consider the ingenuity of King Kalākaua's mele *Kaniakapupu Song* and incorporate the necessary mannerisms that encourage us to "noho a kupa i ke alo" and "noho a kama'āina i ka leo" in order to establish lifelong relationships to kūpuna, community participants, practitioners, and teachers when conducting research. It is in this investment that we are able to recognize "ka hi'ona a ka mana'o" and experience "ka waihona a ke aloha."

NOTES

1. Bishop Museum Lili'uokalani Collection HI.M.7 page 1b notes include: "Signed 'Figg,'" presumably King David Kalākaua.

2. *Journal of the College of Education,* University of Hawai'i at Mānoa.

3. I refer to my kumu hula Kimo Alama Keaulana as "Uncle Kimo" throughout this chapter. "Uncle" is an endearing title for an elder, one who is more knowledgeable and seasoned in age. "Uncle Kimo" is a more personal reference, one used by many including my 'ohana.

4. Uncle Kimo (2003) explained that a mele lei is "a chant used to accompany the presentation of a lei to an ali'i. It is our Hawaiian belief that a lei of flowers and leaves would eventually wilt and die but a lei of poetry would remain fresh."

5. I refer to Uncle Kimo's Kumu Hula Adeline Nani Maunupau Lee as "Aunty Adeline" throughout this chapter. The term "Aunty" is an endearing term for an elder, one more knowledgeable and seasoned in age. "Aunty Adeline" is a more personal reference used by my kumu hula.

6. Ka Waihona A Ke Aloha, Ka Papahana Ho'oheno is an interactive resource center for the promotion, preservation, and perpetuation of mele and mele practitioners. It is part of the Kawaihuelani Center for Hawaiian Language, Hawai'inuiākea School of Hawaiian Knowledge, University of Hawai'i at Mānoa.

BIBLIOGRAPHY

ʻĪʻī, J. P., M. K. Pukui (trans.), and D. B. Barrere (ed.) (1963). *Fragments of Hawaiian History*. Honolulu: Bishop Museum Press.

Kaleiheana, A. K. (1974). *Ka Leo Hawaiʻi. Hui Aloha ʻĀina Tuahine*. Honolulu: University of Hawaiʻi at Mānoa.

Kanahele, G. S. (1979). *Hawaiian music and musicians: An illustrated history*. Honolulu: University Press of Hawaiʻi.

Ka Waihona A Ke Aloha: Ka Papa Mele Kauwela (2006). *Nā Mele No Kauaʻi me Niʻihau*. Hawaiian 483 Ka Papa Mele Wahi Pana. Honolulu: University of Hawaiʻi at Mānoa.

Keaulana, K. A. (1997–2010). Personal conversations: Mele and hula mentorship. Honolulu.

———. (2003). Mele: General information. Unpublished information regarding mele. Honolulu.

Maaka, M. J. (2003). E Kua Takoto te Manuka Tutahi: Decolonization, self determination and education. *Educational Perspectives, 37*(2), 3–31.

The meaning behind the spirit of aloha. Accessed June 25, 2013, from http://lifeintheseislands.com.

Moʻokini, E. (1998). Keōpūolani: Sacred wife, Queen Mother, 1778–1823. *Hawaiian Journal of History*, 27–48.

Nākoa, S. K., W. H. Wilson, S. Merritt, and Ahahui Olelo Hawaii (1979). *Lei momi oʻEwa*. Honolulu: Ahahui Olelo Hawaiʻi.

Porsanger, J. (2004). An essay about indigenous methodology. http://septentrio.uit.no/index.php/nordlit/article/viewFile/1910/1776.

Pukui, M. K. (1983). *ʻŌlelo noʻeau: Hawaiian proverbs & poetical sayings*. Honolulu: Bishop Museum Press.

Pukui, M. K., and S. H. Elbert (1986). *Hawaiian dictionary: Hawaiian-English, English-Hawaiian* (revised and enlarged ed.). Honolulu: University of Hawaiʻi Press.

Queen Liliʻuokalani. "Kaniakapupu Song: This is the second poem in a book of Hawaiian poems written by Queen Liliʻuokalani in her hand." Bishop Museum HI.M. 7 p. 1b. Honolulu.

Smith, L. T. (1999). *Decolonizing methodologies: Research and indigenous peoples*. London: Zed.

Uemoto, S., W. Silva, A. Suemori, and Kalihi-Palama Culture & Arts Society (1984). *Nana i na loea hula* [Look to the hula resources]. Honolulu: Kalihi-Palama Culture & Arts Society.

He Lei Aloha ʻĀina

Mehana Blaich Vaughan

He lei paʻiniu no Kīlauea.
A lei of paʻiniu, signifying that the wearer has visited Kīlauea Crater.

He lei pahapaha no Polihale.
A lei of pahapaha limu, signifying that the wearer has visited Polihale,
Kauaʻi.

Throughout Hawaiʻi, lei symbolize certain places and show that the wearer has
experienced them. Lei offer a way to see and know a landscape because each
lei is unique to the place where it is made. Like the process of making lei, my
research in the field of environmental studies seeks to gather a variety of materials and put them together in stories that build knowledge and ways of seeing
certain ʻāina.

My Tūtū, Amelia Ana Kaʻōpua Bailey, taught me to pay attention to ʻāina,
with a focus on what type of lei could be made from each place. Riding with
Tūtū in the car was an adventure because she was always looking out the window, her eyes tracing the trees, the bank along the side of the road, even the
median strip of the freeway. I remember waiting in the car as she darted across
four lanes of H-1 to pick salmon-colored bougainvillea, a *Times* supermarket
grocery bag trailing behind her. Whether driving the saddle road on Hawaiʻi
Island or the streets of her own Mānoa Valley, Tūtū was watching for flowers.
To her, every landscape offered a tantalizing vision of its own lei just waiting
to be made.

I have a similar craving to weave stories of certain landscapes. Since I was a
child, everywhere I went, I remember wondering, Who are the people of this
place? What did it look like before? What parts of it (plants, views, fish, rock
walls) are still here? Will they be here in the future? Now I address these questions through interdisciplinary environmental research focused on relationships between people and places in rural parts of Hawaiʻi and on how these
relationships have changed over time. Most of my work has centered in the
Haleleʻa moku and Kīlauea area of Kauaʻi, where I grew up. This chapter begins by sharing an experience of one place in Haleleʻa, Lumahaʻi Valley. This
experience inspired me to go back to school at age thirty to pursue a degree in

environmental studies, and continues to shape my approach to research in this field.

Moʻolelo ʻĀina: Stories of a Place

In high school, I moved away from Kauaʻi, then spent nearly fifteen years living away from home, studying sociology in college, traveling, and teaching at a Hawaiian language immersion school on Oʻahu while pursuing a master's degree in Hawaiian education. In 2003, I finally moved home to Kauaʻi, where I had a job running mālama ʻāina education programs at the Waipā Foundation on Kamehameha Schools lands. The foundation works to restore the 1,600-acre ahupuaʻa of Waipā as a community learning center for culturally based stewardship and Hawaiian cultural practice. At Waipā, I worked with students of all ages, including a group of nine local high school students funded to intern with us through Alu Like, a nonprofit to assist native Hawaiians in their efforts to achieve social and economic self-sufficiency. That summer, we had the opportunity to take the interns on a four-day trip to explore possibilities for conservation work at the very back of Lumahaʻi, the large valley that wraps around the much smaller neighboring valley of Waipā, both trust lands of Ke Aliʻi Pauahi. Most of the students grew up swimming regularly in the muliwai on the beach, Hoʻohila, where Lumahaʻi's river lazily meets the sea. However, none of us knew anyone who had ever been to the very back of the 1,600-acre valley, which we planned to reach by helicopter. Though the flight was less than ten minutes just over one ridge, getting us there would require five expensive helicopter trips: three for people and two to sling-load our gear.

My Tūtū, Amelia Ana Kaʻōpua Bailey, preparing lei for a gathering at ʻohana home in Namahana, Kauaʻi, 1980. Photo courtesy of Beryl Leolani Bailey Blaich.

In preparation for the trip, the students began to ask their families what they knew of Lumahai. A few kūpuna had been to the area on hunting trips or recalled older family members who went there, however, knowledge of the place and what it was like was sparse. Our searches of maps and the sources we knew for mo'olelo turned up only a few place names and vague references. The students became aware that they were going to a place that generations of their family members had only heard about, yet somehow still felt connected to and thought of as powerful. They worked hard to prepare, encouraging one another by researching native plants, memorizing place names, practicing getting in and out of the helicopter, packing meals, learning cultural protocol, and making ho'okupu. They scrubbed their boots and froze their clothing so as not to introduce new weeds to the area.

On the helicopter ride, my first, we soared over plunging ravines in every shade of green. When I was able to catch my breath, I noticed clumps of la'ī, ti, planted high on the steep sides of each gully we passed. When the chopper made its descent, dropping suddenly, I looked down and saw no space in which to land. We set down on an uluhe-covered slope, disembarking into a tangled mat of thigh-high scratchy fern quivering in the wind from the chopper blades. Dwarf lehua adorned a spongy bog at the base of towering pali. Five small streams emerged from rocks at the piko of the deep valley below. I was afraid to take a breath, lest I disturb something.

When the sound of the helicopter trailed off, our group offered oli komo, asking to enter. We also addressed Laka, all around us in the dwarf lehua, flowering 'ie'ie, and three different vining maile sisters. As we gave our lei and ho'okupu, I was reminded of one community member's question as we were getting input for the trip: "If you believe in Laka, why go? You don't believe she can handle the forest on her own?" To me, our offerings, our presence in that place were a means of ho'omana, giving strength to Laka, just as she gave strength to our efforts. Still, each step in the bog felt tender, and no matter how carefully we walked, we stomped on the moss, leaving indentations for mosquito puddles. Each sling load that brought tents, cereal boxes, coolers, the wok, and our other gear further flattened uluhe under the weight, sound, and wind of the chopper.

Yet signs of the need for conservation work were everywhere. Invasive Australian tree ferns showered spores on our heads and shoulders as we cut them. Their light green fronds peeked above the tree canopy in every direction, gullies away threatening to spread into an impenetrable sunlight-blocking ceiling. Strawberry guava seedlings sprang by the fistful from clumps of goat dung. Over the next few days the students set to work, scaling ridges to reach those far-off ferns. We climbed down from the bog and into the dryland forest to weed. Soon, uprooted clydimia plants and thimble berry bushes hung roots toward the sky, lacing fallen tree branches. Students counted as they pulled. Only their voices and the shaking bushes gave away their presence amidst the thick vegetation and towering old 'ōhi'a: "One-thousand, four-hundred thirty-seven clydimia, one-thousand, four-hundred thirty-eight clydimia, one-hundred ninety-three thimble berry."

Conservation and research efforts that focus on intact native forests and areas with high concentrations of rare species often assume that these remote and pristine sites—wao akua, realms of the gods—are disconnected from humans. The environmental organization partnering in our work was proceeding on the assumption that this place was untouched and unvisited, because it was upstream of a precipitous cliff and waterfall. After our trip, an archaeological study was conducted to evaluate the feasibility of constructing a helicopter landing zone and camping platform. The first sample pit uncovered a large chunk of mana mana, branch coral, very deliberately carried from the ocean to honor and enhance the mana of this place. Yes, people certainly had been there before.

This trip, unlike many conservation and environmental research efforts in Hawai'i, incorporated means of acknowledging the sacredness of our "work site" and asking its guidance; of accessing people's stories and connection to this place, however tentative and distant; and of reconnecting the place to community by training younger generations descended from the area to take care of it. These three threads gleaned from our trip continue to shape my attempts at 'āina-based research: 'āina as source, 'āina as people, and 'āina as ongoing connection and care.

'Ike 'Āina: Three Strands

Wili, or wrapped, lei are distinct from other styles of lei such as kui (to string with a needle) or hili (to braid one type of material) because they require fiber strands, hau, and, more recently, raffia to wrap and bind the lei. As a child, I often sat on the cold cement steps next to Tūtū's lei table in the garage. The flower refrigerator hummed along under Hawaiian mele on KCCN as I watched the definitive wrap and pull of her wrist. The beauty of lei wili comes from combining materials of different sizes, shapes, textures, and colors. The three-strand raffia structure allows for finesse in the binding. Tūtū's finished lei highlighted each different flower and fern she used, while producing something more beautiful than the sum of these parts.

My efforts at 'āina-based research also draw on varied materials and information gathered through mixed methods—interviews, focus groups, surveys, meeting observations, document analysis, archival work, and ecological monitoring—to create a holistic and, I hope, new view of a place. Like Tūtū's raffia, three unifying strands bind everything together: 'āina as source, the place itself; 'āina as people, those connected to that place; and 'āina as ongoing connection and care, the strengthening of connections between people and place. Here, for each of these three strands or sources of 'ike, I offer lessons to guide the gathering process of research.

'Āina as Source

The stream crossing is so overgrown with hau bush that we have to bend and wade with our bellies against the cold brown water. We hold on to the slippery hau branches, feet skidding on mossy rocks as the stream rushes to plunge over the falls ten feet below. We are already wet from the sodden leaves and branches we pushed through to get here, and it looks as if it will start pouring again any minute. Before stepping into the frothing stream water I motion to Beth, my research assistant, to wait. It is time to offer our oli. Beth, an undergraduate student raised in Seattle, has never been to Hawai'i before this summer internship helping with my research. She stops reaching for the sample bottle in her backpack, straightens up, trying not to scratch the skin between her pants and tennis shoes where a cluster of mosquitos circle angrily, and takes a breath to chant.

We are stream sampling today to build skills and understanding of water systems vital to the community where I was raised. We want to understand the effects of land use change, resulting in erosion and sediment, on streams and ultimately the corals reefs and inshore fisheries still so essential to survival, food security, and the way of life on this coast. We need to collect samples on the rainiest days, the waimea, reddish-water days of swollen café au lait channels clouding the bay, slowly pushing the line between blue and brown farther toward the horizon.

We stand facing the lunging water, teeth chattering, and find our voices. Yet the purpose of this chant is more than just a request for protection. This oli asks permission of this place, of the wai, the water itself, for our work. We explain the purpose of our study, why the water will be used, and how. May we take just a small sample from its home in the kahawai, the stream? Just as a pōhaku, rock, needs to know the function for which it is being selected so that it may lend its mana to the effort, wai should be asked to come along too. Whether my students' work involves collecting wai, pōhaku, leaf litter, fish gonads, or soil, I ask that they learn oli to first ask permission.

Once removed, these aspects of 'āina must continue to be treated with respect. The water samples we are collecting will leave Kaua'i, frozen and packed in dry ice for shipment to California. There, a highly sensitive spectrometer will shine light through the water, measuring the wavelength of emerging beams. Each color will correspond to various nutrient levels. Silica will show the pres-

Tracked, by Maui printmaker Abigail Romanchak, 2010, traces the footsteps of conservationists, wearing GPS trackers, as they moved through one protected native forest over the course of a year. Romanchak enlarged maps of their tracks, carved segments onto plates, and then printed them on rice paper. The prints use reddish paint made of soil from the same Maui forest. *Tracked* earned the most outstanding artist award in the Biennial IX exhibit at the Honolulu Contemporary Museum of Art in 2010. Image courtesy of artist.

ence of groundwater. Calcium is likely from evaporated ocean water returned as rain. Nitrate and nitrite will indicate the presence of fertilizers or possible sewage. Most of the wai in our six-ounce sample bottles is extra, collected in case samples need to be retested. Once they finish the tests, I ask research assistants not to dump this surplus wai down the drain: Instead, carry it out of the lab, water a tree, and give thanks. Where possible, we have shipped unused samples home and returned wai to the spot where it was collected. All environmental research focuses on 'āina, often collecting and analyzing the land itself. In the work I strive to do and encourage my students to do, 'āina should be not only subject but also partner, source, inspiration, and guide.

'Āina as People
I conduct most of my research through interviews and site visits with longtime residents who have multigenerational ties to the places I study. As in Lumaha'i Valley, it is rarely easy to identify the community of people with connections to a place; this community is often unseen. However, every place in Hawai'i has people attached to it who care about and hold deep wisdom of it. These people, worth seeking, offer a vital strand in the lei.

People's connections to places are often built through use. In one example of research conducted to understand human use, I worked with lawaiʻa, or fishermen, of Hāʻena, Kauaʻi, who were engaged in community planning efforts for their local fishery. Our research team had already spent a year and a half counting users of the coastline and thought we had a clear picture of the "community," a handful of fishermen and many recreational users who accessed the area to surf, kite surf, snorkel, sunbathe, and gather shells.

The fishermen wanted to extend our study to understand where fish from the area ended up. We worked together to track what fish they caught, who they gave them to, and where. This work revealed a network of families connected to Hāʻena's coast by receiving gifted māhele, or shares of fish, even though they lived on the other side of the island or even on the mainland. Most of these fish recipients had ancestral ties to the area, but many had moved away due to construction of luxury vacation homes and resulting increases in property taxes. Had the lawaiʻa not wanted to share their catch and giving practices, we could have missed an entire community of fish recipients who remain connected to Hāʻena's fishery. Though easily overlooked in management and policy efforts, this community will nonetheless be affected by such planning. Research like mine, focused on "human dimensions" of the environment, can help illuminate unseen communities and their interactions with a place. This research is much richer if it not only studies but also engages these communities.

ʻĀina as Ongoing Connection and Care

Throughout Hawaiʻi, people are actively engaged in community-based efforts to take care of places they love and are fed by. My students and I aim not only to study but also to strengthen their efforts. I work with mālama ʻāina organizations in my home community and in others that have invited our research team to document their efforts, lessons, and challenges. We try to conduct this research in a participatory way, working as partners with these organizations to develop research questions, collect and analyze data, discern answers to our questions, and decide how to use this information. As much as possible, I attend regularly scheduled community meetings and workdays to get feedback on research progress and share preliminary findings. These sessions usually include food and informal discussion, often yielding valuable insight into whether our findings ring true, potential explanations for them, and future directions for research. I also hold formal community presentations to share research in forms that can be utilized to support community efforts.

One trend in environmental research is the remote collection of large data sets across many sites. In contrast, my research emphasizes helping people add to in-depth knowledge of places where they have kuleana, responsibility. In the ongoing stream monitoring project described earlier, we hire community members to collect water samples, take photos, and conduct visual assessments of stream health using indicators such as water color, flow speed, and vegetation cover on banks. Over time, our goal is to correlate data on nutrient levels obtained through targeted sampling with these more holistic observations, thereby connecting the data we collect to what people already know about the stream system. We aim to strengthen the community's ability to observe and assess stream health using convenient and inexpensive methods, without needing to rely on scientific teams or a laboratory. This effort builds capacity for community-based management and for real-time, day-to-day decision making, such as whether or not it is safe to allow one's children to swim.

Pani a Paʻa: Conclusion

The sky lit gold over the distant glimpse of ocean at the mouth of Lumahaʻi Valley as we walked back up the trail after that long final day of weeding. Likely we had friends and cousins swimming at the river mouth even as we stood here ma uka of its source. Three students said they had decided after this trip they wanted to work in conservation. Returning home, I began to consider doctoral programs in environmental studies, even though I had not taken math since high school and never took chemistry. Now a professor, my motivation remains preparing students for jobs taking care of places they love and are connected to.

Waipā youth mappers and kumu on work trip to the back of Lumahaʻi Valley in the summer of 2003. Left to right: Namolokama Osakoda, Kaui Fu, Titi Giltner, Noe Wong, Kaili Chandler, Olena Asuncion, Kamealoha Forrest, Mokihana Martin, Uncle David Sproat, Adam Hussey, Mehana Blaich Vaughan, and Paʻula Chandler. Photo by Auliʻi George Dudoit, courtesy of Kaui Fu.

'Āina: source, 'aina: people, 'aina: ongoing connection and care—three unifying strands, like the raffia that binds together one of Tūtū's lei wili. Learning from Tūtū's example and teaching, I approach environmental research the way she taught me to gather a variety of materials and to wili lei. My research often comes together in mo'olelo, storytelling, and in poetry, avenues our kūpuna used, like lei, to make beloved places seen and felt. These lei can only be made from the places from which their elements were gathered. Each 'a'ali'i bush is sculpted by a certain direction of wind, the day's length of sun, and weathering of soil on its side of a ridge. Multiple bushes yield a lei entirely different from one made from 'a'ali'i just one ridge over.

In my environmental research, I am guided by Tūtū's informal, mostly unspoken, instruction in gathering for lei. Oli first: Ask and explain the purpose for your gathering. Look. Listen. Take only what you need. Clean your materials before you depart, leaving as much as you can with the plants to rejuvenate and replenish. When the process is complete, and the lei dries, bring it back to this spot or return it to some other 'āina to bring growth.

The poem that follows brings together individual bits of material gathered from the area where I grew up. Woven with three strands—place, people, and the connection between them—I hope this lei tells a textured story of 'āina, ma uka to ma kai (mountains to sea) and the human footprints it bears, both seen and unseen. Research, like lei, should bring growth along with beauty, should weave disparate elements together in a way that shows new perspective and creates new life. Lei are to be given and shared, not to remain the property of the maker. Like any other haku of mele, of inoa, once given, this lei belongs to its recipient: Nou kēia lei. He lei wili 'ia me ke aloha, no ku'u Tūtū, no ka 'āina aloha, aloha nō.

Pu'unahele

WAO NAHELE—UPLAND FOREST, 140 ACRES, TMK #13–531
Name lost
Bird catchers' camp
Where orange lehua once bloomed
Branch coral laid gently on an altar
The place where the hunting dogs froze
Road launching power lines over the mountain
Straightest guava branches for kalā'au
The spot the Pleiades first crest the ridge
In October's crisping dusk

KULA—FLATLANDS, 10.2 ACRES, TMK #13–458
Below Pu'u Māheu, hill-raking winds

Sweet soil for growing 'uala
Sunset view meditation spot
Place to check surf at "Wires"
Night path of the spirits returning from shore
Where we kids used to ride our bikes
The first gated driveway that we'd ever seen
Former route of the sugar cane train
Field #45, best yield per acre
State land-use classification . . . Ag.

KAHAWAI—RIPARIAN ZONE, 1.4 ACRES, TMK #13–172
A taro patch called Nāhiku
'Auwai with 'o'opu mouths big as a fist
First place to flood, now so much less water
Where the cousin on crystal meth hides
Rocks the women scrubbed clothing clean on
Roof dropped there by the tsunami
Perch for the child scaring rice birds
Stand up paddle right out to the beach
Option to construct two ADUs
Vacation rentals with kitchenettes

KAHAKAI—COASTAL LANDS, 0.2 ACRES, TMK #13–890
Kamakau, the long curving hook
Line of shells swept up by first swell
The hill used to kilo, direct them to moi
The space to spread nets out to dry
Two turtle eggs hatching one March morning
Outflow of bagasse from the mill
Shearwater flyway that stopped power lines
Where the sand departs from in the fall
'Āholehole caught for baby's lū'au
Eel circling the spot Uncle cleaned them
Those "champagne pools" the guidebook named
Six visitors swept away this last winter
Private beach view, price $2.7 million dollars
Right where the fishing trail used to descend

GLOSSARY

ADU	additional dwelling unit
'āholehole	fish form of god Lono
'auwai	irrigation ditch

bagasse	fibrous waste product from sugar milling
hoʻokupu	offerings to cause growth and thriving
ʻike	knowledge or insight
kalāʻau	hula implement made of two sticks
kilo	to spot fish, a fish spotter
kūpuna	elders, those who stand at the source
Laka	goddess of the forest and of hula
lehua	Native Hawaiian forest tree used in lei
limu	seaweed
ma uka	upland
moi	Pacific threadfin fish, once reserved for chiefs
moʻolelo	stories, history
muliwai	river mouth
Nāhiku	"the seven"; also the name for the Big Dipper
oli komo	entrance chant
ʻoʻopu	freshwater goby fish
pali	cliff
piko	center
pōhaku	rock
ʻuala	sweet potato
wai	water

Mo'olelo for Transformative Leadership: Lessons from Engaged Practice

Kaiwipunikauikawēkiu Lipe

With contributions from 'Ekela Kanī'aupi'o-Crozier and Mehanaokalā Hind

Aloha nui kāua e ka mea heluhelu! (Greetings, dear reader). I would like to set the stage for this chapter by stating that I recently earned my PhD in education administration from the University of Hawai'i at Mānoa (UHM), a predominantly non-Hawaiian institution (Balutski and Wright 2012).[1] I did so as a Native Hawaiian woman. In particular I negotiated and navigated my graduate school experiences as a Native Hawaiian granddaughter, daughter, sister, wife, mother, and hula dancer.

It was not easy identifying as and being a Hawaiian woman in an overwhelmingly non-Hawaiian university. I often struggled with cultural dissonance (Museus 2008)—the tension and conflict caused by the inconsistencies between my home culture and the university campus culture (Jayakumar and Museus 2012).[2] My university's campus culture—complete with its values, behaviors, and ways of teaching/learning/knowing—did not recognize, acknowledge, and utilize those of my home and personal culture. As a result, one of the many areas in which I struggled with cultural dissonance was in methodologies for learning, teaching, and research.[3]

Early Influences: Hawaiian Cultural Practice

I have been greatly shaped by Hawaiian cultural practices: I was raised by Hawaiian families, educated in Hawaiian culture and language schools, and prepared in Hawaiian hālau hula.[4] One of the many lessons I learned in these various Hawaiian settings is the power and importance of engaging in mo'olelo. Pukui and Elbert (1986) teach us that the term "mo'olelo" is derived from two words. The first is mo'o, which is translated as "succession, series, especially a genealogical line, lineage" (p. 253). It has also been explained to me as each vertebra connecting the spine together. The second word, 'ōlelo, translates into English as "language, speech, word, statement, utterance; to speak, say, converse" (p. 284). Furthermore, Pukui (1983) transcribed a famous Hawaiian proverb, "I ka 'ōlelo nō ke ola, i ka 'ōlelo nō ka make" (p. 129) to mean that in speech there is life and in speech there is death.

Because Hawaiian language was a completely oral language until the mid-1800s (Benham and Heck 1998; Kawai'ae'a, Housman, and Alencastre 2007), it makes sense that 'ōlelo was given so much emphasis and power: The livelihood of the Hawaiian people—our entire knowledge system—depended on the continuity of mo'olelo as spoken and taught to the next generation. Therefore, I grew up learning not only that mo'olelo in its many forms is important but also that it is essential that we share those mo'olelo out loud. I learned that it is critical to listen to mo'olelo as they are told, to share mo'olelo with others, and to use those mo'olelo to learn, teach, connect, and make sense of the world. Here I use the phrase "mo'olelo aku, mo'olelo mai"—to share and receive mo'olelo—to name this engaged practice and methodology for teaching and learning.

Favorite Modes of Mo'olelo
One of my favorite modes of mo'olelo is mele,[5] specifically in oli[6] and hula. When I was little, my mother often taught me chants during long car rides. This helped the time pass and invited me into another realm of Hawai'i. In elementary school, science came to life for me as we learned about the water cycle through the traditional chant *Ka Wai a Kāne*. While learning hula not only did I learn about so many different aspects of my Hawaiian world through mele but I also became the storyteller as I danced and chanted myself. Therefore, by engaging in mo'olelo as mele, I learned about academic subjects, life lessons, histories, genealogies, and identity.

A second of my favorite modes of mo'olelo is 'ōlelo no'eau—Hawaiian proverbs and poetical sayings (Pukui 1983). Since I was a little girl, 'ōlelo no'eau have been both fun and useful. It is always exciting to learn an 'ōlelo no'eau because it usually captures a longer mo'olelo and collection of lessons in one or two easily memorizable phrases: An 'ōlelo no'eau is a secret password or code into a rich, captivating mo'olelo that folks can easily share and refer to. At the same time, an 'ōlelo no'eau is always useful because once it is known and understood, when it is referred to, everyone can automatically connect to the meaning, lessons, and mo'olelo captured within it.

A third of my favorite modes of mo'olelo is narration or storytelling. Storytelling has always been important to me because it allows me to think about and visualize life through another's perspective or to share mine with someone else. A power, a privilege, and also a responsibility are gently but necessarily negotiated during storytelling. Further, a great Hawaiian storyteller is able to weave in mele and 'ōlelo no'eau to add to the richness of the story he or she is sharing. I have sat and listened to both kūpuna (elders) and 'ōpio (youth) share their mo'olelo, in the process learning many lessons and perspectives from them. At the same time, as I am doing in this chapter, I have also learned to share my own moʻolelo for the purpose of imparting a lesson, special memory, or experience with others.

Graduate School: A Stark Contrast

Although I engaged in moʻolelo all my life as foundational forms of teaching and learning methodology, mele, oli, hula, ʻōlelo noʻeau, and storytelling were almost never used or invited into the classroom in the doctoral program I attended in a Western, predominantly non-Hawaiian higher education institution. Being in the classroom stifled my use of my cultural and personal pedagogies and methodologies. Though I tried to bring various forms of moʻolelo into the academy, these efforts were frequently ignored or pushed to the side. I struggled with finding my way as a Native Hawaiian doctoral student, finding it difficult to feel settled within my work and glean meaningful lessons from my research. I often felt discouraged and out of place, and thus slowly but unconsciously stopped engaging in my beloved modes of moʻolelo.

Though I initially struggled, I finally found my way! Therefore, this chapter is dedicated to highlighting some of the tensions I experienced, sharing some ways in which I found my path as a Native Hawaiian researcher in the academy by engaging in moʻolelo as methodology and how I used those lessons to learn about transformation (Eckel, Hill, and Green 1998; Engeström 2001):[7] transforming campus cultures and transformative leadership.

My Doctoral Research

My doctoral research focused on a central question: How can the University of Hawaiʻi at Mānoa (UHM), a predominantly non-Hawaiian university, be transformed into a Hawaiian place of learning? To explore this question, I learned from the stories of eight Native Hawaiian female educational leaders—my kumu (teachers)—who have been transforming spaces into Hawaiian places of learning, both within the academy and in the community, over the past thirty years. Their work and stories were of particular interest to me because they were able to transform spaces into educational kīpuka[8] (Goodyear-Kaʻōpua 2013), despite the contentious and often racist environments (Alfred 2004) that surrounded them. This is significant because UHM is also such a contentious environment.

Survivance

To help guide my study, I began with three frameworks. Of particular importance to this chapter is the framework of survivance. Vizenor (2008) describes survivance as an "active presence" (p. 1) of Indigenous peoples in the world today: It is "found in spirit, cast of mind, and moral courage" and is the "continuance of stories" (p. 1). Survivance is a state of being in which we, as Indigenous peoples, "reject being the victim" (p. 1). Rather than allowing the stories of colonization and victimization to define us, survivance suggests that we move beyond them to focus on the amazing people we are and the tremendous things we do as Indigenous peoples. Dr. Graham Smith (2011) of Aotearoa reminds us that making this shift and recognizing our strengths are important steps in the process of being self-determining. Hence, survivance illuminated the spirit, energy, and work of each of the women in my study.

Beyond Survivance

Though survivance is an incredibly important framework in our journey as Indigenous peoples to reclaim the stories that define us, I could not help but think that for me, as a Native Hawaiian, a kanaka ʻōiwi researcher, someone who has been privileged to be raised in my language and culture, there must be something more. I felt a kuleana (privilege, responsibility) to dig deeper to find a Hawaiian concept from which I could draw a framework for presenting the transformational leadership that the women I learned from had achieved. I thought of Indigenous scholars such as Dr. Graham Smith (2003), who argues that Indigenous peoples must move beyond the terms and processes of decolonization and look to our own traditions and cultures to rediscover what is innately in us. Similarly, I thought of Dr. Pualani Kanakaʻole Kanahele (2012), who reminds us that our ancestors live within us and that the knowledge and experiences of our ancestors are passed down from generation to generation through our DNA. But inviting this ʻike kūpuna (ancestral knowledge) into the academy—and having the confidence to do so—was often difficult and daunting because I was constantly bombarded by Western theory, literature, and methodologies. Little, if any, space was made for Indigenous knowledge systems (Lipe 2013).

While struggling with the realities of the Western academy, I continued to think about the wisdom of Indigenous scholars who directed my attention and gave me confidence to engage in what is innately Hawaiian: moʻolelo. Therefore, I began to listen to and study, over and over again, the narratives of the women in my research, trying to make sense of the richness and immensity of their experiences and stories. The women were so generous with their moʻolelo—sharing triumphs and struggles, as well as the processes and details of their work, and also identifying key experiences, people, and lessons that shaped them.

All the while I was learning from their moʻolelo, I kept asking myself these questions: What are these moʻolelo trying to teach me about transforming campus cultures? What does survivance look and feel like to Hawaiians? I grappled, explored, and reflected on these questions for several months.

Chanting to My Children: A Methodological Tool

During my doctoral journey, as I was constantly thinking about my research—the dozens of hours of recorded stories and the hundreds of pages of raw transcripts I had gathered—and how to make sense of it all, I was also fulfilling my responsibilities as a mother. One of those responsibilities was driving my children to school, an hour-long commute from where we lived. During those car rides, we often chanted and sang Hawaiian songs to pass the time, engaging in the tradition of moʻolelo en route passed down by my mother.

On one particular morning, as I made my way onto H-1 East from Likelike Highway, I happened to be chanting *Māewa i ka Hao Mai a ka Makani* by Kainani Kahaunaele (1997) to my children:

Māewa i ka hao mai a ka makani	*Swaying in the gusts of the wind,*
Puehu wale aʻe nāhi hua ʻaʻaliʻi	*The ʻaʻaliʻi seeds freely scatter*
Kau liʻiliʻi i ka loa a me ka laulā	*Distributed evenly all about,*
Loku iho ka Hāʻao a ao mai ka pō	*The Hāʻao rain pours throughout the night,*
Polapola aʻe kahi hua i ka wai lani	*The seeds sprout in the heavenly water,*
ʻO ka puka aʻela nō ia o ka muʻo	*Immediately the leaf buds emerge*
E kupu ana hoʻi a mohala	*And grow until they blossom*
I ka helu a ka lā; i ka wai o ka ʻōpua	*As the sun scratches the earth; and in the rain*
I pua nō ke ʻaʻaliʻi i keʻekeʻehi ʻia e ka ua-	*The ʻaʻaliʻi unfolds because the rains tread upon*
Māhuahua a manomano a lēʻī	*And they grow strong and abundant*
E lei ana i ke ʻaʻaliʻi kū makani ē	*See, the land is luxuriously adorned with lei of ʻaʻaliʻi*

In the hoʻāeae-style melody[9] that my kumu hula, Manu Boyd, gave to this mele, the ancestral words spoke to me. By engaging in oli and hearing the words out loud, I realized that the moʻolelo of the ʻaʻaliʻi kū makani was the perfect frame, the perfect lens through which to study and learn from the moʻolelo of the women!

The Guidance of ʻŌlelo Noʻeau

Kahaunaele's (1997) oli helped me see the women and their stories as those of ʻaʻaliʻi kū makani because of my connection to, engagement in,[10] and understanding of the ʻōlelo noʻeau that Pukui (1983) recorded for us: "He ʻaʻaliʻi kū makani mai au, ʻaʻohe makani nāna e kūlaʻi" (I am the wind withstanding ʻaʻaliʻi. No wind can topple me over; p. 60). The ʻaʻaliʻi has long been used as a Hawaiian metaphor and model for strength, resiliency, and flexibility because it can survive challenging environments and elemental forces and still bloom to become a beautiful and useful resource. As such, this particular 'ōlelo no'eau is often used to describe a person who embodies such qualities. Therefore, as I came to learn about survivance (Vizenor 2008) and used it as a preliminary framework, engaging in oli and using 'ōlelo no'eau helped me move beyond that concept and return to my own ancestral frames. I realized that Hawaiians *do* have our own concept for survivance: 'a'ali'i kū makani.

Indeed, the women are 'a'ali'i. First, they are deeply rooted in Hawai'i. Then they draw strength from that rootedness and become flexible, resilient, beautiful women who, every day, live into survivance. Specifically, they withstand challenging environments and, using their 'a'ali'i qualities, manage to bloom and transform currently contentious, racist environments *back* into Hawaiian places of learning.

In addition, as Kahaunaele (1997) skillfully weaves together the elements, environments, and genealogies, that feed and give life to the 'a'ali'i in her oli, she directs our attention to the 'a'ali'i's life cycle. As I chanted and internalized the life cycle of the 'a'ali'i, I realized that the mo'olelo of my kumu also tell of life cycles. The 'a'ali'i plant begins as a hua, or a seed. Similarly, the women encounter many beginnings—the beginning of a journey, the beginning of a struggle, or the beginning of a learning process. Then, through the gusts of wind, the seeds are scattered and distributed. By the downpours of rain, the seeds become swollen and sprout. And then the sun shines down and nourishes the blossom until the 'a'ali'i becomes strong and abundant. These components of the life cycle are the genealogies—the people and the critical events and experiences—that make the women strong, that motivate them to get up every day to continue the transformational work they do both in the academy and in the community. Some of these conditions they encounter are indeed harsh and contentious (Alfred 2004). Similarly, sometimes the 'a'ali'i tree must survive high winds or periods of drought. However, these challenging conditions are what make the 'a'ali'i so admirable; they are what empower and inspire us when we utter the 'ōlelo no'eau, "He 'a'ali'i kū makani mai au. 'A'ohe makani nāna e kūla'i!" (Pukui 1983, p. 60).

Connecting Back to the Research

I return to my central research question: How can the University of Hawai'i at Mānoa, a predominantly non-Hawaiian university, be transformed into a Hawaiian place of learning? What I gleaned from engaging and weaving together the different yet connected forms of mo'olelo—including the oli *Māewa* (Kahaunaele 1997), the 'ōlelo no'eau "He 'a'ali'i kū makani mai au, 'a'ohe makani nāna e kūla'i" (Pukui 1983, p. 60), and the mo'olelo of the women—led to my answer, which is at least twofold.

First, to transform UHM into a Hawaiian place of learning, we need to transform ourselves. We need to prepare and transform ourselves into 'a'ali'i kū makani—leaders who are rooted in Hawai'i, who can withstand challenging environments and yet manage to bloom and transform spaces with beauty, strength, flexibility, utility, and resiliency.[11] As I learned from the mo'olelo of the women, becoming 'a'ali'i kū makani is essential because of the enormity of the racism and contention that still exist.

Second, the 'a'ali'i process is ongoing and cyclical, with at least three phases. First, there is He Hua, the many beginnings the women experience. Second is Hao Mai, Iho Mai, Pā Mai—the occasions in which their beginnings are shaped by the many elemental influences. The third phase is Kupu a Mohala, coming into full bloom, in which the women engage in transformational work. I see the recognition of these three phases as an invitation to be purposeful and intentional about creating the conditions for the 'a'ali'i kū makani to grow.

Mo'olelo 'A'ali'i

In this section, I re-present snapshots of the mo'olelo of two of my kumu who were part of my doctoral research.[12] I share these stories for three main reasons. First, I want to demonstrate how the 'a'ali'i kū makani framework, informed by oli and 'ōlelo no'eau, illuminated the 'a'ali'i qualities and life cycle within the mo'olelo of the women. Second, I re-present their stories to demonstrate the importance of mo'olelo aku, mo'olelo mai—sharing and receiving stories—as a methodology, because when we value narratives and take the time to study them, so much can be learned. As each of us reads the mo'olelo of the two kumu, we each glean both similar and unique lessons based on who each of us are and our own life experiences. However, we can only connect to the mo'olelo if we take the time to learn from them, which requires us to first value mo'olelo and then to spend time with them.

Two Beloved 'A'ali'i: An Introduction

I am honored to share parts of the mo'olelo of two powerful, beautiful 'a'ali'i who have been mentors to me and also leaders in our communities, actually transforming spaces into educational kīpuka (Goodyear-Ka'ōpua 2013). The first of these two women is 'Ekela Kanī'aupi'o-Crozier. She is perhaps best known for her role as a beloved Hawaiian language teacher who has taught and inspired thousands of people to not only learn Hawaiian but also to use it as their language of choice. Aunty 'Ekela was also the first director of Native Hawaiian Student Services at UHM, heading a program called Operation Kua'ana through which she touched the lives of countless Hawaiians in their journey at the often overwhelming, non-Hawaiian UHM campus and culture. Indeed, as we see in her story, she is an ʻaʻaliʻi kū makani who used the lessons and genealogies that shaped her over the years to then transform spaces for the betterment of future generations. As expected, Aunty ʻEkela shares her stories ma ka ʻōlelo Hawaiʻi[13] so it is very easy to distinguish her voice.

The second woman whose stories are re-presented here is Mehanaokalā Hind. She has long been an older sister to me, guiding me through college as my academic advisor and then becoming my mentor as I began my own journey as an academic advisor at UHM. In addition to helping me, she has advised, mentored, and guided countless students through multiple degrees at the university. Her impact does not end there, however. In addition to academic advising, her roles in our communities have been many, ranging from grounded cultural practitioner to community facilitator to nation-building leader. Through her moʻolelo, we see how she has been able to carry out her work by internalizing lessons and drawing from her many genealogies.

I re-present parts of both Aunty ʻEkelaʻs and Mehanaʻs moʻolelo next to each other under each of the three phases I identified in the ʻaʻaliʻi kū makani lifecycle. This presentation is purposeful, showing how different the individual moʻolelo are and yet at the same time how they illuminate the phases of the ʻaʻaliʻi life cycle. The presentation of the moʻolelo in this manner is an invitation to you, dear reader, to think about your own moʻolelo—to think about your beginnings, your many shaping genealogies, and the ways you have or can internalize and use those genealogies to engage in transformative leadership.

He Hua: A Beginning
[Here both women are responding to the prompt, "Think back to your first memory of UHM."]

ʻAnakē ʻEkela

He ʻumikūmāmāhiku oʻu makahiki, so ua ʻōpiopio wau no ke komo ʻana i loko.[14] ʻAʻohe oʻu mākaukau iki. No Aiea[15] mai au. ʻAʻole wau ʻike i ka nui o nā papa, ka nui o nā haumāna i loko o nā papa, ka nui o kēlā kula.[16] ʻOiai heluhelu wau "ʻIwakālua kaukani kānaka," ʻaʻole hiki iaʻu ke noʻonoʻo i ka nui o kēlā. Ua ʻike wau he nui. So kēlā lā mua o koʻu hele ʻana, kau wau ma ke kaʻa ʻōhua mai Hālawa a hele i Mānoa. ʻAʻole wau kau mua i ke kaʻa ʻōhua. ʻO ia ka maka mua. Pīhoihoi kēlā. A ua nui nā paʻa kaʻa! A ma waho o Aiea, ʻaʻole mākou ʻike. Hele paha i ka hale pule ma Kalihi. Holoholo ma Ala Moana paha, akā aia i ka ʻauinalā. ʻAʻole i ka lā hana. No laila ʻaʻole wau ʻike i ka nui o nā kaʻa ma ke ala loa. So ua paʻa mākou ma ke ala loa.

Aia kaʻu papa i ka hola ʻeiwa o ke kakahiaka. Papa Philosophy 100. Komo wau i ka papa ma Bilger 152. Ua pūʻiwa wau i ka nui o nā haumāna. I was like, "Wow!" And ma hea ke kumu? Lohe wau i kekahi leo. Oh! Aia ke kumu ma lalo loa. And lohi wau ʻumikūmālima minuke. Hilahila wau. Just hilahila nā mea a pau. ʻAʻole wau ʻike. So komo wau i loko o ka papa. ʻIke wau i kekahi hoa papa mai Aiea. He kepanī. Aia kekahi noho ma kona ʻaoʻao, so ʻōlelo wau, "Hiki ke noho?" ʻŌlelo ʻo ia, "Oh, ae." And *kaʻakaʻa* kona maka. ʻŌlelo ʻo ia, "Oh lohi ʻoe." I was like, "Ew, ok! Yeah, lohi wau." So ʻōlelo wau, "He aha kāna i ʻōlelo ai [ke kumu]?" ʻŌlelo ʻo ia [ka haumāna kepanī], "Shh! Ke ʻōlelo nei ke kumu." So hoʻolohe wau i ke kumu. A ʻōlelo ke kumu, "What is your reality? Because if your reality is that I am here in this class speaking to you, there might not be a place for you." Ua pohihihi wau. Ua noʻonoʻo wau, "He aha kēia ʻano ʻōlelo?"

Nui ka pilikia. Lohi wau. ʻAʻole wau ʻike kahi o ka lumi, ua pilikia kēlā. Ka nui o nā haumāna. Kēia kāne e ʻōlelo ana i kekahi mea. Noʻonoʻo wau ua puhi paha ʻo ia i kekahi mea. Pono kākou a pau e puhi i ka mea like āna i puhi ai i maopopo leʻa iā kākou *kona* reality. I was like, "Hah?"

Ma hope o kēlā papa, ʻeha koʻu naʻau. Noʻonoʻo wau, pehea wau e holomua ai i kēia kula? ʻAʻole maopopo iaʻu kēia kāne, a ʻaʻole ʻo ia ʻōlelo Haole e like me ka poʻe ʻē aʻe. No hea mai ʻo ia? No ka ʻāina ʻē. A ʻo ia kekahi. I koʻu hānai ʻia ma Aiea, ʻaʻohe o mākou kamaʻāina iki i ka poʻe mai ka ʻāina ʻē. Mai Hawaiʻi wale nō. Maybe mai ka pūʻali koa. ʻAʻole kēia mau poʻe mai Kina, mai ʻApelika, mai nā wahi like ʻole. Hopohopo nui wau.

Mehanaokalā

I was a student at Honolulu Community College (HCC) and was introduced to ʻEkela[17] and she told me about Kuaʻana Student Services.[18] I never heard of it before and up until this time, I wasn't really identifying with my Hawaiian-ness. This was right about ʻ92 when everyone was prepping for ʻ93.[19] . . . That was all happening and that was foreign to me. Honestly, I don't think even up to that time, I even heard of the overthrow. It was weird.

So right before I'm ready to transition to Mānoa I thought, "I got to go. I got to do my own tour." So I go up there [UHM], and I'm walking around the campus and I'm looking for Kuaʻana, which was in Moore. But it was funny because I go up there and I go into Moore Hall and I turn the corner and I see your mom[20] walking down the hall and up until that point, I'd only seen her on TV and it freaked me out a little bit. She's walking with her students and she was talking and it was so funny because I remember this scene: She was wearing scarves and she had socks on. She was bundled up. And I thought, "Wow this is a freaky scene. We're in Hawaiʻi so why is this professor all bundled up?" And then I soon realized when I was a student there how freaking cold any of those halls can be. But I thought it was funny and that's how come I remember it so well.

So she was coming down the hall, I turned the corner and saw her and I couldn't breathe. I was blown away a little bit. I didn't know what to do and I don't know why I was afraid and star-struck at the same time. I was afraid she was going to say something to me and I was star-struck like, "Oh my god, this is the person I'd seen on TV." So, I back up into a door that's just open and I didn't know what I was backing up into but I back up into the door and I hold my breath and wait as she's walking past the door. She walks past the door, she turns the corner and she walks out. I can hear the glass doors closing outside and then I breathe. And then I turn around and I was in Kuaʻana Student Services. Kuʻumeaaloha was there, ʻOlani Decker was there. These women were there and I start to ask, I start inquiring. That was my first step onto the campus. My most vivid memory of entering UH was seeing all these women.

So my undergraduate degree was in Liberal Studies. I graduated in Conflict Resolution. That was the title of my degree. I floated around for a little while, which was really good because that was the only way that allowed me to add in my Hawaiian Studies classes. I did spend most of my time up in Poli-Sci [Political Science], but the rest of the campus was kind of trippy because I remember walking around and I was just kind of oblivious to everything that was going on while I was there. It was kind of strange for me. I realized I was living in the matrix. I was living in the surface of all these things that were going on but I wasn't looking at any of them. I wasn't looking at any of the controversies that were going on, wasn't paying attention to any of the issues that were being discussed even though my introduction was post-1993.

After that I was kind of a loner out there. I used to walk around the campus a lot by myself, and I think that's what made me a good advisor later on because I would just wander into places and I would be so nīele.[21] I was wandering around but not really paying attention. It was weird. I remember after I gave birth to him [her son], that's when I started to look at the same spaces and see something totally different.

Hao Mai, Iho Mai, Pā Mai: Elemental Influences
[Here each woman speaks about some of her main influences. In this first conversation with ʻAnakē ʻEkela I asked, "ʻO wai kāu mau kumu ʻōlelo Hawaiʻi ma ke kula nui?" Similarly, Mehanaokalā spoke of her influences.]

ʻAnakē ʻEkela

ʻO Pua[22] kaʻu kumu mua makahiki ʻekolu. A laila Nakoa Wahine me Lale[23] makahiki ʻehā. ʻAʻole wau i komo i ka makahiki mua me ka makahiki ʻelua. Koʻu manaʻo ʻaʻole maikaʻi kēlā. Ua pono wau e komo i ka makahiki mua i maopopo leʻa iaʻu nā pepeke, nā analula. Ke komo ʻoe i ka makahiki ʻekolu, nalo kēlā iā ʻoe. No ka mea, pehea e aʻo ai? ʻŌlelo nā kānaka a pau, "Oh just aʻo aku ʻoe e like me kāu i aʻo ai." ʻAʻale wau ʻike.

'A'ohe kanaka i a'o mai ia'u koe wale ka'u kumu mua i ko'u makahiki 'eiwa. Mai ka makahiki 'eiwa a i ka makahiki 'umikūmāmālima, 'umikūmāmāono paha, aia wau ma ka papa 'ōlelo Hawai'i me Charles Ka'eo. No Ho'okena mai 'o ia. He kahu ha'i 'euanelio ma ko mākou halepule. Hana 'o ia ma ka hale kū'ai puke ma Mānoa. So pili 'o ia me Elbert me Pukui.[24] Kona 'ike 'ana i kā lāua hana,[25] no'ono'o 'o ia, "Eh! Hiki ia'u ke hana i kēia ma ko'u hale pule."

So lilo 'o ia i kumu me ka ha'awina me nā mea a pau a komo mai ka po'e kūpuna i loko o kēlā papa, e like me Libert O'Sullivan. 'A'ole 'o Lunalilo ka mea kēia manawa, kona pāpā. A me kona māmā. A me Elizabeth Ellis, ka māmā o Aunty Betty Jenkins. Nā kūpuna! Hiki iā lākou a pau ke 'ōlelo Hawai'i akā komo lākou i loko o kēia papa.

Pōmaika'i wau. Kēia manawa, ke nānā wau, 'ike wau ke kumu no ko lākou noho 'ana. Na ke Akua i ho'onohonoho iā lākou i loko i maopopo le'a ia'u ka 'ao'ao o ke kūpuna. Kēlā 'ano aloha. Kēlā 'ano kani o ka 'ōlelo. No ka mea na ku'u tūtū i hānai mai ia'u ma ka 'ōlelo Hawai'i akā ua loa'a 'o ia i ka ma'i huki so 'a'ole 'o ia 'ōlelo me ka maika'i. Akā na'e 'o ia wale nō ka 'ōlelo a'u i lohe ai no laila maopopo le'a ia'u kona 'ōlelo akā 'a'ole pēlā ka 'ōlelo maoli o ka po'e a pau. So ma kēlā papa wau i lohe ai i ka 'ōlelo ma'amau, ka 'ōlelo Hawai'i, ma ka halepule. Ha'i wau i ka'u po'e haumāna, "Kēlā 'ano 'ōlelo Hawai'i i loko o ka halepule me kēia po'e kūpuna, 'olu'olu, nahenahe. 'A'ohe 'eha." But maopopo ia'u aia ma ka halepule kēlā 'ano 'ōlelo. Ma waho o kēlā, 'a'ole wau 'ike. E like me ku'u tūtū, 'olu'olu kona 'ōlelo. Ko'u kūpunakāne, like pū. Kēlā 'ano 'ōlelo 'olu'olu, nani wale, nahenahe.

Mehanaokalā

So my son was born in 1996. In 1997 I graduated with my BA. But 1997 was also the first year that 'Īlio'ula[26] came about. Aunty Pua[27] forced the kumu hula [involved in 'Īlio'ulaokalani] at that time to do certain things. The first thing that she said was, "All you folks, all you kumu hula who are involved with us in this movement, need to know your genealogies." So of course, what do good kumu hula do? They turn back around, go to their hālau and say, "All you folks need to know this." So my kumu hula made us all learn our personal genealogies.

I come from a family of genealogists. We have these big fat genealogy books in my family. So my kumu gives us this assignment. At the same time I'm taking classes because we're all prepping to go to Aotearoa, so I'm taking chant classes with Kumu Lake.[28] That's a no-no in hālau. You don't take classes from another kumu. But again, I was oblivious. I wasn't *that* into hālau where I understood all the rules. I was there all the time but I was always "my mother's daughter." Nobody knew my name. The aunties knew my name, but I was still always "my mother's daughter." I was nameless in hālau.

I'm taking classes from Kumu Lake because all of us who are going to New Zealand are learning this set repertoire. Kumu Lake teaches us all the basics: Kūnihi ka Mauna, E Hō Mai, Nā 'Aumākua.[29] When 'Īlio'ulaokalani starts up, this whole political movement, one of the ha'awina[30] they get is you need to know your genealogies and you need to learn these chants. Wow! It just so happens to be the same chants Kumu Lake already taught me. So now I'm the only one in hālau who knows all of these chants.

In hālau we get this genealogy assignment. For me, that basically means I just open my family book that's already written, and I'm just memorizing the names back. I memorized ten generations. My kumu tells everybody we need to memorize at least five generations. I memorize ten.

One night at hālau my kumu says, "Okay everybody. Stand up and go one by one." I go last. I'm scared shitless. I go last. I do my genealogy. After that moment, I'm now Mehanaokalā, no longer "my mother's daughter." Everybody knows me. All of a sudden, overnight, I get elevated to this whole other level of expectation by everybody in there. I now sit right next to my kumu in this whole 'Īlio movement, and I'm also starting to be around people my age who all sit right next to all of their kumu.

We start having to do things. We have to go testify at different things. We have to now do presentations all throughout the islands. So within a really short amount of time, I had to get akamai[31] to all the issues that were important to us. I had such a sharp learning curve, and I had to couple that with learning the culture stuff really fast because wherever we did things, our kumu's expectations of what we had to do and the kind of level of protocol was [sic] so high that you just knew you just had to be on it. We would learn chants in the car from the airport to wherever and then have to execute them, or we'd have to know what communities we were interacting with before we'd go so that we knew how to behave. It was the most stressful yet awesome time in my life. In a short amount of time I learned a ton of stuff about our people, our ways, our language. Whatever it was, I had to learn it.

Couple that with coming back to work and to school with your mom and the people who were in my generation like Lani, Kahi, Lokelani Kenolio, and Kinohi[32] who were ready to move. They were ready to go, and they did it all with this enthusiasm and love for everything. They weren't haters. So that was the trigger; it was having that cultural life mix with that political life mix with my academic life. Then that became my life. That became who I am today. People try to break that apart and I don't even know how. That's just my life and it involves academics, politics, and culture. And the way I learned it, you cannot take it apart; it's inseparable. They don't function, in my way of life, separately anymore. I cannot just go to a place and say that this is just cultural. Every chant that I do is a political statement. Every political statement that I make is a reflection of my culture. And all of that is a reflection of the intelligence that I grew from books, from people, and from interactions that I had at the university, and it just all molded this person that I am in that really kind of short amount of time. I am so shaped by everybody who shaped me; who purposefully shaped me. It wasn't an accident. I wasn't just around. No. They were conscious about it. I was lucky.

Kupu a Mohala
[These stories are in response to my question about how they fulfilled their kuleana in their work. In these examples they tell stories of their work at UHM.]

'Anakē 'Ekela

I ia manawa a'u e alaka'i ana i ka'u papahana Student Services, a'o aku wau i ka 'ōlelo Hawai'i kekahi ma ke kula nui. I kēlā wā, just hana! 'A'ole 'oe no'ono'o "'A'ole hiki." Just maopopo iā 'oe 'a'ohe ou 'ike, but hiki, hiki!

So ua hai wau i nā haumāna no ka mea ua loa'a ke kālā no ka peer advisors. But 'a'ole loa'a ke kālā no ke kākau 'ōlelo, no kekahi mea mālama i ke kālā, so ua pono wau e a'o i nā mea fiscal, nā policy o ke kula nui no ka Office of Student Affairs.

A 'ōlelo wau i nā peer advisors, "Well, pono kākou e ho'onui i ka pākeneka o ka Hawai'i ma Mānoa." No laila, 'o ka mea mea mua ho'ouna 'ia nā haumāna Hawai'i mai ke kula nui, ho'ouna 'ia lākou i nā wahi like 'ole, kakahiaka nui, hapalua hola 'elima paha. Pono lākou e hele i Wai'anae, Waimānalo, Hau'ula, Kahana, a kū ma kahi kū ka'a 'ōhua a kali i nā haumāna. A 'ōlelo lākou, "He aha ka hana?" 'Ōlelo wau, "Just kali 'oe ma 'ō a ke hele mai lākou, aloha aku iā lākou. Ha'i iā lākou 'Mai hopohopo, e hele ana kākou i ke kula nui' and you make it as fun as it can be. I no care how early it is!" But ua hau'oli lākou no ka mea ua huli mākou i ko mākou 'ohana e hele mai i ko mākou kula.

Kau lākou ma ke ka'a 'ōhua me kēia po'e keiki, nā po'e seniors paha, a holo i ke kula nui, a lilo i alaka'i no kēlā hui māka'ika'i i ke kula nui. Komo i ka ballroom ma Campus Center, nānā i nā haumāna Hawai'i a pau, pi'i ma ke kahua a 'ōlelo lākou, "'O mea mea ko'u inoa. I'm from Waia'anae, my major is . . ." Ua hiki ke 'ike kā kākou po'e haumāna i hele mai me ke kāhāhā, "Wow po'e Hawai'i e like me a'u mai ko'u 'āina!" And just kū ha'aheo i pili i kēlā alaka'i cause ua launa a mālama i ka pilina mai kā lākou 'āina a i Mānoa a puni o ke kula nui a ho'i ana me lākou. Ua hele a kama'āina he kaina a he kua'ana.

Mehanaokalā

The only reason I could do what I do is because of all those women who gave me the tools by which to do it. They gave me a sense of fearlessness. At the same time, what I learned at Nā Pua No'eau from Loke Kenolio and Uncle David Sing is to be the ultimate team player. The first thing we did was find out who the Hawaiians were in Student Services. We made sure we knew who they were and we would call on them all the time, whether it be in Financial Aid or Records or wherever. And if there weren't any Hawaiians in different places, we were just always available.

We participated in everything. The mentality was, "Oh that office is having a financial aid fair; let's go down. We have the tables, so we can lend you guys our tables. You need supplies? We have supplies." Beyond just building partnerships with any of the Hawaiians, whether they liked it or not, we were always around because we're not going to just keep asking you for help; we're going to be there to offer it.

UH is a monster of a bureaucracy so it was hard busting down those walls. There were many there who just did not want to deal with another subgroup of students. Their mentality was, "Everyone's the same and they just run through the same processes." But we were like, "No. That's not true." We realized the more foreign the environment was, the more we had to make things happen for us by finding collaborators. We maintained a constant presence, and we had to do everything better than everyone else and happier than everyone else. That was how we convinced people whatever their stereotypes were about Hawaiians, to change it.

We needed people who weren't Hawaiian to be on our side so we formed relationships. Uncle David would say, "You wanna carry this off, then form your partners; then your one dollar goes way further; then your one person running that program will go way further, because when you need them they'll come and help you. So every time you can go and help them, help them. Just do it. Don't complain about it. It's just the way we do things around here." Those relationships were key for me because when I began working in an academic unit, I still had to be with those people in Student Services at different times in order to get my students' needs and potential heard throughout the rest of the university. So that presence was really good and really helped us to make change for our students.

[As a reader, take a moment to let their moʻolelo settle within you . . .]

Final Reflections

I learn something new and feel inspired in a new way every time I read the words of the women just cited and the other kumu I had the privilege to learn from. I also feel both proud and humbled because by returning to engagement in moʻolelo and inviting those moʻolelo to teach me, I too became an ʻaʻaliʻi kū makani and transformed myself beyond the average Western-trained researcher and scholar. I became the Native Hawaiian scholar who is innately in me.

Coming full circle, the goal of this chapter was to share at least three moʻolelo of my own. First, I wanted to share my personal struggles with being a Native Hawaiian graduate student and researcher in a Western academic institution. Though I was raised in Hawaiian environments with Hawaiian ways of teaching, learning, and knowing through moʻolelo, I did not always remember to use that ʻike kūpuna in the Western academy because I was not invited to do so. The absence of engagement in moʻolelo made it difficult for me to find my way in graduate school.

Second, though I struggled finding my path as a Native Hawaiian researcher in a Western academy, I finally did recognize my way when I returned to the roots of my Hawaiian cultural practices. As I engaged in moʻolelo through oli, ʻōlelo noʻeau, and moʻolelo aku/moʻolelo mai, I reconnected with my Hawaiian ways of knowing. Further, those Hawaiian ways of knowing opened me up to the ʻike kūpuna that was awaiting me and thus guided my learning from the moʻolelo of the women. Returning to moʻolelo, in its many forms, saved me both academically and personally in my mission to write my dissertation and earn my doctorate.

Third, through actively engaging in moʻolelo, the ʻaʻaliʻi kū makani framework revealed itself to me. This framework, though ancestral and commonly used in Hawaiian contexts, has helped me to better understand the contemporary process of transforming spaces into Hawaiian places of learning. The women's moʻolelo, in light of the ʻaʻaliʻi kū makani framework, have taught me that, in order to transform spaces, we must first prepare and transform ourselves.

Implications

I highlight these three points because they direct us to some important implications in our future work as students, researchers, teachers, and leaders. First, we need to invite different methodologies and epistemologies into our work. When we do so, students feel validated, alternative and additional frameworks can be realized, and thus new lessons can be gleaned and implemented. As teachers, we need to invite students to bring their personal and cultural methodologies into the academy. As students, we need to become fearless and bring those methodologies and ways of knowing into our classrooms and research. We need to help our professors see the value of such ways of knowing as we engage in important research.

Second, we need to engage in our cultural practices, such as moʻolelo. For those of us who are already connected to a cultural practice, we need to continue to engage, even when we are in the middle of coursework and thesis/dissertation writing in predominantly non-Hawaiian/Indigenous institutions. The lessons and frames that we learn from our cultural practices are too

important to be cast aside. For those of us who are not engaged in cultural practice, the 'a'ali'i kū makani framework reminds us that there are multiple beginnings. We are constantly shaped. Therefore, it is never too late to start or return
to a cultural practice in which we previously engaged.

Third, many of us today want to transform spaces into Hawaiian places of
learning, into educational kīpuka (Goodyear-Ka'ōpua 2013). However, these
spaces, whether in the academy or in the community, are indeed contentious
grounds (Alfred 2004). Therefore, the first step to transforming those spaces is
our own personal preparation and transformation into 'a'ali'i kū makani by
drawing on the many genealogies that feed us to make us both strong and
resilient to engage in the necessary work. Many of those genealogies are
connected to learning and sharing mo'olelo that teach us critical lessons. So
I invite you, dear reader, to sing, chant, dance, and tell stories—and as you do
so, listen to the 'ike your kūpuna are gifting you.

NOTES

1. I use the term "predominantly non-Hawaiian institution" to describe University
of Hawai'i at Mānoa because Native Hawaiians make up less than 4 percent of faculty,
1 percent of administration (Native Hawaiian Advancement Task Force 2012), 15.8 percent of undergraduates, and 12.5 percent of graduate students (Balutski and Wright
2012).

2. I use the term "campus culture" as Jayakumar and Museus (2012) do: It "takes
into account the historical context, rituals and traditions, and other symbolic components of a campus's identity, as well as both the observed and unobserved values and
assumptions that shape perspectives, behaviors, and the way education is approached
and delivered" (p. 5).

3. According to *The Greenwood Dictionary of Education* (Collins III and O'Brien 2003),
the term "methodology" is defined as "the application of principles, practices, and procedures to a problem, project, course of study, or given discipline" (p. 220). Similarly,
Tuhiwai Smith (2012) states, "Methodology in its simplest definition generally refers to
the theory of method, or the approach or technique being taken, or the reasoning for
selecting a set of methods" (p. ix).

4. Hālau hula: Hula school (common translation).

5. Mele: "Song, anthem, or chant of any kind; poem, poetry" (Pukui and Elbert 1986,
p. 245).

6. Oli: "chant that was not danced to, especially with prolonged phrases chanted in
one breath" (Pukui and Elbert 1986, p. 285).

7. I draw from two sources when I use the term "transform": First, Eckel, Hill, and
Green (1998) define transformational change as that which "alters the culture of the
institution by changing select underlying assumptions and institutional behaviors,
processes, and products; is deep and pervasive affecting the whole institution; is intentional; and occurs over time" (p. 3). I also draw from Engeström's (2001) discussion
on transformation in which an activity or institution can be "reconceptualized to em-
brace a radically wider horizon of possibilities than in the previous mode (p. 137).

Therefore, in my use of the term "transformation," I am referring to the breadth and depth of change that creates space for a variety of ontologies, epistemologies, and pedagogies to emerge and affect people on campus, as well as the families, communities, and natural environments surrounding institutions of higher education.

8. Dr. Noelani Goodyear-Ka'ōpua (2013) uses the term "educational kīpuka" to describe "zones of indigenous cultural growth" (p. 7). Further, Pukui and Elbert translate kīpuka as "variation or change of form, as a calm place in a high sea, deep place in a shoal, opening in a forest, openings in cloud formations, and especially a clear place or oasis within a lava bed where there may be vegetation" (1986, p. 155). Therefore, I use the term "educational kīpuka" as a Hawaiian term to describe Hawaiian places of learning that have grown and flourished despite the variety of challenging conditions around them.

9. Ho'āeae style of chanting is very melodic and particularly extends the vowels at the end of the lines. It is often used in chants of love and wooing (M. Boyd, personal communication, ongoing).

10. The name of my hālau hula is Hālau o ke 'A'ali'i Kū Makani (Kumu hula Manu Boyd). Because it is the name of our hālau, we have a close relationship with the plant, its uses, metaphors, and symbols. Further, we often say this particular 'ōlelo no'eau out loud to remind us of our innate strength and ability to be flexibile and persevere.

11. The 'a'ali'i can be transformed from a tree into many important things for many different uses. For example, the wood can be used for weapons, tools, and house posts. The flowers are used for lei. The leaves are used for medicine. The fruit are used for medicine, dye, and in lei (Bishop Museum 2014).

12. Because of space limitations, I have selected snapshots of the mo'olelo of just two women. To read the full mo'olelo of all eight women, I invite you to read my dissertation (Lipe 2014).

13. Ma ka 'ōlelo Hawai'i: in the Hawaiian language. I want to honor the first language of mo'olelo in Hawai'i and the transformational work Aunty 'Ekela has done to help revive the Hawaiian language so that we can continue to learn from the ancestral mo'olelo of Hawai'i. It is for this reason that I include her Hawaiian language story here. Also, I do not translate her story in this chapter, though her full story is translated as an appendix in my dissertation.

14. I loko o ke Kula Nui.

15. Pela 'o 'Anakē 'Ekela iā "Aiea" me ka 'okina 'ole.

16. 'O ia ho'i ke Kula Nui o Hawai'i ma Mānoa.

17. It is interesting here that Mehanaokalā's story and Aunty 'Ekela's mo'olelo are connected through shared genealogies of teaching, learning, and service. These are important connections that we make when we engage in mo'olelo aku, mo'olelo mai.

18. Kua'ana Student Services was a program set up to help recruit and retain more Native Hawaiian students at UH Mānoa.

19. She is referring to the 1993 Hawaiian sovereignty march that marked the 100th year since the illegal overthrow of the Hawaiian monarchy. Approximately 18,000 people marched through downtown Honolulu to 'Iolani Palace. For more information on the march, see Kame'eleihiwa (1993).

20. My mother is Dr. Lilikalā Kame'eleihiwa, a professor of Hawaiian Studies at UHM.

21. Nīele: "curious, inquisitive" (Pukui and Elbert 1986, p. 265).

22. Pua Hopkins.

23. Lale Kimura.

24. He mau alaka'i 'ōlelo Hawai'i 'o Samuel Elbert me Mary Kawena Pukui.

25. E a'o ana lāua i ka 'ōlelo Hawai'i ma loko ko ka lumi papa.

26. The 'Īlio'ulaokalani Coalition was formed in 1997 by a group of cultural practitioners to take action on legal and policy matters affecting Hawaiians. For more information, visit http://www.ilio.org and http://artofresistanceshow.wordpress.com/2008/05/16/ilioulaokalani-coalition/.

27. Dr. Pualani Kanaka'ole Kanahele is a kumu hula and Hawaiian scholar.

28. Kumu John Keola Lake was a well-respected kumu hula.

29. These three chants have become "basics" in the sense that they are fairly well known by members of the Hawaiian community.

30. Ha'awina: "lesson, assignment" (Pukui and Elbert 1986, p. 45).

31. Akamai: "smart, clever, expert" (Pukui and Elbert 1986, p. 13).

32. Lani Waiau, Kahi Brooks, Loke Kenolio, and Kinohi Gomes are all peers of her generation who have been active in bringing about change in the Hawaiian community, especially through education.

BIBLIOGRAPHY

Alfred, T. (2004). Warrior scholarship: Seeing the university as a ground of contention. In D. A. Mihesuah and A.C. Wilson (Eds.), *Indigenizing the academy: Transforming scholarship and empowering communities* (pp. 88–99). Lincoln: University of Nebraska Press.

Balutski, N., and K. Wright (2012). *2012 Native Hawaiian student profile*. Unpublished manuscript, Native Hawaiian Student Services, Hawai'inuiākea School of Hawaiian Knowledge, University of Hawai'i at Mānoa, Honolulu.

Benham, M. K. P., and R. H. Heck (1998). *Culture and educational policy in Hawai'i: The silencing of native voices*. Mahwah, NJ: Erlbaum.

Bishop Museum (2014). *Hawaiian Ethnobotany Online Database*. Retrieved on November 1, 2014, from http://data.bishopmuseum.org/ethnobotanydb/ethnobotany.php?b=d&ID=aalii.

Collins III, J. W., and N. P. O'Brien (2003). *The Greenwood dictionary of education*. Westport, CT: Greenwood Press.

Eckel, P., B. Hill, and M. Green (1998). *En route to transformation*. Washington, DC: American Council on Education.

Engeström, Y. (2001). Expansive learning at work: Toward an activity-theoretical reconceptualization. *Journal of Education and Work, 14*(1), 133–156.

Goodyear-Ka'ōpua, N. (2013). *The seeds we planted: Portraits of a native Hawaiian charter school*. Minneapolis: University of Minnesota Press.

Jayakumar, U. M., and S. Museus (2012). Mapping the intersection of campus cultures and equitable outcomes among racially diverse student populations. In S. Museus and U. M. Jayakumar (Eds.), *Creating campus cultures: Fostering success among racially diverse student populations* (pp. 1–27). New York: Routledge.

Kahaunaele, K. (1997). *Māewa i ka hao mai a ka makani*. Unpublished manuscript.

Kameʻeleihiwa, L. K. (1993). "The Hawaiian Sovereignty Movement: January-August 1993." *Journal of Pacific History—Political Chronicles, 28*(3), 63–72.

Kanahele, P. K. (February 4, 2012). *Hoʻomālamalama o nā wahine kapu.* Presented at ʻAha Wahine, Windward Community College, Kāneʻohe, HI.

Kawaiʻaeʻa, K., A. Housman, and M. Alencastre (2007). Pūʻā i ka ʻōlelo, ola ka ʻohana: Three generations of Hawaiian language revitalization. *Hūlili, 4,* 183–237.

Lipe, D. (2013). *Diversifying science: Recognizing Indigenous knowledge systems as scientific worldviews* (Doctoral dissertation). Retrieved from ProQuest (1430284238).

Lipe, K. (2014). *Aloha as fearlessness: Lessons from the moʻolelo of eight Native Hawaiian female educational leaders on transforming the University of Hawaiʻi at Mānoa into a Hawaiian place of learning* (Doctoral dissertation).

Museus, S. D. (2008). Focusing on institutional fabric: Assessing campus cultures to enhance cross-cultural engagement. In S. Harper (Ed.), *Creating inclusive campus environments for cross-cultural learning and student engagement* (pp. 205–234). Washington, DC: NASPA.

Pukui, M. K. (1983). *ʻOlelo noʻeau.* Honolulu: Bishop Museum Press.

Pukui, M. K., and S. H. Elbert (1986). *Hawaiian dictionary.* Honolulu: University of Hawaiʻi Press.

Smith, G. H. (October 2003). *Indigenous struggle for the transformation of education and schooling.* Paper presented at the Alaska Federation of Natives Convention, Anchorage. Retrieved on July 20, 2012, from http://ankn.uaf.edu/Curriculum/Speeches/Graham_Smith.

———. (July 2011). *Transforming education and schooling: Re-centering language, culture and identity.* Paper presented at the 2011 Pacific Educational Conference: Cultivating and Preserving Pacific Identities "in" and "through" Education, Pohnpei State, Federated States of Micronesia. Retrieved on August 1, 2012, from http://www.prel.org/media/186751/pec_opening_19th%20july%202011_dr%20smith.pdf.

Tuhiwai Smith, L. (2012). *Decolonizing methodologies* (2nd ed.). London: Zed Books.

Vizenor, Gerald. (2008). *Survivance: Narratives of native presence.* Lincoln: University of Nebraska Press. Retrieved May 30, 2012, from http://lib.myilibrary.com.eres.library.manoa.hawaii.edu?ID=195840.

Ka Wai Ola: The Life-Sustaining Water of Kanaka Knowledge

Katrina-Ann R. Kapā'anaokalāokeola Nākoa Oliveira

The Flood Waters

It was a bright sunny summer day in Kahakuloa, Maui. Off in the distance the mountains were overcast, but the sky was not noticeably dark or heavy with rain. Kahakuloa was bustling with activity and the sound of 'ōlelo Hawai'i (Hawaiian language) echoed throughout the valley as nearly thirty participants from Mauiakama, an 'ōlelo Hawai'i immersion summer camp, put the finishing touches on four restored lo'i (wetland taro fields) near the stream. Within seeing distance, a young Kanaka[1] girl approximately six years old was about to cross the calm and narrow stream as her father waited for her on the opposite bank. A few feet away from the girl, a Kanaka man in his twenties was just about to bathe in the refreshing waters of the cool, clear stream. Suddenly, large banana stumps and other debris began floating downstream, and dirt churned in the water. The Kanaka man backed away, and bystanders shouted at the little girl to move away from the stream for fear she would be swept up by the flash flood. About fifty yards away, Kahakuloa residents who were preparing to leave the valley had no choice but to wait until the water receded. Within an hour, it was safe to cross the stream by truck. By the next morning, the water was once again transparent; it had been cleansed by the previous afternoon's flash flood.

Like the Kahakuloa stream, the Hawaiian language program at the University of Hawai'i at Mānoa (UHM) has, for the past two decades, maintained a steady course. It has been relatively uneventful since the last major 'ōlelo Hawai'i flash flood of 1995 when protestors stormed Bachman Hall, home of the office of the president of the University of Hawai'i system, to demand that the university abandon plans to cut the Hawaiian language program's budget by nearly 60 percent.[2] Although the protest may have come as a surprise to the administration, there were ominous hō'ailona (signs) that the Kanaka community was in a state of unrest. Like a flash flood that builds as a result of the momentum gained by multiple sources of water running off the land and converging at a stream, protestors from various walks of life from the Kanaka community— including preschool children, cultural activists, and university 'ōlelo Hawai'i students and professors—converged at the system administrative offices at

Mānoa to voice our concerns. We argued that ʻōlelo Hawaiʻi is an official language of the state of Hawaiʻi. Moreover, attempts to revitalize the mother tongue of Hawaiʻi would be crushed if ʻōlelo Hawaiʻi was silenced in the halls of Mānoa where most of the Hawaiian immersion teachers were being prepared to teach. By the end of the day, the administration acceded to the demands of the protestors, and Mānoa's Hawaiian language program budget was fully restored.[3] The flood waters receded.

While UHM has enjoyed relatively calm and clear waters over the past two decades with respect to its Hawaiian language and Hawaiian studies programs, in recent years, its academic landscape has passed some major milestones in terms of the advancement of ʻōlelo Hawaiʻi. In 2006, Kerry Laiana Wong completed the first doctoral dissertation written solely in Hawaiian.[4] In 2007 Leilani Basham became the first person to complete both her master's thesis and doctoral dissertation in Hawaiian.[5] Since 2006, several theses and dissertations have been written ma ka ʻōlelo Hawaiʻi (in the Hawaiian language). In 2010, Kerry Laiana Wong and I were the first faculty members in the UH system to submit promotion and tenure dossiers ma ka ʻōlelo Hawaiʻi. And recently I attended the World Indigenous Peoples Conference on Education held in Honolulu, Hawaiʻi, where I was pleasantly surprised to hear a presentation that was unapologetically delivered ma ka ʻōlelo Hawaiʻi by a Kanaka academic, Ron Kekeha Solis. Delivering conference presentations and writing master's theses, doctoral dissertations, and tenure and promotion dossiers ma ka ʻōlelo Hawaiʻi are examples of acts designed to normalize ʻōlelo Hawaiʻi in the academy. Each of these successes represents a source of water running toward the stream of Kanaka knowledge, ready to break forth as a flash flood to cleanse the university of paradigms and stereotypes that pigeonhole Kanaka knowledge systems. By writing ma ka ʻōlelo Hawaiʻi and by writing in English using frameworks aligned with our customary traditions, Kanaka scholars are creating new arenas where Kanaka ways of knowing are both appreciated and respected.

ʻElua ʻAuwai

My scholarship may be likened to ʻauwai, irrigation ditches that divert some of the water from the stream into loʻi and then channel it back to the stream. Infused by the nutrients in the loʻi, the water from the ʻauwai enriches the ecosystems in the stream. As a Kanaka scholar who writes both in ʻōlelo Hawaiʻi and in English, my work parallels two ʻauwai on either side of the stream that eventually return water to the same enriched stream of Kanaka knowledge.

As a Kanaka, especially one writing in dual languages, I have learned many lessons about the obstacles that Kānaka face when writing in an academic institution. On the one hand, to be taken seriously we must demonstrate to the academy that our research is just as, if not more, rigorous than other disciplines at our institution. Simultaneously, and perhaps even more importantly, we as Kanaka scholars must ensure that our research meets the standards of and receives the approval of our community. This chapter explores some of the efforts by various Kanaka scholars to advance Kanaka methodologies. Although it discusses Kanaka methodologies with particular emphasis on ʻōlelo Hawaiʻi methodologies, this chapter is intentionally not written ma ka ʻōlelo Hawaiʻi in order to reach a broader audience, especially other Kānaka interested in ʻōlelo Hawaiʻi research methodologies, but who are not yet fluent ma ka ʻōlelo Hawaiʻi. It is my hope that we will soon reach a critical mass of ʻōlelo Hawaiʻi speakers so that issues related to Kanaka research methods and epistemologies may be conducted ma ka ʻōlelo Hawaiʻi and enjoy a large readership. Until we reach that tipping point and attain the critical mass necessary for the next cleansing flash flood, I will continue to write in both languages.

Not only do I write in two languages but my complementary academic backgrounds also inform my scholarship. As a geographer by training and a kumu ʻōlelo Hawaiʻi by profession, I have faced the dual challenges of writing ma ka ʻōlelo Hawaiʻi about non-Kanaka constructs such as "mapping" and "cartographic representations" and writing in English while liberally incorporating ʻōlelo Hawaiʻi terms. How does one write ma ka ʻōlelo Hawaiʻi about non-Kanaka concepts? How does one write about Kanaka mapping practices, for instance, when the word for *map*, "palapala ʻāina" (land document), reflects a non-Kanaka construct? That is, although ancestral Kanaka did have methods for locating themselves on the landscape, these methods did not include two-dimensional line drawings on paper until postcontact times. Before their use of maps, Kānaka employed "performance cartographies" or what I like to call "wisdom maps."[6] Through hula, mele (poetry), moʻolelo (historical accounts), and other modes of performance, ancestral Kānaka were able to embed in the minds of their audience an image of the places celebrated in the hula, mele, and moʻolelo.

To further complicate the issue, if the generally accepted term for "map" is palapala ʻāina and the whole crux of my thesis statement is that ancestral Kānaka did not have maps before contact, how do I as a scholar writing journal articles solely ma ka ʻōlelo Hawaiʻi begin to explain Kanaka "mapping" practices once I have openly acknowledged that "palapala ʻāina" insufficiently describes Kanaka ways of locating ourselves? Another dilemma is selecting an ʻōlelo Hawaiʻi term that approximates the notion of "performance cartography" while taking into consideration that "hōʻike honua" (to show the earth, performances related to the earth), a logical option, is already more commonly translated and understood to mean "geography." Thus, before I can even begin my discussion about performance cartographies and Kanaka "mapping" practices, it is necessary for me to define the 'ōlelo Hawai'i terminologies that I will be employing. This additional layer of research would not be as complicated if I were to write in English. Of the terms "geography," "map," and "performance cartographies" perhaps only "performance cartographies" would need to be defined for my English readership.

Methodological Strategies for Crossing the Stream

As previously stated, as Kanaka scholars within the academy, we have the responsibility to meet the standards of our community, as well as of our academic institution. Kanaka academics—including but not limited to Isabella Abott, Naleen Andrade, Nanette Judd, Lilikalā Kame'eleihiwa, George Kanahele, Jonathan Osorio, Abraham Pi'ianaia, Noenoe Silva, Haunani-Kay Trask, Sam No'eau Warner, Kerry Laiana Wong, and Kanalu Young—are notable Kanaka pioneers in their respective academic fields. Each of these scholars have been able to fuse the ancestral wisdom and knowledge systems of their kūpuna with their fields of expertise in the academy, thus demonstrating the relevance of ancestral practices and understandings in a modern context.

In recent years, Kanaka scholars, writing ma ka 'ōlelo Hawai'i and in English alike, have incorporated various techniques to indigenize methodological approaches within the academy. Scholars such as Leilani Basham, Kahikina de Silva, and Keawe Lopes have used mele as the foundation for their thesis statements and methodological approaches.[7] In some cases these scholars have used the first line of a mele as the title of each of their chapters. Sometimes authors purposefully begin each of their book chapters with a poignant mele as a foundation for the rest of the chapter. In other cases, key lessons learned from a mele serve as the research methodology for their scholarship. Other Kanaka scholars such as ku'ualoha ho'omanawanui and Alohalani Brown are known for their scholarship based on mo'olelo, whereas Kekeha Solis is well known for his use of 'ōlelo no'eau (proverbs) as a methodological approach. Another common methodological device is to weave metaphors throughout scholarly publications (see the chapters by Goodyear-Ka'ōpua, Saffery, and Vaughan in this book series). Still others allow the 'āina to speak for itself through 'ōlelo Hawai'i place names and 'ōlelo no'eau related to place.[8]

A common link among these varied methodological styles is the effortlessness with which Kanaka scholars are able to marry their academic scholarship with their customary practices and traditions. In doing so, these and other Kanaka scholars are demonstrating the germaneness of ancestral knowledge systems in a contemporary context. Moreover, they are asserting that our ancestral knowledge may stand up to the same rigorous standards as those applying to other authors writing in the same fields and for the same publications.

The complexity of Kanaka thought embedded in ʻōlelo Hawaiʻi adds another layer of kuleana for the Kanaka scholar. Inasmuch as Kanaka research is often conducted *in* communities and *for* communities *by those with kuleana* to those very communities, sometimes it takes a community to complete a research project. Our work is often strengthened by the collective knowledge, skill sets, and experiences of others. I am so humbled to work with an awesome community of Kanaka scholars at UHM. In my earlier publications, I reached out to experienced artists and publishers to draw exceptional illustrations and create elaborate genealogical charts to accompany my written text. I even hired a well-respected Kanaka copy editor well versed in ʻōlelo Hawaiʻi to review my manuscript before I submitted the manuscript to the publishing press. Rather than attempting to learn these skill sets, I sought out extremely talented professionals within my community with the expertise that I admittedly lacked.

On other occasions, I have relied on my academic community to discuss issues with which I was grappling. For instance, due to the kaona intentionally embedded in Kanaka poetry, mele and other forms of poetry can be particularly difficult to interpret. Because overlapping and intersecting meanings are celebrated in Kanaka knowledge systems, the Kanaka scholar often has multiple layers of information to consider when reading ʻōlelo Hawaiʻi literature or listening to oral histories.

Community of Scholars Methodology

An approach that appreciates and honors these multiple layers of meaning is what I call the "community of scholars methodology." In my experience, this methodological approach is highly effective when colleagues who have mutual admiration and respect for one another's research engage in continued and sustained discussions. Through this process, colleagues are able to discuss various topics collectively based on each person's research interests, which often offer a multiplicity of interpretations of the same text.

I have used this approach in collaboration with fellow colleagues in an attempt to unravel the layers of meaning embedded in ancestral poetry. As repositories of cultural and linguistic knowledge, mele, oli (chants), and hula are excellent sources of native intelligence. In addition to using the *Hawaiian Dictionary*, we also used scientific publications to glean insights about the geological formation of islands, animal behaviors, and other information that might relate to the mele we were researching. We also researched other mele and moʻolelo that might contain similar material related to the mele we were studying. At times we even used the internet to search for images that might shed some light on the meaning of the poetry. In *Mele a Pakui* for example, it is stated,

"He panina Kaula. O ka Mokupapapa." In my discussions with fellow colleagues we wondered whether Ka'ula was being described as a flat island (moku papapa) or if Mokupapapa was the name of another island. A quick search of images of Ka'ula revealed that it is a crescent-shaped flat island. For 'ōlelo Hawai'i scholars interested in conducting research, these multiple techniques serve as a powerful tool for researching 'ōlelo Hawai'i terms and concepts.

Through discussions with 'ōlelo Hawai'i colleagues, we are able to discuss variations that exist among the same mo'olelo recorded by different Kanaka scholars in their primary texts. In some cases, rather than wholeheartedly accepting the work of well-respected Kanaka scholars, the conversation may take an unexpected turn as we attempt to determine whether or not a typographical error was made by the typesetter. On more than one occasion, I have had discussions with my colleagues about whether an "n" or a "u" was the correct letter in a word (e.g., Makalina, Makaliua) because it is possible for a typesetter to accidently invert either letter.

By the nature of the community of scholars approach, all participants render themselves vulnerable to a "peer review" process in which their ideas are constantly analyzed and scrutinized by others in the group. Unlike the academy's double-blind process that protects the anonymity of both the reviewer and the author, Kānaka have a long history of peer reviewing one another openly and publicly. There are numerous examples of public debates in which ka'ao, mo'olelo, and mo'okū'auhau that had previously been only committed to memory and recited orally were published in written form in 'ōlelo Hawai'i newspapers and open to public scrutiny. Just as peers provide feedback on refereed journal articles, in these public spaces those whose scholarship is praised are celebrated for their intelligence, whereas those whose scholarship is substandard or questionable are challenged.

Hale Nauā

In the community of scholars methodological approach, Kānaka come together to discuss research questions in much the same way as the Hale Nauā (House of Wisdom, Temple of Science) might have done in the past to link ancestral Kanaka observations with modern scientific theories. Whereas the original Hale Nauā of Kamehameha I's era primarily met to scrutinize claims to royal genealogies, the Hale Nauā Society founded by King Kalākaua in September 1886 had a much broader function. Its purpose was to revive and advance ancestral Kanaka knowledge systems in areas including astrology, divination, science, art, and literature. Comprised of both male and female Kanaka members, the Hale Nauā Society conducted its proceedings ma ka 'ōlelo makuahine (in the mother tongue) of this pae moku (archipelago). It continues to serve as a model for collaborative Kanaka research methodologies.

Papakū Makawalu Methodology

Given that the Hale Nauā is a well-known ancestral example of a meeting of the minds of highly respected Kanaka scholars, it comes as no surprise then that Kanaka methodologies such as Papakū Makawalu are being used to examine oral and written Kanaka histories from multiple angles and perspectives. The Papakū Makawalu methodological approach appreciates the layers of wisdom in ancestral scholarship. In this "methodical presentation of a holistic preview of the Hawaiian universe," scholars deconstruct layers of embedded meaning.[9] This is accomplished by examining oral and written 'ōlelo Hawai'i histories collaboratively and through close observation, especially by capturing images in the form of digital photographs.

Sense Abilities Methodology

As a Kanaka scholar, I have a deep appreciation for close observation when conducting research. Like contemporary scientists, ancestral Kānaka formed hypotheses and conducted extensive investigations to acquire new knowledge or refine previous knowledge. Through close observation, ancestral Kānaka were able to make many breakthroughs (e.g., non-instrument navigation, pharmaceutical remedies, astronomical observations) that are only now being acknowledged and validated by the scientific community.

In recognition of the fact that my kūpuna were stellar observers and scientists in their own right, I too rely heavily on the use of my "sense abilities" or the use of my senses as a methodology for comprehending the world around me and examining my research topic from multiple perspectives. I recognize at least nine sense abilities that I believe all Kānaka are born with: sight, listening, taste, touch, smell, na'au, kulāiwi, au 'āpa'apa'a, and mo'o.

Sense Ability of Sight

'Ike means "to see" and "to know"; the sense ability of sight assists us in comprehending visual clues. Kanaka navigators, for example, describe how the sight of certain birds provides clues about the location and proximity of a landmass. An apprentice navigator relayed to me a story about how his navigation mentor, Nainoa Thompson, on his first voyage saw a land bird flying and mistakenly assumed that the landmass was in the opposite direction. Thompson believed that the bird was departing the island in search of food. What Thompson did not notice, however, was that the bird was carrying a fish in its bill. The bird was not flying *away* from the island in search of food; rather, the bird was flying *toward* the island to feed its chicks. Thompson's own navigation mentor correctly prophesized that if the canoe maintained its course it would make landfall in two hours.

Sense Ability of Listening

Because we as researchers may learn a great deal by listening to others, especially elders and master practitioners, the sense ability of listening is commonly used in indigenous communities as a methodology. Researchers often conduct interviews, both formal and informal, and transcribe what they hear. Linda Smith refers to a form of informal interviews as "kitchen table discourse."[10] In this interview style, although the researcher has a research goal in mind, he or she does not prepare a preset list of formal interview questions, but rather the inquiry is organic in nature, driven by the course of the conversation.

In more traditional contexts, sense abilities involve a lifetime of learning gleaned through conversations between apprentice and master. These conversations are particularly important for apprentices learning an ancestral practice such as lomilomi (massage), navigation, or hula. Their conversations with their mentors are built on mutual respect, trust, and admiration and may continue for the duration of their lives.

Sense Ability of Taste

Academic researchers may not necessary appreciate the applicability of the sense ability of taste when conducting archival research. Yet, at times, something as simple as tasting a new variety of limu (seaweed) may lead to an epiphany. A researcher might taste the limu to better understand a mele written by his great-grandmother about the delicacies of her ancestral homeland.

Sense Ability of Touch

The sense ability of touch can have a profound impact on archival researchers. Touching the actual documents written by one's ancestors or by highly respected Kanaka scholars who have long since passed can serve as an inspiration for contemporary scholars who are eager to piece together knowledge of the past. When I take my graduate students to archives to conduct research, the students often remark that they "get chicken skin" when they touch the same piece of paper once held by Kanaka royalty.

Similarly, mele and other forms of Hawaiian poetry such as ʻōlelo noʻeau may speak to the characteristics of winds and rains. However, only when someone actually travels to that place and experiences the winds and rains of that location will she or he truly understand the mele. The first time I traveled to Kohala, Hawaiʻi, I vividly remember my astonishment at the strength of the wind. However, after recalling the song "Maikaʻi ka Makani o Kohala" (The Wind of Kohala Is Good), I was reminded that Kohala is a place noted for its strong winds.

Field researchers might have similar experiences. A few years ago, a kupuna explained how he had found a small stone along a path in Kahakuloa. He then looked around and placed it on a groove on a much larger stone along the path; the smaller stone fit perfectly. The kupuna explained that the small stone once held the light that lit that path at night. For me, being able to see and touch both stones was an awesome feeling because it reminded me that, as I walk on the landscape, I am walking in the footsteps of my kūpuna.

Sense Ability of Smell
Just as the feel of the wind on the skin jars the memory and recalls times past at certain locales, so too can certain places be noted for their scents. Maui residents sometimes use scents, both pleasant and unpleasant, as landmarks. I can think of two places on Maui that are known for their stench. One is in Puʻunēnē where there is an open ditch for irrigating the sugar plantation. Another is past Waiheʻe Valley near Camp Maluhia where there is a pig farm.

Sense Ability of Naʻau
The sense ability of naʻau is often referred to as the sixth sense. It is an innate sense and knowledge base with which Kānaka are born. The sense ability of naʻau honors our intestines as the center from which our instincts and feelings emanate. Sometimes researchers instinctually sense danger or know the answer to a question they are seeking simply because of a feeling in their naʻau.

Sense Ability of Kulāiwi
The sense ability of kulāiwi values our longstanding relationships with our ancestral homelands. It appreciates the unique local knowledge systems that we refine over generations by residing on the same lands. It honors the fact that within the Kanaka community there are subcommunities of people who have developed local practices and knowledges that differ from those of Kānaka residing elsewhere in the pae moku. A quick survey of loʻi kalo (wetland taro gardens) throughout the pae moku indicates that kalo farming practices vary from place to place depending on resources, topography, and climate.

Sense Ability of Au ʻĀpaʻapaʻa
The sense ability of au ʻapaʻapaʻa honors Kanaka methods of timekeeping such as our moon calendars. This method is an ancestral science and intelligence gathered by observing the life cycles of living organisms and other timeless constants in our natural environment.

Sense Ability of Moʻo
The sense ability of moʻo is based on knowledge systems created and refined over thousands of years. It acknowledges the Kanaka community as a whole for technological advances such as the creation of fishponds, loʻi systems, and

non-instrument navigation. It is an understanding that the knowledge we create today serves as a legacy for succeeding generations of Kānaka.

Serendipitous Methodology

Another methodology that I have sometimes encountered while conducting research is what Kanaka scholar Kerry Laiana Wong refers to as the "serendipitous" method.[11] In this approach, information that the researcher is seeking exposes itself suddenly and unexpectedly. I have engaged in numerous conversations with fellow colleagues who believe that their kūpuna guide them as they conduct research and then reveal the answers that they have been seeking. Although I do indeed believe that my kūpuna have guided me in directions that I did not have the cognitive capacity to dream up for myself, I also believe in Oprah Winfrey's assertion that "there's no such thing as luck. It's preparation meeting opportunity." For example, the sun, moon, and stars rise and set every day, yet many of us do not know how to harness this knowledge to navigate across the Pacific Ocean because we have not been trained to do so. Similarly, I can think of several examples during my genealogical and archival research when the answers for which I was so desperately searching had been right before my eyes. It was not until I was prepared and able to recognize the answers that I finally understood that those very answers had been there all along.

Conclusion

As Kānaka who carry the family names and genealogies of our kūpuna, we are a reflection of all of our ancestors and our ancestral homelands; thus, we have an obligation to conduct our research in a way that is ethical, culturally appropriate, and beneficial to our community. Sometimes when I have unanswered questions regarding ancestral knowledge systems or archival research, I try to imagine myself in my kūpuna's shoes. What might my kūpuna have done to solve this same problem given the resources available to them in their time and environment? One day as I reflected on the fact that Kānaka used kukui nuts for light and that each kukui nut kernel burns within a couple of minutes, I thought about how my kūpuna had to devise a method of cracking the kukui nut shells at a rapid rate to make the effort worth their time. By putting myself in their shoes, I reasoned that my kūpuna likely roasted their kukui nuts and may have even submerged the hot nuts in cold water to ensure that the shell of the nuts broke, thereby exposing the kernels inside with minimal effort.

Although I am comforted by the fact that my kūpuna lived and worked on the same ancestral lands that I walk on today, I sometimes feel as though I am swimming upstream against the current as a contemporary Kanaka scholar seeking to add to the knowledge systems of my kūpuna. What contributions can I possibly make to the incredible legacy of thousands of years left behind by my kūpuna? At times, observing hōʻailona in my environment provides a sense of relief from this enormous kuleana. Like the unseen nutrients that enter the stream through the ʻauwai, some impacts made by contemporary scholars enrich the ecosystem of Kanaka knowledge yet remain undetected by many.

Other impacts such as the publication of peer-reviewed journal articles and books may be more visible indicators of the advancement of Kanaka scholarship within the academy. When I first attended the University of Hawaiʻi at Mānoa in the early 1990s, only two Native Hawaiian professors, Haunani-Kay Trask and Lilikalā Kameʻeleihiwa, were published book authors. The Hawaiian language program was a section within the Department of Hawaiian and Indo-Pacific Languages and Literature. The Center for Hawaiian Studies comprised four offices within the School of Pacific Islands Studies. Much has changed over the past two decades. Today, Kawaihuelani Center for Hawaiian Language and Kamakakūokalani Center for Hawaiian Studies are companion programs within the Hawaiʻinuiākea School of Hawaiian Knowledge. The Hawaiian studies building, built in the late 1990s, is bursting at the seams. And more than a dozen other Native Hawaiian academics have published books on various topics related to Kanaka knowledge.[12] Each scholar's contribution to the field is like a source of water originating from his or her place of strength on the landscape and flowing into the larger body of Kanaka knowledge. This stream of knowledge is enhanced and enriched by each contribution.

NOTES

1. Kanaka is used throughout this chapter to refer to a singular Native Hawaiian. Kānaka references Native Hawaiians in the plural form. I have intentionally not used the term "Hawaiian" because it was not used by my ancestors prior to western contact.

2. Fernandes, "UH Tries to Cut 14 Classes." *Ka Leo o Hawaiʻi*, May 1, 1995.

3. "Protesters Besiege Bachman Hall." *Ka Leo o Hawaiʻi*, May 1, 1995.

4. Wong, "Kuhi Aku, Kuhi Mai, Kuhi Hewa Ē: He Mau Loina Kuhikuhi ʻĀkena no ka ʻŌlelo Hawaiʻi."

5. Basham, "He Puke Mele Lāhui: Nā Mele Kūpaʻa, Nā Mele Kūʻē a me Nā Mele Aloha o nā Kānaka Maoli"; Basham, "I Mau ke Ea o ka ʻĀina i ka Pono: He Puke Mele Lāhui no ka Lāhui Hawaiʻi"; de Silva, "Killer Mele"; Lopes, "Ka Waihona A Ke Aloha: Ka Papahana Hoʻoheno Mele: An Interactive Resource Center for the Promotion, Preservation and Perpetuation of Mele and Mele Practitioners."

6. Louis, "Hawaiian Place Names: Storied Symbols in Hawaiian Performance Cartographies."

7. Basham, "He Puke Mele Lāhui"; Basham, "I Mau ke Ea o ka ʻĀina i ka Pono"; de Silva, "Killer Mele"; Lopes, "Ka Waihona A Ke Aloha: Ka Papahana Hoʻoheno Mele."

8. Andrade, *Hā'ena: Through the Eyes of the Ancestors;* Freitas, personal communication; Louis, "Hawaiian Place Names: Storied Symbols in Hawaiian Performance Cartographies."

9. http://www.edithkanakaolefoundation.org/current-projects/papaku-makawalu/.

10. Smith, *Decolonizing Methodologies: Research and Indigenous Peoples.*

11. Wong, "Huli ka Lima i Lalo a Kaomi i ke Pihi."

12. Aikau, *A Chosen People, A Promised Land: Mormonism and Race in Hawai'i;* Andrade, *Hā'ena: Through the Eyes of the Ancestors;* Beamer, "Na Wai Ka Mana?: 'Ōiwi Agency and European Imperialism in the Hawaiian Kingdom"; Goodyear-Ka'ōpua, *The Seeds We Planted: Portraits of a Native Hawaiian Charter School;* ho'omanawanui, *Voices of Fire: Reweaving the Lei of Pele and Hi'iaka Literature;* Iaukea, *The Queen and I: A Story of Dispossessions and Reconnections in Hawai'i;* Kanahele, *Ka Honua Ola: 'Eli'eli Kau Mai;* McGregor, *Nā Kua'āina: Living Hawaiian Culture;* Meyer, *Ho'oulu: Our Time of Becoming: Collected Early Writings of Manulani Meyer;* Oliveira, *Ancestral Places: Understanding Kanaka Geographies;* Osorio, *Dismembering Lāhui: A History of the Hawaiian Nation to 1887;* Silva, *Aloha Betrayed: Native Hawaiian Resistance to American Colonialism;* Tengan, *Native Men Remade: Gender and Nation in Contemporary Hawai'i.*

BIBLIOGRAPHY

Aikau, Hokulani. *A Chosen People, A Promised Land: Mormonism and Race in Hawai'i.* Minneapolis: University of Minnesota Press, 2012.

Andrade, Carlos. *Hā'ena: Through the Eyes of the Ancestors.* Honolulu: University of Hawai'i Press, 2008.

Basham, Leilani. "He Puke Mele Lāhui: Nā Mele Kūpa'a, Nā Mele Kū'ē a me Nā Mele Aloha o nā Kānaka Maoli." Master's Thesis in Political Science, University of Hawai'i at Mānoa, 2002.

———. "I Mau ke Ea o ka 'Āina i ka Pono: He Puke Mele Lāhui no ka Lāhui Hawai'i." PhD Dissertation in Political Science, University of Hawai'i at Mānoa, 2007.

Beamer, B. Kamanamaikalani. "Na Wai Ka Mana?: 'Ōiwi Agency and European Imperialism in the Hawaiian Kingdom." PhD Dissertation in Geography, University of Hawai'i at Mānoa, 2008.

Blaich, Mehana. "Mai Uka a i Kai: From the Mountains to the Sea, 'Āina-Based Education in the Ahupua'a of Waipā." Master's Thesis in Education, University of Hawai'i at Mānoa, 2003.

Cashman, Kimo A. "Still Looking in the Hole with My Three-Prong Cocked: Fire the Pōhaku Cannon." *AlterNative: An International Journal of Indigenous Peoples* 5, no. 2 (2009): 28–45.

de Silva, Kahikina. "Killer Mele." Master's Thesis in English, University of Hawai'i at Mānoa, 2005.

Goodyear-Ka'ōpua, Noelani. "Rebuilding the 'Auwai: Connecting Ecology, Economy and Education in Hawaiian Schools." *AlterNative: An International Journal of Indigenous Peoples* 5, no. 2 (2009): 46–77.

———. *The Seeds We Planted: Portraits of a Native Hawaiian Charter School.* Minneapolis: University of Minnesota Press, 2013.

Goodyear-Ka'ōpua, Noelani, Willy Kauai, Kaleilehua Maioho, and 'Īmaikalani Winchester. "Teaching amid U.S. Occupation: Sovereignty, Survival and Social Studies in a Native Hawaiian Charter School." *Hūlili: Multidisciplinary Research on Hawaiian Well-Being* 5 (2008): 155–201.

ho'omanawanui, ku'ualoha. *Voices of Fire: Reweaving the Lei of Pele and Hi'iaka Literature.* Minneapolis: University of Minnesota Press, 2014.

Ho'oulumāhiehie. *Ka Mo'olelo Hiwahiwa o Kawelo.* Honolulu: Bishop Museum Press, 2008.

Iaukea, Sydney L. *The Queen and I: A Story of Dispossessions and Reconnections in Hawai'i.* Berkeley: University of California Press, 2012.

Kame'eleihiwa, Lilikalā. *Native Land and Foreign Desires: Pehea La E Pono Ai?* Honolulu: Bishop Museum Press, 1992.

Kanahele, Pualani Kanaka'ole. *Ka Honua Ola: 'Eli'eli Kau Mai.* Honolulu: Kamehameha Publishing, 2011.

Kaomea, Julie. "A Curriculum of Aloha? Colonialism and Tourism in Hawai'i's Elementary Textbooks." *Curriculum Inquiry* 30, no. 3 (Fall 2000): 319–344.

———. "Indigenous Studies in the Elementary Curriculum: A Cautionary Hawaiian Example." *Anthropology and Education Quarterly* 36, no. 1 (2005): 24–42. doi:10.1525/aeq.2005.36.1.024.

Lopes, Robert Keawe. "Ka Waihona A Ke Aloha: Ka Papahana Ho'oheno Mele: An Interactive Resource Center for the Promotion, Preservation and Perpetuation of Mele and Mele Practitioners." PhD Dissertation in Education, University of Hawai'i at Mānoa, 2010.

Louis, Renee Pualani. "Hawaiian Place Names: Storied Symbols in Hawaiian Performance Cartographies." PhD Dissertation in Geography, University of Hawai'i at Mānoa, 2008.

MacKenzie, Melody Kapilialoha. *Native Hawaiian Rights Handbook.* Honolulu: Native Hawaiian Legal Corporation, 1991.

McGregor, Davianna. *Nā Kua'āina: Living Hawaiian Culture.* Honolulu: University of Hawai'i Press, 2007.

Meyer, Manulani Aluli. *Ho'oulu: Our Time of Becoming: Collected Early Writings of Manulani Meyer.* Honolulu: 'Ai Pōhaku Press, 2003.

Oliveira, Katrina-Ann R. Kapā'anaokalāokeola Nākoa. *Ancestral Places: Understanding Kanaka Geographies.* Corvallis: Oregon State University Press, 2014.

Osorio, Jonathan Kamakawiwo'ole. *Dismembering Lāhui: A History of the Hawaiian Nation to 1887.* Honolulu: University of Hawai'i Press, 2002.

———. "'What Kine Hawaiian Are You?': A Mo'olelo About Nationhood, Race, History, and the Contemporary Sovereignty Movement in Hawai'i." *Contemporary Pacific* 13, no. 2 (2001): 359–379.

Silva, Noenoe K. *Aloha Betrayed: Native Hawaiian Resistance to American Colonialism.* Durham: Duke University Press, 2004.

Silva, Noenoe K., and Iokepa Badis. "Early Hawaiian Newspapers and Kanaka Maoli Intellectual History, 1834–1855." *Hawaiian Journal of History* 42 (2008): 105–134.

Simpson, Leanne. *Dancing on Our Turtle's Back: Stories of Nishnaabeg Re-creation, Resurgence and a New Emergence.* Winnipeg: Arbeiter Ring Publishing, 2011.

Smith, Linda Tuhiwai. *Decolonizing Methodologies: Research and Indigenous Peoples.* London: Zed Books, 1999.

Sproat, D. Kapua'ala, and Isaac Moriwake. "Ke Kalo Pa'a O Waiāhole: Public Trust as a Tool for Environmental Advocacy." In *Creative Common Law Strategies for Protecting the Environment,* 247–284. Washington, DC: Environmental Law Institute, 2007.

Stillman, Amy K. "No ka Po'e i Aloha i ka 'Āina: Poetics of the Hula Ku'i." Honolulu, July 26, 1994.

———. "Of the People Who Love the Land: Vernacular History in the Poetry of Modern Hawaiian Hula." *Amerasia Journal* 28, no. 3 (2002): 85–108.

Tengan, Ty P. Kawika. *Native Men Remade: Gender and Nation in Contemporary Hawai'i.* Durham: Duke University Press, 2008.

Trask, Haunani-Kay. "The Birth of the Modern Hawaiian Movement: Kalama Valley, O'ahu." *Hawaiian Journal of History* 21 (1987): 126–153.

———. *From a Native Daughter: Colonialism and Sovereignty in Hawai'i.* Revised edition. Honolulu: University of Hawai'i Press, 1999.

———. *Light in the Crevice Never Seen.* Revised edition. Corvallis, OR: Calyx Books, 1999.

———. *Night Is a Sharkskin Drum.* Honolulu: University of Hawai'i Press, 2002.

Warner, Sam L. No'eau. "Kuleana: The Right, Responsibility, and Authority of Indigenous Peoples to Speak and Make Decisions for Themselves in Language and Cultural Revitalization." *Anthropology and Education Quarterly* 30, no. 1 (1999): 68–93. doi:10.1525/aeq.1999.30.1.68.

———. "The Movement to Revitalize Hawaiian Language and Culture." In *The Green Book of Language Revitalization in Practice,* edited by Leanne Hinton and Ken Hale, 133–146. San Diego: Academic Press, 2001.

Wong, K. Laiana. "He Hāwa'e Kai Nui a Kau Ma Kula." *Educational Perspectives* 37, no. 1 (2004): 31–39.

———. "Huli ka Lima i Lalo a Kaomi i ke Pihi." *AlterNative: An International Journal of Indigenous Peoples* 5, no. 2 (2009): 14–27.

———. "Kuhi Aku, Kuhi Mai, Kuhi Hewa Ē: He Mau Loina Kuhikuhi 'Ākena no ka 'Ōlelo Hawai'i." PhD Dissertation, University of Hawai'i at Mānoa, 2006.

Wright, Erin Kahunawaika'ala. "'Education for the Nation': Forging Indigenous Hawaiian Identity in Higher Education." PhD Dissertation, University of California at Los Angeles, 2003.

Young, Kanalu. "Kuleana: Toward a Historiography of Hawaiian National Consciousness, 1780–2001." *Hawaiian Journal of Law and Politics* 2 (2006): 1–33.

Ka ʻIkena a ka Hawaiʻi: Toward a Kanaka ʻŌiwi Critical Race Theory

Erin Kahunawaikaʻala Wright
and Brandi Jean Nālani Balutski

A process of decolonization.
Helped me shift paradigms.
Looking for an answer to my questions.
You had been on a long, hot, dry hike or run.
All of a sudden someone gives you this ice-cold water.
It just quenched a thirst.
Made me understand why I was angry.
I need to know who I am and where I come from, learn for myself.
I was playing catch-up. I should have learned all this before.
Gave this language to things that I had seen or thought about but didn't
   know how to speak about.
We could make this kīpuka.
Passionate professors. Influential. Inspiring.
Formal learning but also a part of changing or influencing.
Didn't imagine I would be part of a movement.
It's okay to make mistakes, it's okay to be scared, but just keep going.
Larger goal very clear, well-being and advancement of the lāhui.
Laser focused and unified.
Determined the entire course of my life.
Solidified my kuleana.
Where I found my voice.
Hawaiian Studies gave me values on improving myself to help the
   larger whole.
Power of one person being a part of something bigger.
You could change an issue dramatically.
I felt really empowered.
Mindset always on nationhood.
What is our legacy?
Our kuleana is to advance and advocate.
Our kūpuna did impossible things, if they can do these crazy incredible
   things, we can do it too.
Other people believe in you . . . you better too.[1]

Ma Ka Hana Ka 'Ike: Contemplating the Praxis of Research

I wouldn't even say encouraging engagement, but like it was just expected like you had to do something. Think and then act. You know, it wasn't just think.[2]

The ways in which we have conducted research have been guided by this principle, "ma ka hana ka 'ike": In doing work, there is knowledge. This principle reflects our kūpuna's (elders, ancestors) infinite wisdom in truly understanding that careful observation, practice, and reflection are integral to refining praxis. For us, the meditative practice of research brings to our attention many ordinary yet vital lessons such as the importance of proper preparation, strategizing, active listening, and teamwork. This practice has also underscored the significant need for theoretical frameworks and methodologies generated from Kanaka 'Ōiwi[3] and for culturally grounded orientations to more fully identify, understand, and articulate the experiences of Kanaka 'Ōiwi maneuvering through U.S.-imposed higher education.

As illustrated by the poetic transcription that opens our chapter, Kanaka 'Ōiwi higher educational journeys are formulated and expressed in rich and varied mo'olelo (narrative, story, history) that often feature 'āina (land), kuleana (responsibility, privilege, concern), mo'okū'auhau (genealogy), 'ike Hawai'i (Hawaiian knowledge), ea (sovereignty, breath), and mo'olelo as key elements. How can we best understand and share the richness of these mo'olelo? Moreover, how can we best use these mo'olelo to guide transformative thinking and action in higher education for Kanaka 'Ōiwi?

Over the last several years, we have primarily used critical race theory (CRT) and tribal critical race theory (TribalCrit) (Brayboy 2005) as analytical tools to think about the mo'olelo of Kanaka 'Ōiwi and their implications for higher education praxis. Although not culturally grounded in a literal sense, CRT and TribalCrit are grounded in the realities of U.S. racism and colonialism and their intergenerational impacts on communities of color that we have found relevant and useful. By foregrounding the consequences of racism, colonialism, and occupation on communities of color and (re)imagining ways to realize transformational change, these theories have been particularly beneficial in helping us examine and understand the complexities, possibilities, and outcomes of participating in higher education for Kanaka 'Ōiwi. They enable us to name the oppression, whether structural, normative, or overt, while helping us reframe the issues and build equitable educational environments. Yet even with the advent of very valuable education research using CRT in the last decade and a half, we still find these frameworks insufficient to fully express the mo'olelo of Kanaka 'Ōiwi.

Inspired by Ladson-Billings and Tate's (1995) initial articulation of CRT for education, Brayboy's (2005) groundbreaking piece advancing his ideas for TribalCrit, and our 'ike kūpuna of "ma ka hana ka 'ike," we now find ourselves exploring and sifting through the complexities and nuances of delineating a Kanaka 'Ōiwi–focused CRT ('ŌiwiCrit). Our methodological underpinnings for 'ŌiwiCRT emerge from two epistemological foundations: CRT and what we refer to as Hawaiian critical consciousness. The purpose of this chapter is three-fold. First, it provides a general background on CRT and the ways it has been articulated by others as we see and understand it through a Hawaiian critical consciousness lens. Second, it humbly offers our emerging ideas on developing an 'ŌiwiCrit based on a variety of data pieces and ongoing analysis, including our interviews with Kanaka 'Ōiwi participants in higher education, conversations with our peers and colleagues, our positionalities as Kanaka 'Ōiwi women working in higher education in U.S.-occupied Hawai'i (particularly in the field of student affairs), and our own growing praxis in 'ike kūpuna, 'ike Hawai'i, and emerging higher education research, methods, and methodologies. Finally, it presents our thoughts on how this approach to expressing and understanding Native Hawaiian higher education mo'olelo helps guide our research. Again, the ideas we pose in this emerging theoretical counter-narrative are tentative and malleable and require more research, vetting, and serious reflection.

Ka 'Ikena a ka Hawai'i: Kanaka 'Ōiwi Critical Consciousness

I learned to be more compassionate . . . have a greater respect for my kūpuna.

The image that most times we had seen of Hawaiians in terms of the main-stream media was evictions . . . the idea that Hawaiians are not the ones who are decision makers, they're not educated, the picture of a Hawaiian back then was an uneducated blue-collar worker, you know, and so to be a part of this experience for me was really empowering.

We fully and gratefully acknowledge that our work is a result of the broader legacy or mo'okū'auhau of our 'ike kūpuna and of contemporary Kanaka 'Ōiwi intellectuals (organic and otherwise), whose work in our communities and in the academy we have come to rely on as our philosophical foundation. We think of this legacy as our 'ike Hawai'i grounding, and it informs the ways in which we make sense of the world, including our research. We have been profoundly influenced and inspired as students and professionals in higher education by our mākua Kanaka 'Ōiwi scholars such as Haunani-Kay Trask, Kekuni Blaisdell, Jon Osorio, Kanalu Young, Lilikalā Kame'eleihiwa, Noenoe Silva, Julie Ka'omea, Rona Halualani, Hannah Tavares, Maenette Benham, and No'eau

Warner—as well as our kaikua'ana in scholarship such as by Noelani Goodyear-Ka'ōpua, Kapā Oliveira, Kehaulani Kauanui, Hōkūlani Aikau, Kaleikoa Kā'eo, and Ty Kāwika Tengan.[4] The majority of these scholars are not in the field of education, but collectively their work attends to power dynamics/relationships using 'ike kūpuna, Indigenous, and transdisciplinary frameworks, methods, and methodologies to understand their impacts on contemporary Kanaka 'Ōiwi society, as well as the ways in which our disciplines, our lāhui, and our society in general may be imagined, reimagined, and actualized. Collectively, their work and the work of many, many other important scholars/organic intellectuals/artists/activists (Kanaka 'Ōiwi, Indigenous, non-Indigenous) who go unnamed here push us to think more deeply about the experiences of our people in the context of U.S. higher education and other Indigenous peoples internationally and, in turn, problematizing these experiences in the name of, as Goodyear-Ka'ōpua (2011) says, "lāhui-hood."

Again, for us as Kanaka 'Ōiwi researchers, our work is about more than naming that which is inequitable and critiquing structures such as colonialism and racism that reinforce and replicate oppression; like our scholarly mākua and kaikua'ana, we also do this work in hopes of contributing to a reconceptualization of our collective futures in ways that fully nurture the tremendous potential and 'ike of our lāhui for the betterment of Hawai'i.

Ka 'Ike Kumu: Critical Race Theory

> *The capacities, the skills, just the confidence sometimes to be involved to make a difference, to speak, to struggle, to fight.*

Originally developed as a counter-narrative to "positivist and liberal legal discourse of civil rights" (Ladson-Billings 1998), CRT has seen a tremendous development and diverse application over the last three decades. Matsuda, Lawrence, Delgado, and Crenshaw (1993, pp. 6–7) identify six foundational tenets of CRT guiding the analysis:

1. CRT asserts that racism is endemic to American society.
2. CRT expresses skepticism at dominant legal claims of neutrality, meritocracy, and color-blindness.
3. CRT challenges ahistoricism and insists on a contextual and historical analysis of the law.
4. CRT insists on the recognition of the experiences of people of color and communities of color in analyzing law and society.
5. CRT is interdisciplinary.
6. CRT scholarship works toward eliminating racial oppression as part of the broader goal of ending all forms of oppression.

CRT is a useful analytic for examining and understanding the racialization of Kanaka ʻŌiwi because it foregrounds race, racism, and power; challenges and interrogates intersections of various forms of oppression; and centers the experiences of Kanaka ʻŌiwi in the analyses of power (Labrador and Wright 2011; Wright and Balutski 2013). In our work, for example, CRT brings to the fore questions that highlight the inequities that surface for Kanaka ʻŌiwi around historically and consistently low completion, persistence, and retention rates at the University of Hawaiʻi at Mānoa (Balutski and Wright 2011, 2012; Balutski, Freitas, and Wright 2008, 2010). We appreciate the honesty that CRT engenders about race, racism, and the inherent inequalities in U.S. projects such as education. As Freire (1970, p. 29) writes,

> To surmount the situation of oppression, people must first critically recognize its causes, so that through transforming action they can create a new situation, one which makes possible the pursuit of a fuller humanity.

Although Kanaka ʻŌiwi may not describe themselves as "oppressed," the idea advanced by CRT and education scholar-practitioners such as Freire is the necessity of first understanding the root causes of inequality before we can authentically address the symptoms of an inequitable system; in that way we can avoid reproducing those structures. Furthermore, CRT employs culturally relevant approaches to identifying and presenting data through, for example, counter-narratives, storytelling, and auto-ethnography, and it challenges researchers to examine the complexities of these experiences by using tools such as narrative analysis (Delgado and Stefancic 2001).

The utility of CRT has resulted in the generation of several theoretical sub-branches that focus on particular intersectionalities[5] and go beyond the Black-White binary in which CRT was largely theorized and applied; for example, LatCrit (Gonzales and Portillos 2007; Solórzano and Villalpando 1997), Asian-Crit (Sue et al. 2009), QueerCrit (Carbado 2000; Pinar 2003), critical race feminism (Berry 2009; Thompson 2004), and TribalCrit (Brayboy 2005). As mentioned, CRT's spirit is anticolonial and liberatory and is therefore foundationally well suited for not only examining the ways in which traditionally marginalized communities have been silenced and oppressed but also for providing the space to challenge the oppressive and dominant structures that enable such oppression.

Brayboy (2005) extends the work of CRT to include the political conditions and historical circumstances of Indigenous peoples in the United States, particularly American Indians, in TribalCrit. He outlines nine additional tenets of

TribalCrit, five of which we present here because they are most applicable to our discussion (p. 429):

1. Colonization[6] is endemic to society.
2. U.S. policies toward Indigenous peoples are rooted in colonialism, White supremacy, and a desire for material gain.
3. Indigenous peoples occupy a liminal space that accounts for both the political and racialized natures of their identities.
4. Indigenous peoples constantly seek ways of expressing self-determination, sovereignty, and autonomy.
5. Reframing culture, knowledge, research, and power through an Indigenous perspective is imperative.

Brayboy's analysis, especially around these five tenets, is relevant to examining Kanaka 'Ōiwi higher educational journeys in the context of U.S. colonialism and imperialism in the Pacific. Articulating Hawai'i-specific colonialism is vital to our research because of its intergenerational impacts on the current socioeconomic and sociopolitical conditions of Kanaka 'Ōiwi, including participation in U.S.-occupied or, as Goodyear-Ka'ōpua (2013b) terms it, "state sanctioned," education. It acknowledges and incorporates the historical and contemporary context of the United States' treatment of Indigenous people as well as the occupation of Hawai'i into the analysis of Kanaka 'Ōiwi educational journeys. TribalCrit has guided us to think through the ways colonialism and neocolonialism have altered Kanaka 'Ōiwi relationships with our 'āina, our economies, our governance, our ways of learning and teaching, our relationships with each other, and even ourselves. For example, we have considered the ways in which Kanaka 'Ōiwi liminality[7] is expressed in higher education. But although these tenets are indeed very applicable to our framing and analysis—in terms of understanding the Kanaka 'Ōiwi–specific consequences of racialization and colonialism, for example, on participation in higher education—they are still insufficient to fully articulate Kanaka 'Ōiwi mo'olelo.

Ladson-Billings and Tate (1995) have also applied this framework to the field of education. They hold that CRT becomes a salient framework for education given the permanence of race in the United States, the role of race in educational inequity, and the absence of the theorizing of race in education. In a later piece, Ladson-Billings (1998) reinforces the idea of not only theorizing race in education but also committing to "exposing racism *and* propos[ing] radical solutions for addressing it" (p. 22). Solórzano's contributions to the development of a CRT in education and LatCrit also provide us with ways to think about a Kanaka 'Ōiwi CRT framework in higher education, especially because he has

Kanaka ʻŌiwi Critical Consciousness

Colonization, prolonged and illegal occupation, and Asian settler colonialism is endemic to Hawaiʻi society

Critiques of multiculturalism

Liminality is complicated by self-determination

Tourist industry influences all aspects of Hawaiʻi

Hawaiian identity development is nuanced and non-linear

Applicability to examine theory and practice of sovereignty and self-determination in multiple contexts

Critical Race Theory & Tribal Critical Race Theory

Colonization & racism are endemic to society

Critiques of neutrality, meritocracy, and color-blindness

Liminality

Assimilation is problematic

Transforming structures that maintain subordination

Applicability to examine inequalities in education

Kanaka ʻŌiwi CRT

Educational structures are reflections of colonialism and occupation

How do broader socio-historical and socio-political contexts influence Hawaiian educational journeys?

How do colonial structures influence Hawaiian educational journeys?

How do Hawaiians articulate these journeys?

How are Native Hawaiians racialized in education?

How can we reconceptualize higher education?

Theoretical Influences for Kanaka ʻŌiwi CRT

conducted research in multiple educational settings, including K–12, higher education, and among faculty. Solórzano (1998) describes CRT in education as "a framework or set of basic perspectives, methods, and pedagogy that seeks to identify, analyze, and transform those structural, cultural, and interpersonal aspects of education that maintain the subordination of scholars of color" (p. 122).

Based on these epistemological foundations of Hawaiian critical consciousness and CRT, we have thought about the ways in which these knowledges can be used together to build our approach and understanding of Native Hawaiian higher educational mo'olelo.

Ka 'Ike Laulā: Toward a Kanaka 'Ōiwi Critical Race Theory

I had this thirst . . . but you know as you start drinking it then you're like wow, this thirst is way deeper than I realized, or this is so much more satisfying than I could have imagined.

We have come to consider how a Kanaka 'Ōiwi critical race theory (or 'ŌiwiCrit as we have dubbed it) may differ from CRT, TribalCrit, and other CRT-inspired frameworks. As the chapter subtitle suggests, our thinking is broad. Although we dislike using durable, inflexible words like "framework" and "tenet," we find ourselves currently at a loss for a more applicable metaphor to describe our thinking, given the emerging, dynamic, and organic nature of our thoughts in developing 'ŌiwiCrit. Therefore, we have decided to talk about these budding ideas as themes that together have informed our approach and analysis of Native Hawaiian higher education mo'olelo. The following themes have emerged from our work thus far:

- The consequences of colonialism and occupation are pervasive and unique to Hawai'i in their exploitation of 'āina and appropriation of identity, particularly in the areas of local identity and settler colonialism, tourism, and de/militarization.
- Aloha 'āina (love for the land and nation) is fundamental to the expression and analysis of educational journeys for Kanaka 'Ōiwi.
- It is important to recognize and honor hūnā (sacred, hidden) of mo'olelo. Unlike western notions of research, not everything is free and open, and sometimes what is shared may only be understood by a few.
- Mo'okū'auhau (connections to people, places, and spaces) can be used to describe and understand the diverse pathways and relationships that individuals have with respect to different contexts.

- Kuleana (right, responsibility, privilege, concern, authority) is the culmination of Kanaka ʻŌiwi moʻolelo about their educational journeys and the ways in which they enact agency.

We map out the developing conceptual intersectional relationships between these themes in the figure below. "External Forces" are the contextual factors that influence Kanaka ʻŌiwi educational journeys, "Identity Conscious Articulations" are the intentional, culture-based ways in which these educational experiences are understood and expressed, and "Kuleana" is the theme that relates to the self-reflexive and praxis-oriented aspects of the educational journey. The arrows represent the interactions or relationships between the themes. External forces influence articulations, whereas articulations are also reframed by broader sociocultural and sociopolitical circumstances. Articulations also

External Forces Impacting Kanaka ʻŌiwi Educational Moʻolelo

The consequences of colonialism and occupation are pervasive and unique to Hawaiʻi in its exploitation of ʻāina and appropriation of identity.Examples include local identity and settler colonialism, tourism, and de/militarization and occupation.

Identity Conscious Articulations of Kanaka ʻŌiwi Educational Moʻolelo

Aloha ʻĀina

is fundamental to the expression and analysis of educational journeys for Kanaka ʻŌiwi.

Recognizing and honoring hūnā of moʻolelo

Unlike Western notions of research not everything is free and open and sometimes what is shared may only be understood by a few.

Utilizing moʻokūʻauhau

to describe and understand the diverse pathways and/or relationships individuals have with respect to different contexts.

Kuleana

is the culmination of Kanaka ʻŌiwi moʻolelo about their educational journeys and the ways in which they enact agency.

Kanaka ʻŌiwi CRT Emerging Thematic Intersections

influence the understanding of kuleana, while kuleana also informs the ways in which articulations are framed.

Of course, these ideas are not new for our community, but as Solórzano articulates in his study on Chicana/Chicano scholars, "collectively, they represent a challenge to existing models of scholarship" (p. 123) and, for our research, scholarship in higher education. Because of space limitations, we limit our discussion here to three themes: (1) the consequences of colonialism and occupation, (2) aloha 'āina, and (3) kuleana. These emergent themes originate from the corpus of our research and, of course, are not as strictly or easily delineated as we describe them here. For example, aloha 'āina, mo'okū'auhau, and kuleana are interrelated and demonstrate their own intersectionalities. But at this point in our processing, we present them somewhat simply, again with the intent to think, practice, read, and write more. It is important to note that, although we use a grounded approach situated in data gathered from the higher educational mo'olelo of Kanaka 'Ōiwi, we believe that these themes also apply to the general experiences of Kānaka 'Ōiwi navigating non-Hawaiian educational structures.

Consequences of Colonialism and Occupation in Hawai'i

Analysis of sovereignty and politics and stuff that, just on another level that really kind of spoke to me. That was the very first time that I ever heard the word sovereignty, and something about how they spoke about it and what not just made it seem like wow that's it. They have identified what the problem is and what we need.

I remember being mad all the time because there were a lot of people there [at a non-Native serving institution on the U.S. West Coast] from Hawai'i . . . but they were trying to differentiate themselves from those who are of other ethnicities. . . . So, they sort of throw off this identity like they're Hawaiian. I know that used to really piss me off back then, but I didn't understand it or I didn't know why I was getting so angry back then.

Contextual factors (past and present) play a significant role in the experiences of Kanaka 'Ōiwi higher educational mo'olelo, especially because educational structures are reflective of the broader society (Durkheim 1956). Currently, Kanaka 'Ōiwi are engaging in deep discussions and thoughtful actions around (de)colonization and (de)occupation in several arenas, including culture, 'āina, economies, and governance. As described earlier, we understand "colonialism" and "occupation" in context-specific ways and not in particular legalistic terms.[8] A CRT lens enables us to recognize the very real sociocultural and sociopolitical impacts of U.S. hegemony on Kanaka 'Ōiwi people and Hawai'i. Therefore,

to further complicate the context underlying Kanaka ʻŌiwi educational journeys, we have identified three interrelated areas in which the consequences of
colonialism and occupation are particularly felt: local identity and settler colonialism, tourism, and militarism. These areas speak to the many ways in which
dominant power structures are socially and economically reinforced in Hawaiʻi
and how they also permeate our educational structures and the higher education journeys of Native Hawaiians.

Disrupting "Local" Identity

CRT appropriately critiques liberalism, including its color-blindness and its advocacy of "especially equal treatment for all persons, regardless of their different histories or current situations" (Delgado and Stefancic 2012, p. 26). Hawaiʻi
is often paraded as the multicultural model for the United States, if not the world
(Grant and Ogawa 1993). However, Hawaiʻi as a "multicultural paradise" ob-
scures deep-seated historical and contemporary racism. This dominant narrative glosses over Hawaiʻi's history—including the genocide of Kanaka ʻŌiwi,
Asian peonage, and the overthrow of the Hawaiian nation—with an oversim-
plified analysis of seemingly positive modern race relations based on points
such as Hawaiʻi's high rate of intermarriage and multiethnic population, shared
foods, and people of color in prominent political, social, and economic positions
(Okamura 1998). Furthermore, because Hawaiʻi is so diverse, racism is often de-
clared as nonexistent. Instead, "local" identity becomes the salient, dominant
identity, thereby creating tension with "mainlanders."[9] Akin to the CRT critique
of multiculturalism and ahistoricism, Fujikane (2008, p. 26) writes,

> Attempt[ing] to redeem the settler state by casting it as a multicul-
> tural nation, Asian settler historiography in Hawaiʻi is also premised
> on a linear employment of history that celebrates the multicultural,
> mixed-race "local" society as a corrective to both Hawaiʻi's colonial
> "past" and the "divisiveness" of Hawaiian nationalism.

Pushing against the paradigm of Hawaiʻi as a "multicultural paradise" and
racism as a Black-White binary (or even an Indigenous-White binary), Trask
(2000) asserts that local identity is a mechanism to mask Asian American racism in Hawaiʻi and the subjugation of Kanaka ʻŌiwi. She terms this phenomenon "Asian Settler Colonialism." Like other settler states, Asian Americans in
Hawaiʻi are complicit in perpetuating this multicultural myth to justify and reinforce their positions of power. Fujikane (2008, p. 3) explains,

> Asian political and economic "successes" in Hawaiʻi have been rep-
> resented as evidence of Hawaiʻi's exceptionalism as a multicultural

state, proof that Asians have been able to overcome the racist treatment and policies of the American sugar planters to form what several scholars have described as "harmonious multiculturalism." Many historians employ a developmental narrative that begins with the colonization of Hawaiians and ends with multicultural democracy in Hawai'i. The story of multiethnic diversity is thus cast as the triumphant "resolution" to Hawai'i's colonial "past."

Delgado and Stefancic (2012) further warn of the consequences of binary thinking: It "can cause a minority group to go along with a recurring ploy in which Caucasians select a particular group—usually a small, nonthreatening one—to serve as tokens and overseers of the others" (p. 81).

Asian Settler Colonialism in Hawai'i relies on the concept of multiculturalism and the construction (and maintenance) of local identity. We have considered the influence of this legacy on higher education in Hawai'i for Kanaka 'Ōiwi, given the history of the University of Hawai'i. A review of the University of Hawai'i's leadership—the primary higher education pathway for Native Hawaiians, we would argue—reveals a severe lack of Native Hawaiian representation. For example, of the fourteen presidents of the university in its 106-year history, only one was non-White (Fujio Matsuda, the first Asian American university president in the United States) and one was a woman (University of Hawai'i 2014). At the flagship campus at Mānoa, its executive leadership team (i.e., chancellor, vice chancellors, associate/assistant vice chancellors, deans, associate/assistant deans, and directors) is predominantly White or Asian and male, with only three Native Hawaiians (all women) among its nearly ninety individuals (University of Hawai'i at Mānoa 2014). As such, we find settler colonialism to be a major influence in Hawai'i public higher education.

Corporate Tourism

An integral means of reifying and reinforcing this "multicultural paradise" image of Hawai'i is mass-based corporate tourism,[10] the largest industry in Hawai'i (State of Hawai'i Department of Business, Economic Development, and Tourism 2014). Hawai'i and Kanaka 'Ōiwi have been commodified and racialized to suit the tourist industry. Hawai'i has been marketed as a beautiful and exotic (but not too exotic) location with happy natives ready to serve tourists' every whim. Trask (1999) notes, "To most Americans, then, Hawai'i is theirs: to use, to take, and, above all, to fantasize about long after the experience" (p. 136).

In 2012, Hawai'i was visited by nearly eight million tourists (six times as many Hawai'i residents), resulting in more than $14.4 billion in revenue (Hawai'i Tourism Authority 2014). In addition to appropriating our cultural capital (i.e., hula, language, traditional symbols and images) and draining our natural resources, tourism also reproduces a service-based economy for Hawai'i in which Kanaka 'Ōiwi and Hawai'i residents alike are economically bound to the instability of a tourist economy. Tourism is part of the larger context of living in Hawai'i that may have direct or indirect impacts on Kanaka 'Ōiwi educational journeys: directly, as individuals (or their families) work in the tourist industry, or indirectly, as influencing Kanaka 'Ōiwi identity. So although tourism is an incredibly profitable industry, at what cost does that come?

Military Occupation

Militarism is inextricably tied to the colonization and occupation of the Pacific and, in this case, of Hawai'i.[11] The allure of Hawai'i as a strategic military location was solidified during King Kalākaua's reign in the 1880s, a century after initial western contact in 1778 with the arrival of Captain James Cook and then the 1820 arrival of Calvinist missionaries from Boston. World War II was a watershed era in the U.S. military's control over the Pacific, especially in Hawai'i. Trask (1999) explains, "As the preeminent military power in the world, the U.S. has dealt with the Pacific as if it were an American Ocean" (p. 48). From establishing bases on various Pacific Islands to executing military exercises (such as nuclear testing), the U.S. military and its allies have had a profound influence on the cultural, economic, political, and environmental geographies of the Pacific. In Hawai'i, the military presence is seen as a natural part of the environment.

Particularly since World War II, the U.S. military has treated the Pacific as its personal weapons testing laboratory. From 1946 to 1948, sixty-six atomic and hydrogen bombs were tested in the Marshall Islands, leaving many islands uninhabitable because of the radiation levels and forcibly exiling people from their homelands, such as Bikini and Rongelap Islands (Robie 1990). In Hawai'i, the U.S. military built nearly twenty military bases and seized the island of Kaho'olawe on December 8, 1941, the day after the Japanese bombed Pearl Harbor. From then until 1990, the U.S. and its allies used Kaho'olawe to test torpedoes, bombs, surface explosions, and other weapons, virtually destroying the island's natural geography—including its freshwater table—and causing massive erosion that, in turn, decimated the island's reef ecosystem.

In 1976, Protect Kaho'olawe 'Ohana, a Kanaka 'Ōiwi–led grassroots organization, filed suit in federal court to stop the U.S. Navy's bombing. Finally in 1990, the island was conveyed to the state of Hawai'i, along with its leftover unexploded and exploded ordnance materials and other kinds of trash. Kanaka 'Ōiwi and their allies continue to clean up, heal, and care for the island physically (i.e., by replanting native plants), culturally/spiritually, and educationally.

Today, the United States Pacific Command (USPACOM) is headquartered in Hawai'i. USPACOM comprises a fleet of nearly 700,000 civilians, contractors, and soldiers, representing one-fifth of the total U.S. military strength and two-thirds of the total U.S. Marine Corps' combat strength. The USPACOM's vision and motto are summed up in its slogan: "Partnership, presence, and military readiness." Unfortunately, this partnership is an imposed, not a collaborative one, and is in the form of neocolonial political arrangements (i.e., statehood, protectorate, territory) in which the lure of U.S. funding, protection, and liminal citizenry is often negotiated at the expense of Indigenous control over lands and resources.

Struggles and protests such as that over Kahoʻolawe, as well as other demilitarization demonstrations, such as those in Mākua Valley, are testament to Kanaka ʻŌiwi's ongoing battles to reclaim stewardship over our ancestral lands. Like tourism and settler colonialism, militarism plays an integral role in Hawaiʻi's economic, political, physical, and cultural landscape. Bringing these critiques into our work is vital, as demonstrated by participants who have discussed the positive role that learning about these struggles has played in their own higher educational journeys. In our student affairs practice, holding the space for Kanaka ʻŌiwi students to engage in conversations about demilitarization, sovereignty, and occupation provides unique opportunities to introduce them to concepts of power and how to critique such structures. Creating spaces of resistance provides a venue for students to share in a collective struggle—creating bonds, feelings of belonging, and organic agency around nation-building.

Aloha ʻĀina

My mom is from Kipahulu on Maui. My dad is from Waiāhole. I grew up in Kuliʻouʻou Valley. . . . My family has been there since 1912, the old homestead . . . lived on nine acres of homestead land. Each acre was given to nine children of my great-grandmother and -father.

My mom is from Hilo, Hawaiʻi. . . . She came here to Mānoa and stayed with her relatives in Papakōlea.

Born and raised on Maui, I'm the second oldest in a family of eight. I was raised by my dad's grandmother, who was pure Hawaiian, and his aunt. . . . They watched me when I was a baby to school age and in Hālawa, where the stadium lies . . . their land was condemned.

My mom's side of the family is from Kaimuki . . . before that . . . Kalihi . . . before that . . . North Hilo. My dad's from New York.

I was able to be out there in the pastures and have fun . . . raised by my tūtū. I was born on Oʻahu, raised on Oʻahu and Maui.

'Āina is foundational to providing a shared context to talk story about experiences as Hawaiian people, as well as about experiences in higher education. Identifying 'āina as a central organizing concept for Kanaka 'Ōiwi narratives is not anything new. Oliveira (2014, p. 92) writes,

> The fact that Kānaka had a very close connection to the 'āina in ancestral times is evident in our 'ōlelo makuahine. Terms such as 'āina, aloha 'āina (love for the land), and kua'āina (the people who carry the burden of land on their backs) all reflect an undeniable bond between the 'āina and Kānaka. Kānaka knew their places so intimately that they were able to describe their kulāiwi apart from other places.

Our participants often spoke at length about 'āina in different ways. On the surface, they used it to provide a literal mapping of place and time. 'Āina described the places they were born and raised; most prominently discussed were place names and the quality of being 'āina momona (rich, abundant). They also used 'āina to retrace the journeys of their 'ohana throughout the generations as they traversed Hawai'i and went abroad for work, school, adventure, family, and love.

As we conducted more interviews, we began to think of an expansive role of 'āina in their narratives and started to unpack the other ways participants talked about 'āina and the influences it had on their making sense of their identities and educational journeys. 'Āina evoked powerful sensory and emotional connections as they associated certain 'āina with particular activities (e.g., learning, fishing, planting, gathering, eating), with family members or relationships (e.g., grandmother's house, uncle's pond, fishing with grandfather), or events (e.g., land being condemned, seeing evictions, first time going to Kaho'olawe). More importantly, they shared how those 'āina-based experiences made them feel—motivated, empowered, inspired, curious, angry, unhappy, or dissatisfied—which they then reconnected to their educational journeys.

They also used 'āina as a metaphor to describe their educational journeys or aspects of their educational journeys. Although not unique to Kanaka 'Ōiwi (the use of metaphor is typical in the Hawaiian oral tradition), the kaona (hidden meaning) of the metaphor and the specific metaphors used provide additional insight into conveying a particular idea, feeling, or sense about their journey. For example, one participant describes how her peers sustained her while she was attending a non-Native university:[12]

> *So even though [institution] wasn't a real Hawaiian place, we could make this kīpuka of our own just by hanging out amongst ourselves.*

On the surface, we could say that this participant felt supported by her peers in what we can infer was a generally unsupportive higher educational institution. Yet, she uses the word "kīpuka." Kīpuka (Pukui 1983, p. 155) is defined as "a calm place in a high sea, deep place in a shoal, opening in a forest, openings in cloud formations, and especially in a clear place or oasis within a lavabed where there may be vegetation"; it can also be defined as a "short shoulder cape; cloak, poncho" or even "a loop, lasso; snare." Our participant ascribed her ability to survive an inhospitable environment to her peer group as they created their own safe, nurturing environment, similar to the role a kīpuka plays in the natural environment.

We have come to think of this multifaceted theme as "aloha ʻāina." Trask (1993), Goodyear-Kaʻōpua (2013b), and Oliveira (2014) describe aloha ʻāina not only as a feeling of aloha, or love, for the land but also the relationship in aloha ʻāina is familial and practice based, extending back to time immemorial. Oliveira (2014) notes that the term "ʻāina" is most commonly translated as "land," but that the root of the word "ʻai" is "eat." She writes, "Ai emphasizes that people do not only *live* on the land but also *eat* off of its resources" (p. 140), an idea clearly evident in their moʻolelo: The connection goes beyond a physical space; it is integral to their lives. Goodyear-Kaʻōpua (2013a) adds that aloha ʻāina goes beyond a feeling or affection for the land; it is a very real practice. Kanahele (2005, p. 23) states simply, "I am this land, and this land is me"—a sentiment shared in the literature and in our participants' moʻolelo. Reinforcing the concept that it is a practice, not just an idea, "aloha ʻāina" is also associated with sovereignty and self-determination movements to express the loving resolve that Kanaka ʻŌiwi have for our land and our identities as people, something that is inextricably tied to our land and our unique connection to it.

Kuleana

Ultimately my tūtū told me that I needed to promise her that I would learn my genealogy. Because she said when I learn my genealogy, I'll know who I am and what I have to do.

We were raised with the expectation that we were all going to college.

It's just . . . and I think that does something it was about you have kuleana and you better get out there and figure out how you can frickin' fulfill it.

I feel like that's part of my kuleana, too, is to support others . . . especially Native Hawaiians.

It was more about because you made it here now you have a responsibility or that kuleana to give back.

The importance of connecting new generations through education through our daily life to all of that wealth is, I think, a big part of what I see as my kuleana.

Affirming that as a kanaka I had a kuleana to come home at some point, but also leaving that freedom like you have to listen to your na'au.

I wanted to learn everything and anything about nā mea Hawai'i.

I knew I wanted to learn . . . whoever was teaching Hawaiian things, I wanted to learn.

I wanted my education to be about learning but also . . . doing.

Kuleana (right, responsibility, authority, privilege, burden) is another feature of traditional society that plays a significant role in the contemporary lives of Kanaka 'Ōiwi. After the privatization of land in Hawai'i, the word "kuleana" was used to describe the lands set aside for the maka'ainana (common people) to continue subsistence agricultural practices, as outlined in the Kuleana Act of 1850 as part of the 1848 Māhele (Kame'eleihiwa 1992). Garovoy (2005, p. 527) writes, "Deeds executed during the Māhele conveying land contained the phrase 'ua koe ke kuleana o na kānaka,' or 'reserving the rights of all native tenants,' in continuation of the reserved tenancies which characterized the traditional Hawaiian land tenure system." Using the word "kuleana" to describe these lands demonstrates, if not reinforces, the strong familial bond Kanaka 'Ōiwi had with the 'āina (versus the western notion of ownership) because of the enormous responsibility, privilege, and burden of caring for it.

Among our participants, kuleana was a significant theme. Although kuleana was used to describe different kinds of responsibilities at a variety of levels (e.g., personal, family, community), it was most meaningfully used to describe the culmination of their educational journeys. In particular, their mo'olelo provided clarity on the depth of the meaning of kuleana (i.e., the dual nature of kuleana as privilege and burden) to them and on discovering their personal kuleana to the lāhui. For example, one participant said,

I don't think I could work in a regular job because I mean I think, I have to have this sense of purpose and this sense of sort of enacting change for the betterment of our people, and you know other people too but first and foremost for our people.

Similarly, Goodyear-Kaʻōpua (2013a, p. 154) shares the idea of using kuleana as a pedagogical tool: "Kuleana can be a concept that drives learning when posed as a question (what is my kuleana?) and when the learner is open to deep self-reflection." For our participants, part of the moʻolelo of their educational journeys included continuous deep reflection "not to find finished answers but to continue asking the questions in each new context and moment on kuleana at different points in time" (p. 155), which, in turn, affected their perceptions of their educational journeys and professional aspirations:

> *You heard the speech, but to me when you got to Hawaiian Studies it was more about now you have a kuleana, now you have a responsibility to give back because you were one of the ones who made it here and those that really care. So it's not just the Kamehameha speech of oh you should count your blessings because you made it here and so ten others didn't. It was more about because you made it here now you have a responsibility or that kuleana to give back.*

Like aloha ʻāina, kuleana is certainly not a new concept/practice, but it continues to play a vital role in the ways in which Kanaka ʻŌiwi make sense of their educational journeys and life aspirations.

Our Way Forward

I found my voice.

We have much more work ahead to fully develop our thinking about ʻŌiwi CRT. As demonstrated here, our work using CRT and Native Hawaiian critical consciousness to approach and analyze the higher educational journeys of Kanaka ʻŌiwi advances scholarship in ways that are culturally oriented, anticolonial, and meaningful in theory and practice to Kanaka ʻŌiwi and other Indigenous peoples in similar contexts. Identifying and understanding these nuances are integral to the ways in which we expose racism and other forms of subordination to both transform existing institutions, models, and processes and imagine new ones in support of Kanaka ʻŌiwi success. Furthermore, our approach also features the successes experienced by Native Hawaiians in higher education to illuminate best praxis and shift the deficit-based discourse to success-based learning.

We end this chapter with the following prophecy from Kapihe, a kanaka who lived during the time of Kamehameha I:

E iho ana o luna,   That which is above will rise up,
e piʻi ana o lalo,   that which is below will come down,

| e hui ana nā moku, | the islands will come together, |
| e kū ana ka paia | the walls will stand up.[13] |

Like many Kanaka ʻŌiwi, we view Kapihe's prophecy as foretelling of a time when our lāhui Hawaiʻi will once again be pono (balance, harmony). Like our kūpuna, we hope to continue to contribute to praxis to help us restore balance to our community.

NOTES

1. Nālani created a poetic transcription from the transcripts of one of our studies on Kanaka ʻŌiwi in higher education. In this composition, at least one quote from each of the participants is included to string together an overall story from the interviews conducted to date. Glesne (1997) defines a poetic transcription as "a creative analytic practice in which the researcher fashions poem-like pieces from the interviewees" (p. 282).

2. Participants' quotes, set in italics and used in this chapter, are from thirty-two interviews we conducted with Kanaka ʻŌiwi college graduates for two projects we are working on about Kanaka ʻŌiwi in higher education. Each section features a quote or several quotes from these participants to set the tone for the subsequent section. Our participants were a cross-section of Kanaka ʻŌiwi college graduates, so they were very diverse in terms of geography, demographics, academic performance, and so on. Additionally, we each conducted interviews with Kanaka ʻŌiwi who were not part of these studies; these interviews have also informed our perspectives.

3. We use the terms "Kanaka ʻŌiwi," "Hawaiian," and "Native Hawaiian" interchangeably in this chapter to describe the Indigenous people of Kō Hawaiʻi Pae ʻĀina (Hawaiian archipelago).

4. We are being University of Hawaiʻi at Mānoa–centric!

5. "Intersectionalities" refers to the examination of the ways in which different identities (e.g., gender, race, class, sexuality) interact with each other. It exposes the multiple ways in which these relationships affect individuals and communities.

6. Our operational definition of colonialism in this chapter comes from Trask (1999, p. 251): "Behaviors, ideologies, and economies that enforce the exploitation of Native people in the colonies."

7. Brayboy describes liminality as an "in betweenness." Indigenous peoples are both political and racialized beings (which are also interrelated, of course). We can think about Kanaka ʻŌiwi liminality in a similar way as being historically and legally/politically "race-d" (Labrador and Wright 2011). For example, Kanaka ʻŌiwi are legally defined by blood quantum ("native Hawaiian" is 50 percent blood quantum) and are simultaneously criminalized (Keahiolalo-Karasuda 2010).

8. For expert analyses discussing Hawaiʻi as a colony or occupied nation-state, please see B. K. Beamer (2014), *No mākou ka mana: Liberating Hawaiʻi*. Honolulu: Kamehameha Schools Publishing; D. K. Sai (2008), *The American cccupation of the Hawaiian Kingdom: Beginning the transition from occupied to restored state*, Unpublished dissertation, University of Hawaiʻi at Mānoa, Honolulu, HI; and K. Vogeler (2014), "Outside Shangri La: Colonization and the US occupation of Hawaiʻi," in Goodyear-Kaʻōpua, Hussey, and Wright (2014).

9. People in Hawaiʻi often refer to the continental part of the United States as the "mainland." Typically, the word also refers to negatively perceived behaviors such as moving quickly, speaking loudly, or not observing "local" social norms like removing footwear before entering a home. Jonathan Okamura has written extensively and critically on local identity. Please see J. Y. Okamura (1992), *Why there are no Asian Americans in Hawaiʻi: The continuing significance of local identity,* retrieved from http://www2.hawaii.edu/~okamuraj; and (2008), *Ethnicity and inequality in Hawaiʻi* (Philadelphia: Temple University Press).

10. Our understanding of "tourism" comes from Trask (1999, p. 139): "My use of the word 'tourism' in the Hawaiʻi context refers to a mass-based, corporately controlled industry that is both vertically and horizontally integrated such that one multi-national corporation owns an airline, the tour buses that transport tourists to the corporation-owned hotel where they eat in a corporation owned restaurant, play golf and 'experience' Hawaiʻi on corporation-owned recreation areas, and eventually consider buying a second home built on corporation land. Profits, in this case, are mostly repatriated back to the home country. In Hawaiʻi, these 'home' countries are Japan, Taiwan, Hong Kong, Canada, Australia, and the United States."

11. Again, we are not engaging in a full discussion on the military in Hawaiʻi but instead are providing an overview.

12. In higher education research on underrepresented populations, most students of color attend what are called "predominantly white institutions" or PWIs. PWIs are defined as higher learning institutions with 50 percent or greater enrollment of Whites (Brown and Dancy 2009). We have opted to use the term "non-Native colleges and universities" (NNCUs) to describe those institutions that represent mainstream or PWIs (Shotton, Lowe, and Waterman 2013). Even though the particular institution in this case, the University of Hawaiʻi at Mānoa, does not meet the 50 percent mark, its largest single population is White.

13. This is one of the most common versions of Kapihe's prophecy to Kamehameha I; other versions exist with different interpretations (Charlot 2004).

BIBLIOGRAPHY

Balutski, B. J. N., A. Freitas, and E. K. Wright (2008). *Native Hawaiian student profile.* Annual Report on the Status of Native Hawaiian Students in the University of Hawaiʻi System Using Institutional Data. Released through Kōkua a Puni, U.S. DOE Title III Strengthening Institutions.

———. (2010). *Native Hawaiian student profile.* Annual Report on the Status of Native Hawaiian Students in the University of Hawaiʻi System Using Institutional Data. Released through Kōkua a Puni, U.S. DOE Title III Strengthening Institutions.

Balutski, B. J. N., and E. K. Wright (2011). *Native Hawaiian student profile.* Annual Report on the Status of Native Hawaiian Students in the University of Hawaiʻi System Using Institutional Data. Released through Kōkua a Puni, U.S. DOE Title III Strengthening Institutions.

———. (2012). *Native Hawaiian student profile.* Annual Report on the Status of Native Hawaiian Students in the University of Hawaiʻi System Using Institutional Data. Released through Kōkua a Puni, U.S. DOE Title III Strengthening Institutions.

Berry, T. R. (2009). Women of color in a bilingual/dialectical dilemma: Critical race feminism against a curriculum of oppression in teacher education. *International Journal of Qualitative Studies in Education, 22*(6), 745–753.

Brayboy, B. M. J. (2005). Toward a tribal critical race theory in education. *Urban Review, 37*(5), 425–442.

Brown II, M. C., and T. E. Dancy II (2009). Predominantly white institutions. In K. Lotomey (Ed.), *Encyclopedia of African American education,* pp. 524–527. Thousand Oaks, CA: Sage.

Carbado, D. W. (2000). Symposium: Race and the law at the turn of the century: Black rights, gay rights, civil rights. *UCLA Law Review, 47,* 1467–1519.

Charlot, J. (2004). A note on the Hawaiian prophecy of Kapihe. *Journal of Pacific History, 39*(3), 375–377.

Crenshaw, K. (1989). Demarginalizing the intersection of race and sex: A black feminist critique of antidiscrimination doctrine, feminist theory and antiracist politics. *University of Chicago Legal Forum,* 139.

Delgado, R., and J. Stefancic (2001). *Critical race theory: An introduction.* New York: New York University Press.

———. (2012). *Critical race theory: An introduction* (2nd ed.). New York: New York University Press.

Durkheim, E. (1956). Education and society. In *Power and ideology in education.* New York: Oxford University Press.

Freire, P. (1970). *Pedagogy of the oppressed.* New York: Herder & Herder.

Fujikane, C. (2008). Introduction. In C. Fujikane and J. Y. Okamura (Eds.), *Asian settler colonialism: From local governance to the habits of everyday life in Hawai‘i.* Honolulu: University of Hawai‘i Press.

Garovoy, J. B. (2005). "Ua koe ke kuleana o na kanaka" (reserving the rights of native tenants): Integrating kuleana rights and land trust priorities in Hawaii. *Harvard Law Review, 29,* 523–571.

Glesne, C. (1997). That rare feeling: Re-presenting research through poetic transcription. *Qualitative Inquiry, 3*(2), 202–221.

Gonzales, J. C., and E. L. Portillos (2007). The undereducation and overcriminalization of U.S. Latinas/os: A post-Los Angeles riots LatCrit analysis. *Educational Studies: A Journal of the American Educational Studies Association, 42*(3), 247–266.

Goodyear-Ka‘ōpua, N. (2009). Rebuilding the ‘auwai: Connecting ecology, economy, and education in Hawaiian Schools. *AlterNative, 5*(2), 46–77.

———. (2011). Kuleana lāhui: Collective responsibilities for Hawaiian nationhood in activists' praxis. *Affinities: A Journal of Radical Theory, Culture, and Action, 5*(1), 130–162.

———. (2013a). *The seeds we planted: Portraits of a Native Hawaiian charter school.* Minneapolis: University of Minnesota Press.

———. (2013b). Sovereign pedagogies. Presented as part of the "Sovereign Pedagogies on Settler Colonialism in Hawai‘i and Palestine Panel," New York University. Retrieved July 15, 2014, from http://www.indigenouspolitics.com/?p=115 (Episode #7: Settler colonialism in Hawai‘i).

Goodyear-Kaʻōpua, N., I. Hussey, and E. Kahunawaikaʻala Wright (Eds.) (2014). *A nation rising: Hawaiian Movements for Life, Land, and Sovereignty.* Durham: Duke University Press.

Grant, G., and D. M. Ogawa (1993). Living proof: Is Hawaii the answer? *Annals of the American Academy of Political and Social Science, 530*(1), 137–154.

Hawaiʻi Tourism Authority (2014). Retrieved from http://www.hawaiitourismauthority .org/default/assets/File/reports/visitor-statistics/2012%20ANNUAL%20RE PORT%20(Table%2041%20Revised).pdf.

Kameʻeleihiwa, L. K. (1992). *Native lands and foreign desires: How shall we live in harmony: Ko Hawaiʻi ʻĀina me na koi puumake a ka poʻe Haole: Pehea lā e pono ai.* Honolulu: Bishop Museum Press.

Kanahele, P. (2005). I am this land, and this land is me. *Hūlili: Multidisciplinary Research on Hawaiian Well Being, 2*(1), 21–30.

Kaomea, J. (2001). Dilemmas of an Indigenous academic: A Native Hawaiian story. *Contemporary Issues in Early Childhood Education, 2*(1), 67–82.

———. (2009). Contemplating kuleana: Reflections on the rights and responsibilities on the non-Indigenous participants. *AlterNative, 5*(2), 78–99.

Keahiolalo-Karasuda, R. (2010). A genealogy of punishment in Hawaiʻi: The public hanging of Chief Kamanawa II. *Hūlili: Multidisciplinary Research on Hawaiian Well-Being, 6*, 147–167.

Labrador, R. L., and E. K. Wright (2011). Engaging the Indigenous in Pacific Islander Asian American studies. *AmerAsia Journal, 37*(3), 135–147.

Ladson-Billings, G. (1998). Just what's critical race theory and what's it doing in a *nice* field like education? *Qualitative Studies in Education, 11*(1), 7–24.

Ladson-Billings, G., and W. F. Tate IV (1995). Toward a critical race theory for education. *Teacher's College Record, 97*(1), 47–64.

Matsuda, M., C. R. Lawrence, R. Delgado, and K. Crenshaw (Eds.) (1993). *Words that wound: Critical race theory, assaultive speech, and the First Amendment.* Boulder, CO: Westview Press.

Okamura, J. Y. (1998). The illusion of paradise: Privileging multiculturalism in Hawaiʻi. In D. G. Gladney (Ed.), *Making majorities: Constituting the nation in Japan, Korea, China, Malaysia, Fiji, Turkey, and the United States,* pp. 264–339. Stanford: Stanford University Press.

Oliveira, K. R. K. N. (2014). *Ancestral places: Understanding Kanaka geographies.* Corvallis: Oregon State University Press.

Pinar, W. F. (2003). "I am a Man": The queer politics of race. *Cultural Studies Critical Methodologies, 3*(3), 271–286.

Pukui, M. K. (1983). *ʻŌlelo noʻeau: Hawaiian proverbs & poetical sayings.* Honolulu: Bishop Museum Press.

Robie, D. (1990). *Blood on their banner: Nationalist struggles in the South Pacific.* Atlantic Highlands, NJ: Zed Publishing.

Shotton, H. J., S. C. Lowe, and S. J. Waterman (2013). *Beyond the asterisk: Understanding native students in higher education.* Sterling, VA: Stylus Publishing.

Solórzano, D. G. (1998). Critical race theory, race and gender, microaggressions, and the experience of Chicana and Chicano scholars. *Qualitative Studies in Education, 11*(1), 121–136.

Solórzano, D. G., and O. Villalpando (1997). Critical race theory, marginality, and the experience of students of color in higher education. In C. A. Torres and T. R. Mitchell (Eds.), *Sociology of education: Emerging perspectives*, pp. 211–224. Albany: State University of New York.

State of Hawaii, Department of Business, Economic Development, and Tourism (2014). Retrieved from http://dbedt.hawaii.gov/economic/library/faq/faq08/.

Sue, D. W., J. Bucceri, A. I. Lin, K. L. Nadal, and G. C. Torino (2009). Racial microaggressions and the Asian American experience. *Asian American Journal of Psychology, S*(1), 88–101.

Thompson, A. (2004). Gentlemanly orthodoxy: Critical race feminism, whiteness theory, and the APA Manual. *Educational Theory, 54*(1), 27–57.

Trask, H. K. (1993). *From a Native daughter: Colonialism and sovereignty in Hawai'i*. Monroe, MA: Common Courage Press.

———. (1999). *From a Native daughter: Colonialism and sovereignty in Hawai'i* (2nd ed.). Honolulu: University of Hawai'i Press.

———. (2000). Settlers of color and "Immigrant" hegemony: "Locals" in Hawai'i. *Amerasia Journal, 26*(2), 1–24.

University of Hawai'i. (2014). *Past Presidents of the University of Hawai'i*. Retrieved from http://www.hawaii.edu/about/pastpresidents.html.

University of Hawai'i at Mānoa (2014). *Executive & managerial personnel*. Retrieved from http://www.manoa.hawaii.edu/admin/executive-managerial.html.

Warner, S. L. N. (1999). Kuleana: The right, responsibility, and authority of Indigenous peoples to speak and make decisions for themselves in language and cultural revitalization. *Anthropology & Education Quarterly, 30*(1), 68–93.

Wright, E. K., and B. J. N. Balutski (2013). The role of context, critical theory, and counter-narratives in understanding Pacific Islander Indigeneity. In S. D. Museus, D. C. Maramba, and R. T. Teranishi (Eds.), *The misrepresented minority: New insights on Asian Americans and Pacific Islanders and their implications for higher education*, pp. 140–158. Sterling, VA: Stylus Publishing.

He Ala Nihinihi Ia A Hiki I Ka Mole: A Precarious Yet Worthwhile Path to Kuleana Through Hawaiian Place-Based Education

Maya L. Kawailanaokeawaiki Saffery

Preserving and then passing down living narratives from one generation to the next have been part of our tradition as Kānaka since our origins. Whether they take the form of mele (poetry, songs, chants) composed and performed, or of moʻolelo (stories, histories) told and retold first orally and then in written form, many of these histories focus on the kanaka-ʻāina connection because it is this relationship that ultimately defines us as a people and allows us to live a pono (balanced, sustained, nourished) life. Kānaka understand that we come from the land itself (Beckwith and Luomala 1972; Fornander and Thrum 1999; Johnson 1981; Kamakau 1869–1871, 1964, 1991; Kameʻeleihiwa 1992; Kanahele 2005; Liliuokalani 1997; Malo 1987). We believe that the land, the sea, the sky, and all creatures that exist in the universe are all our kūpuna as much as are our human grandparents. Decades of colonization have attempted to sever this relationship, but the roots that tie us to our places, practices, and people run so deep that they can never be completely dissolved. Our kūpuna appreciated the importance (and difficulty) of sustaining meaningful, reciprocal, productive connections to the ʻāina, and they made sure to document these epistemologies in mele, moʻolelo, moʻokūʻauhau, ʻōlelo noʻeau, inoa ʻāina,[1] and the like, so that subsequent generations of Hawaiians would be able to share, celebrate, and learn from our histories; apply lessons learned and practices perfected to our constantly changing world; and begin to create contemporary narratives of our own.

In an attempt to honor this storytelling tradition of my kūpuna as well as give context and background to the research methodology that I elaborate on later, I open this chapter with a moʻolelo or history about one of the most beloved aliʻi nui of Hawaiʻi, ʻEmalani Kaleleonālani Naea Rooke, and her empowering journey to the summit of the highest mountain in Hawaiʻi and the entire Pacific: Maunakea[2] or Mauna a Wākea. After losing the 1874 election for the throne to King David Kalākaua, Queen Emma struggled to find a way to organize a unified opposition to the king for the next election. While her opponent was traveling around the world, Queen Emma quickly chose to respond to what she called "his tour of pleasure and self-praise"[3] by going to Maunakea, the piko of the Hawaiian world. There she immersed herself in the mountain lake, Waiau, "the sacred, regenerative waters of her ancestor-god Wākea" (de Silva 2006, p. 2) for whom the mountain is named, "the wondrous liquid point of union from which all kānaka descend" (p. 3). This trip cleansed and reinvigorated Queen Emma physically and spiritually, strengthened her relationship with her ancestors and their teachings, validated her seniority of rank and ancestral lineage, and, furthermore, reaffirmed her kuleana (right, responsibility, capability, and privilege) to rule the nation of Hawai'i. We are fortunate to have a legacy of eight mele composed by the queen's companions, as well as the oral history of a descendant of Queen Emma's guide[4] on that journey, which together commemorate this 1881[5] expedition from Mānā up Maunakea and back.

One of the recurring images in these mele is of the long, steep, unsteady trail that Queen Emma traveled—both physically and spiritually—to reach her destination, enabling her to return to, restore, and sustain her kuleana as a Kanaka and ali'i nui. Her trip up the ala 'ūlili or steep mountain trail was particularly difficult not only because of the terrain but also because it followed an overwhelmingly painful time in her life after the sudden deaths of both her son, Prince Albert Kahakuohawai'i, in 1862 and then her husband, Kamehameha IV Alexander 'Iolani Liholiho, in 1863; it took place during an uncertain time in her political career after she lost the 1874 election to Kalākaua and was working to mount her second campaign against him; and it occurred on the cusp of one of the most devastating and tumultuous times in our nation's history with the 1893 overthrow of our monarchy and the 1898 illegal annexation by the United States just around the corner. In the mele, "A Maunakea 'o Kalani,"[6] the last, in geographical sequence, of the eight mele commemorating this journey (de Silva 2006), there are many lines that contribute to this ala or pathway imagery—perhaps, most notably, the following:

He ala nihinihi ia   It is a narrow, precarious trail
A hiki a i ke Mole.[7]   That leads back to Kemole/the base.

In these two lines of poetry we uncover a layered description of Queen Emma's many paths—past, present, and future; literal and figurative; political and personal. Kīhei de Silva, noted Hawaiian scholar of hula and mele who has done extensive research on Queen Emma, interprets the lines this way: Although her paths may be "narrow and precipitous (nihinihi) at times, . . . careful footwork (nihi) and circumspect behavior (nihi) will ultimately take her back to Kemole," a hill and "gulch on the western slope of Maunakea at about the halfway point on Emma's journey from Waiau back to Mānā" (2006, pp. 4–5) and to ka mole— her base, taproot, foundation, and source; in other words, her people.

These two lines inspired the title for my chapter—"He Ala Nihinihi Ia A Hiki I Ka Mole: A Precarious Yet Worthwhile Path to Kuleana Through Hawaiian

Place-Based Education." Just like the haku mele (composer) of "A Maunakea 'o Kalani" used the pathway image to convey the significance of Emma's journey to reclaiming and sustaining her kuleana as ali'i nui, I likewise find the pathway image extremely powerful when evaluating the significance of a place-based graduate exchange between indigenous programs at the University of Hawai'i at Mānoa (UHM) and the University of Victoria in British Columbia (UVIC) as a part of my dissertation research on Hawaiian place-based education.[8] This highly experiential program immerses students in place- and project-based activities and scholarship around the themes of decolonization, cultural revitalization, sustainable self-determination, and indigenous resurgence through the experiences of Native Hawaiians and First Peoples of Canada. The exchange is a two-week intensive graduate seminar that is alternately hosted by UHM's Indigenous Politics program (UHIP) in Hawai'i and by the University of Victoria's Indigenous Governance program (IGOV) in Canada. The ala imagery or metaphor from Queen Emma's mele and mo'olelo allowed me to recognize the different pathways that emerged and converged during the 2012 UHIP-IGOV place-based graduate exchange, those that were rediscovered, those that were newly cleared, and those that led to both ancestral and new indigenous knowledge and practice. The most significant pathway revealed during my evaluation was the sometimes precarious yet always worthwhile path to restoring and sustaining kuleana for the benefit of our places, our communities, and our people. What I found was that successful and effective Hawaiian place-based education can and should play an important role in helping us as students recognize and begin to navigate our own pathways to kuleana (i.e., our rights and responsibilities to our people, places, and communities). Just as Queen Emma carefully navigated the sometimes narrow and precipitous pathway to Waiau, all of us, her descendants, continue to struggle to find and then negotiate our own way along this same path. Nāna i waele i ke ala, ma hope aku mākou: She cleared the path and we follow.[9]

With this mo'olelo and mele for Queen Emma and Maunakea in mind, I share in this chapter my journey to understanding, recognizing, and conceptualizing the indigenous methodology that underpins my doctoral research on effective methods and goals for successful Hawaiian place-based education programs. It was the evaluation data I collected during the 2012 UHIP-IGOV place-based graduate exchange, which took place in part on the islands of Kaho'olawe and Moloka'i, that led me back to the mele and mo'olelo of Queen Emma, with which I opened this chapter. And it was her mele and mo'olelo that inspired the development of my research methodology, a process of reflection and rediscovery of my many genealogies that ultimately helped me to see my hālau hula as my first experience with Hawaiian place-based education.

Situating the Research Within My Own Genealogies

Wahi a kahiko[10]: "I ulu nō ka lālā i ke kumu—the branches grow because of the trunk," meaning that "without our ancestors we would not be here" (Pukui 1983, p. 137). I present this saying of my kūpuna to introduce the concept of genealogy, which contextualizes my research and, more specifically, my decision-making process in terms of methodology and method. In essence, I see my research as being informed by and situated within my many genealogies as a Kanaka, hula practitioner, educator, and emerging scholar. Honoring the many kumu who have contributed to my growth and learning (in all its many forms) and "rediscover[ing] fragmented, subjugated, local and specific knowledge" (Kaomea 2006, p. 334) by reflecting on my many histories with these kumu have led me down the path to conceptualizing and implementing the research methodology I present in this chapter.

The 'ōlelo no'eau (wise, poetical saying) that opens this section uses the metaphor of the tree to articulate the undeniable tie we have as Kānaka to our ancestors. Hawaiian scholar Kekuewa S. T. Kikiloi (2012) examines in depth this genealogical connection in his groundbreaking research on the island of Mokumanamana, which is located on the axis of northwest and southeast in the Hawaiian archipelago, the gateway between pō and ao, and has been the site of significant transformation and reproduction for Hawaiian society and religion over the generations. Kikiloi brings to the fore the concept of the 'aha (braided cordage and a spiritual and political ceremony of our ali'i nui) as a symbolic connection between ancestors and descendants. He explains that the 'aha or "the twisting coir[11] braided cord was a powerful symbol that evoked the imagery of 'binding,' 'connecting,' and 'linking' people and ancestors and focusing them in common purpose—essentially increasing their strength through collective and cohesive action. The cord was the genealogical connection between past, present, and future" (pp. 98–99). Images, sayings, and practices such as the two explained earlier (kumu and 'aha) bring into focus the importance of genealogy to Hawaiians and reaffirm the active role that our ancestors continue to play in our lives even after they have returned to the spiritual realm of pō. We are further reminded of the ongoing presence of our kūpuna by the words of kumu hula and Hawaiian scholar Pualani Kanahele (2005, p. 28): "Even those grandparents who have died are still wonderful to us, because they have left us clues as to how our life should be lived today. We still live in the same space they did, and a lot of things have not changed."

Genealogy has and always will be a cornerstone of our Hawaiian worldview. It is through genealogy that my ancestors articulated the creation of the world from darkness to the coral polyps, the creatures of the ocean and land, the gods, and eventually the first human. It is through genealogy that my people understand our familial and reciprocal relationship to the natural world including the land, sea, sky, and all creatures that live in these environments. It is through genealogy and spiritual practices that the great chiefs of Hawaiʻi validated their authority to rule and questioned the authority of their rivals. It is through genealogy that the histories of our ancestors are remembered, reenacted, and readjusted in present time by their descendants for the purposes of acquiring mana and strengthening identity (Kameʻeleihiwa 1992; Kikiloi 2012). It is through genealogy that knowledge, practices, and traditions are perpetuated and passed down from one generation to the next. And it is through genealogy that we can tap back into and reawaken those parts of us that have been buried by layers of colonization and marginalization.

One word for genealogy from our native language is "moʻokūʻauhau." Embedded within it is the word "moʻo," which refers to "succession, series, especially a genealogical line, lineage" (Pukui and Elbert 1986, p. 253). The succession of generations within one's moʻokūʻauhau can be created by a human ancestral lineage. However, we are all a part of many moʻokūʻauhau beyond those of our families, including genealogies of places, organizations, and movements that include individuals, groups, natural creatures and phenomena, and so on. One becomes a part of these many moʻokūʻauhau not only through familial ties but also through sustained practice, presence, and commitment to people, places, and causes. In her inspiring book, *The Seeds We Planted*, Hawaiian educational and political scholar Noelani Goodyear-Kaʻōpua (2013) situates "the Hawaiian charter school movement and the specific work of classroom teachers at one school in the context of longer genealogies of Hawaiian survivance" (p. 6). She recognizes that the Hawaiian "genealogy of struggle [for cultural persistence, political power, and land] opened the space for schools like Hālau Kū Māna to exist in the first place" (p. 12). Furthermore, the school's curriculum helps students and teachers "to see themselves as important actors within a genealogically situated movement for self-determination and sovereignty" (p. 13).

Similar to how people can become a part of the genealogy of a movement through their participation in it, as did the founders, teachers, and students of Hālau Kū Māna, people can also become a part of one another's genealogy through the fundamental kumu-haumāna (teacher/mentor-student) relationship. Renowned Maori scholar Linda Tuhiwai Smith (1999) says her political awareness and activism or her "dissent lines come down through [her] tribal lines but also through [her] experiences as a result of schooling and an urban background" (p. 13). Through years of working together, learning from one another, and exchanging knowledge and experience, kumu and haumāna become genealogically tied, whether or not they are genetically related. In his contribution to this book, Hawaiian language scholar, musician, and kumu hula

Robert Keawe Lopes Jr. analyzes the words of King David Kalākaua's mele titled "Ua Noho Au A Kupa I Kō Alo"[12] to conceptualize this relationship further and draw connections between the attitudes and methods required for indigenous research to those described in the mele. He explains that by sitting in reverence (noho) at the feet of our mentors, both literally and figuratively, and staying there until we are accustomed (kupa) to their presence (alo) and they are accustomed to ours (he alo a he alo) and until we are familiar (kama'āina) with their voices (leo), we eventually gain access to their teachings (mana'o), which are contained in their repository of love (waihona a ke aloha). I have been fortunate enough to develop and sustain several relationships like this with kumu from both my cultural/personal life and my academic/professional life. In the next section I introduce two incredible kumu who have welcomed me into their genealogy through the practice and perpetuation of traditional[13] hula, oli, and mele.

He lālā au no ku'u kumu

In the 'ōlelo no'eau I shared earlier—*I ulu nō ka lālā i ke kumu*—the connection between ancestor and descendant is described through the metaphor of a kumu or tree, whose lālā or branches grow from, are supported and sustained by, and are forever connected to its trunk. However, our understanding of genealogy is expanded by the works of the indigenous scholars discussed earlier that explain that our kumu are not only our biological ancestors but also our teachers and mentors. Just as lālā or branches sprout forth from a tree, so do students grow from their teachers. We are forever connected to one another, rooted in the teachings and traditions that are shared and perpetuated through this important relationship. This saying was most likely the inspiration for a mele I learned as a child from one of my first teachers. I learned this mele (only two stanzas are shown here) and its accompanying hula when I was nine years old as a haumāna of my kumu hula, Māpuana de Silva. Each verse begins with the phrase "He lālā au no ku'u kumu/I am a branch of my teacher," and I can say with no hesitation that I am indeed a branch of my many teachers—He lālā nō au no ku'u po'e kumu.

Ku'u Kumu

He lālā au no ku'u kumu	I am a branch of my teacher
Nāna au e ko'o mai	Who supports me
Inā ikaika ka makani	If the wind is strong
Nāna au e a'o mai	(S)he teaches me
Luliluli, luliluli	Sway, sway
A la'i mālie hou	Until all becomes calm again.

He lālā au no ku'u kumu	I am a branch of my teacher
Nānā au e paipai mai	Who encourages me
Inā ikaika ka ua nui	If the rain is heavy
Nānā au e a'o mai	(S)he teaches me
Uē ka lani, uē ka lani,	The heavens weep, the heavens weep
A ola ka honua	And the earth lives.[14]

One of the most significant and sustained sites of growth and learning for me has been my hālau hula (hula school), Hālau Mōhala 'Ilima. It is there that I became a part of a new genealogy beyond my family roots—my hula genealogy. Just as I am a lālā of my kumu, Māpuana de Silva, she is also a lālā of her kumu, Maiki Aiu Lake, Sally Naluai, Lani Kalama, and Patience Namaka Bacon—who are lālā of their kumu, Lokalia Montgomery and Mary Kawena Pukui, just to name a few. It is through my kumu and the relationship I developed with her that I am connected to her kumu and all my hula ancestors who came before.

I began studying traditional hula in 1989 at the age of nine when my mother signed me up for Hālau Mōhala 'Ilima, which is based in Ka'ōhao, Kailua, Ko'olaupoko, O'ahu. There I learned hula, oli, and mele that honor our gods, our royalty, our sacred places, and our histories. I have since traveled throughout ka pae 'āina 'o Hawai'i,[15] across the Pacific, and to the North American continent, sharing hula and connecting with others who are committed to perpetuating their own forms of cultural expression. I have applied my training to participate in ceremonies and exchanges with other indigenous groups from New Caledonia and Tahiti to Peru and the Pacific Northwest. My mo'o, or succession of learning, practicing, and sharing, has continued without interruption for twenty-five years, strengthening my mo'okū'auhau and leading to my two 'ūniki 'ai lolo[16]—graduating as an 'ōlapa (dancer) in 2005 and most recently as a ho'opa'a (drummer and chanter) and kumu hula (teacher) in 2012. The words I continue to give voice to and the motions I continue to give life to are the same words and motions that my kūpuna practiced for generations and that I continue to perpetuate into the future. I agree with Lopes (2010) that "the only way one can validate his or her status as being a true student is to produce in the present, performances that include manifestations of one's mentor's mana'o, that represent the lineal relationship to one's knowledge" (p. 129). One of the highest compliments 'ōlapa can receive is for observers to recognize the style and teachings of their kumu in their own work, which is not limited to dancing but also how they carry themselves in different situations, how they interact with kūpuna and other indigenous peoples, and, in my case, how I design, conduct, and present my research.

Although some may not see the connection of my hula genealogy to my work as an academic, I see them as intimately related. For one, we learn in our hālau that hula cannot be separated from the history, language, values, and other spiritual and cultural practices of our ancestors. In fact, it was instilled in us early that learning and presenting hula and mele involve much more than memorizing words and motions. They involve traveling to the places for which these mele and hula were written and presenting them in context as a way of honoring, communicating, and engaging with the kūpuna (seen and unseen) of those places once again. They also involve hours of research on the mele themselves—remembering the ones who protected their integrity over the generations and eventually passed them down to us; acknowledging the original composers of these mele; taking into account the times, places, and reasons these mele were written; uncovering the layered meanings of their sometimes mistakenly perceived simple lines of poetry; and eventually recognizing the lessons embedded in them as revealed through careful analysis of the interconnectedness of all these many contexts. This kind of in-depth research informs our presentations of these mele as a hālau. Simultaneously, our practice of returning to the sites of origin for these mele and presenting them in place informs our research and understanding of them. It is a cyclical process of research and practice.

In my role as an indigenous educator and researcher, I am now realizing additional levels of impact that my hula genealogy is having on my current work. In particular, I have been greatly influenced by this ongoing, cyclical process of research informing practice and practice informing research, which was modeled for me throughout my twenty-five years in the hālau by my kumu hula, Māpuana de Silva, and her husband, Kīhei de Silva. There is no doubt that Uncle Kīhei is one of the premier, if not the premier scholar of Hawaiian mele and hula alive today. In some ways, he can also be seen as a Hawaiian "portraitist"[17] (Lawrence-Lightfoot and Davis 1997), who understands the importance of the many contexts in which mele exist and how the interplay of these contexts with our position as Hawaiian practitioners and researchers shapes our understanding of the mele. Portraitists see "context as a collage of multiple sources of data" (p. 65): physical, historical, cultural, ideological, metaphorical, symbolic, and personal. Goodyear-Kaʻōpua (2013) was drawn to portraiture as a research approach because she says that it "acknowledges that scholarly writing is an art form that takes a situated perspective and should include attentiveness to the aesthetics of the finished piece" (p. 43). If you would ever have the opportunity to read one of Uncle Kīhei's factsheets for the mele and hula we present at the Merrie Monarch Hula Festival every year, you would undoubtedly agree that they are pieces of art. Many in our community recognize them as mini-dissertations full of invaluable research for as many as fourteen different mele and oli each year.

In 2006, one of the mele that Uncle Kīhei researched for our Merrie Monarch factsheet was a hula noho with 'ili'ili written for Queen Emma's trip to Maunakea. Aunty Māpu had learned the mele and hula from Aunty Pat Namaka Bacon, and they had chosen it for our hula kahiko presentation that year. That mele was "A Maunakea 'o Kalani." It was at that time that I learned this mele and hula, presented it in public, and fell in love with it. Since then, I have presented it in many different contexts, from the lantern-lit pā hula (outdoor hula platform[18]) on the island of Kaho'olawe in Hawai'i to the dirt floor of a traditional Coast Salish longhouse in British Columbia to the piko of the island of Mo'orea in our ancestral land of Kahiki. It was Uncle Kīhei's research on the mele in 2006 that enabled me to understand the themes and concepts embedded in the mele well enough to know when it would be appropriate to present it again in new contexts in my own life. As genealogy led Queen Emma back to ka piko o Wākea in 1881, it is my genealogy that has led me back to this mele when analyzing and interpreting the evaluation data collected during the 2012 place-based graduate exchange between the Indigenous Politics program at UHM and the Indigenous Governance program at UVIC. As a result, my understanding of the diverse data came into focus, and my understanding of the mele I had been dancing and chanting for six years expanded and deepened. Although "Hawaiian genealogies are the histories of our people" (Kame'eleihiwa 1992, p. 19), they are also "more than just contextual information but still a form of Hawaiian intellectual production" (Goodyear-Ka'ōpua 2013, p. 45). When we recognize and reflect on our mo'okū'auhau and how they have shaped us, we become "most clear about [our] own kuleana, [our] learning objectives, and [our] visions of potential futures" (p. 45)—thereby facilitating the production of new knowledge that can be added to the intellectual waihona of our people and used to envision healthy and prosperous futures for our lāhui (the Hawaiian people and nation).

Indigenous Epistemology and Methodology

Mele practiced and perpetuated in hālau hula, preserved and passed down in family collections, stored and cataloged in the archives, and recorded and disseminated in nūpepa 'ōlelo Hawai'i (Hawaiian language newspapers) all make up the vast waihona mele of our lāhui. As I explained earlier, mele are just one form of living narrative that our kūpuna used to remember significant events and people, honor and express our aloha 'āina, document ingenious cultural practices, record important lessons learned through the histories of our people, and outline proper ethical and spiritual protocols on which to model our behavior. In other words, our native texts are our sources of Hawaiian epistemology. Here are just a few examples of the many complex ways mele embody and reveal Hawaiian ways of knowing and existing in the world.

One of my mentors and hula sisters, kumu hula and Hawaiian language and political scholar Leilani Basham, has written extensively about mele in the political context, specifically "mele lāhui, or mele written in honor of the lāhui, the Hawaiian people and nation" (2008, p. 152). She describes the many reasons our kūpuna wrote and used mele:

> Mele, which are poetry, music, chants, and songs, have been a foundational part of the histories and lives of the Kānaka Maoli of Hawai'i. We have used mele to record and recount our histories and stories, as well as our ideas about the lives of our people and our land. Mele have been a vital part of our cultural belief systems and practices, our connection to our 'āina, our land base, as well as our formal religious practices and our informal daily practices. Mele have also been vital to our political theories, ideas, and practices. (p. 152)

Basham's (2007) appreciation of the complexity of mele and their integral connection to our mo'olelo is informed in part by the writings of Hawaiian intellectuals of the late nineteenth and early twentieth centuries. In "Ka Moolelo Hawaii Kahiko" published in *Ka Na'i Aupuni*, Joseph M. Poepoe (1 Pepeluali 1906) wrote, "Ua piha ko kakou mau mele me na hoonupanupa ana a ia mea he aloha; piha me na keha ana no na hana koa a wiwo ole a ko kakou poe ikaika o ka wa kahiko; ka lakou mau hana kaulana; ko lakou ola ana ame ko lakou make ana" (p. 1).[19] In "Ka Moolelo o na Kamehameha" published in *Ka Nupepa Kuokoa*, Samuel Manaiakalani Kamakau (21 Kēkēmapa 1867) described the art of composing mele and the treasured secrets about our lāhui contained therein:

> O ka haku mele kekahi hana akamai a naauao o ke poe kahiko, a ua kaulana loa ia poe ma ia hana. . . . He nui ke ano o na mele a he nui no hoi ka waiwai i loaa ma loko o na mele a ka poe kahiko i haku ai. Ua hanaia ko ka lani, ko ka lewa, ko ka moana, ko ka honua, ko ka la, ka mahina, na hoku a me na mea a pau. Ua hanaia na mele me na waiwai huna i loko o ka lehulehu loa. He nui na loina a me na kaona i loko.[20] (p. 1)

Both of these short excerpts elevate mele and their composers to their rightful place as great literary and historical accounts by skilled scholars and authors who not only knew about the events and people of our past but also understood the power mele had to communicate our values, perspectives, and beliefs about the world (our epistemology) to those who were conscious enough to find them woven within their beautiful lines of poetry.

Celebrated Hawaiian musician and Hawaiian language educator Kainani Kahaunele (2014) emphasizes the importance of learning, singing, and composing mele in our time: "Mele is a common denominator that inspires and supports activism and activists"; "mele amplify our spirit, our minds, our potential, and our existence"; and "if there's anything any Hawaiians can do to their mana gauge, tool box, or mental rolodex, it is to know Hawaiian mele, for therein lie invaluable lessons and knowledge of our heritage" (p. 56).

Often mele (and oli and pule) are used to communicate with the spiritual realm to access knowledge because they are seen as one of the highest forms of communication. Nuu-chah-nulth scholar E. Richard Atleo's (2004) "theory of tsawalk (everything is one)" suggests that "while the human mind is necessary for human cognition and for accessing and acquiring information, it can also be a conduit for spiritual information that can complement or complete or further illuminate our understanding of existence" (pp. xix–xx). He further explains that "the human orientation, wherein the experience is initiated from the physical realm through the usual means of fasting, meditating, ritual cleansing, praying, petitioning, waiting, and chanting" (p. 72), is one of two orientations that make up what he calls "the oosumich method, the necessity of spiritual protocols, and the necessity of ritual cleansing in order to acquire knowledge" (p. 71).

Beyond the act of acquiring knowledge, many indigenous scholars also talk about the power of mele to help us communicate with and actually shape our environments that in turn shape us. Goodyear-Kaʻōpua (2013) calls this notion and practice "land-centered literacies." She writes, "If healthy relationships entail communication, then the practice of aloha ʻāina must include facility in multiple languages, human and nonhuman" (p. 35). She goes on to list examples of such land-centered literacies, including "offering chant in our own human language and then observing and finding meaning in the responses of winds, rains, birds, waves, or stones" (p. 34). Tewa scientist and educator Gregory Cajete (2000) of Santa Clara Pueblo, New Mexico adds,

> Native cultures talk, pray, and chant the landscape into their being.
> This is the animating power of language inherent in the spoken word
> that connects the breath of each person to the breath of the world.
> Native languages invest their homeland with their presence through
> the active verb-based process of "talking the land," that is, naming its
> places, singing its virtues, and telling its stories. (p. 184)

Finally, in Kikiloi's (2012) research about the ʻaha ceremony and its relationship to the northwestern Hawaiian islands of Mokumanamana and Nihoa, he quotes Kelsey's (n.d.) understanding of mele koʻihonua: "The earth, as a royal genealogy, was adzed open, as it were, by genealogical chant called mele koʻi honua (mele literally means chant; koʻi means adze; and honua means earth). In sum, it means to carve or shape the earth" (p. 27). Literally and figuratively, voicing mele can provoke a response from our environment, thus changing the landscape and us in return.

When I reflect on my time in my hālau hula, I remember countless times in which we used mele to interact with our place and communicate with our kūpuna in the ways described earlier. In fact, the number of times I presented oli, mele, or hula on stage in competition is dwarfed by the number of times I offered oli, mele, and hula on pā hula in the pouring rain, on the top of mountains in dense cloud cover, on steep ledges overlooking vast valleys, on the soggy ground of mountainous bogs, perched high on towering sea cliffs, on the rocky shores of streams and lakes, in the company of our indigenous cousins, and in the presence of our kūpuna seen and unseen. In many ways these memories are much more vivid and meaningful than any Merrie Monarch performance I ever participated in. It was through these experiences that I was reminded over and over again that our kūpuna are very much still with us, and they are listening. I was also reminded that our contexts are dynamic, "not static and that the actors are not only shaped by the context, but that they also give it shape" (Lawrence-Lightfoot and Davis 1997, p. 57). We are taught at Hālau Mōhala ʻIlima that mele and their accompanying hula are the best ways to engage with and communicate with our ancestors (human, deity, land, etc.).

All of these examples reinforce the idea that mele are sources of Hawaiian epistemology, and many indigenous researchers have published about the significance of indigenous epistemologies to the development of indigenous methodologies. Margaret Kovack (2005), of Plains Cree and Saulteaux ancestry, describes indigenous epistemology as "fluid, non-linear, and relational" in which "knowledge is transmitted through stories that shape shift in relation to the wisdom of the storyteller at the time of the telling." She says plainly, "An Indigenous epistemology is a significant aspect of Indigenous methodology and suggests an Indigenous way of functioning in the world" (p. 27). Kanaka scholar and philosopher Manulani Meyer (2001) takes this a step further when she says our epistemology "is the sword against anthropological arrogance and the shield against philosophical universalism. How one knows, indeed, what one prioritizes with regard to this knowing, ends up being the stuffing of identity, the truth that links us to our distinct cosmologies, and the essence of who we are as Oceanic people. It is a discussion of place and genealogy" (p. 125). Thus, not only are our epistemologies shaped by our ʻāina and moʻokūʻauhau, but relying on them to inform our methodologies is also a form of native resistance and resurgence. In the field of geography, Renee Pualani Louis (2007) maintains that "embracing Indigenous epistemologies is a critical element of Indigenous methodological research" (p. 133). In the field of education, Smith (2005) calls for "epistemic self-determination" (p. 94) in which "Indigenous epistemologies rather than say, pedagogical styles, can lead to a different schooling experience and produce a different kind of learner" (p. 95). She has inspired other indigenous researchers and educators with this idea. Goodyear-Ka'ōpua (2013) references "epistemic self-determination" in her book when talking about Hawaiians taking back "the power to define what counts as knowledge and to determine what our people should be able to know and do" (p. 29); Sarah-Jane Tiakiwai, writing within the context of teacher education at Te Wānanga o Aotearoa, also cites "epistemic self-determination" when she purports that "repositioning and reconceptualizing education in this way recognizes the innovation that exists within indigenous communities and the desire to search within these cultural frameworks and understandings to consider alternative ways of making a difference in the education of indigenous communities" (O'Malley and Tiakiwai 2010, p. 3).

Although turning to indigenous epistemologies when conceptualizing indigenous research methodologies is essential to our credibility, validity, and success as indigenous researchers, it is no simple task. For one, the narratives that contain our epistemologies are not as easily accessible today as they once were. Agents of settler colonialism have attempted (and continue to attempt) to bury, erase, silence, and destroy anything that contains traces of our ways of knowing and existing in the world and to replace it with their own dominant perspectives and value systems (Kauanui and Wolfe 2012; Kosasa 2008; Wolfe 2006). But they have not been completely successful: "Whilst our knowledge systems have been fractured and ruptured they are durable and timeless enough for us to resurrect them for use in our daily lives as living practices" (Edwards 2013, p. 43). The following quote from kumu hula Pualani Kanahele (2005) should be a reminder to us all that our people and our 'ike (epistemologies) are "relentless, strong, and still here" (Kovack 2005, p. 34):

> We have to pay attention to our Hawaiian native intelligence and experiences. We should be able to look for them, define them—because nothing is lost. In fact, we still have a lot of knowledge that was left to us by our ancestors. It's still there; we just have to go and look for it. That's what we are all about—research. (p. 27)

Aunty Pua encourages us to take up the work of research and redefine it for ourselves because all we need to know about ourselves still exists, just beneath the surface, waiting to be acknowledged and honored once again. Many of us Hawaiians venturing into the realm of research strive to follow Aunty Pua's instructions, but the tragic history that surrounds this phenomenon known as "research" in our indigenous communities requires our special care and reflection along the way so as to not repeat the atrocities of this history. "The term research is inextricably linked to European imperialism and colonialism" (Smith 1999, p. 1), thus making the job of entering the world of research as indigenous peoples that much more challenging. Traditionally, research has been "an encounter between the West and the Other" (p. 18) where research was largely conducted on the Other by the West with damaging consequences. In fields such as anthropology, native people were the "objects" of the research, and their ʻike (knowledge) was the "data" to be extracted and analyzed by Western researchers for their own promotion and profit. Developing and applying "theory" and "methodology" based on the "data" they mined from native communities was what white researchers did. In the Western model of research, our people were not involved in this process of "theorizing" or "analyzing" because they were not seen as equals; they were largely the objects of the research and occasionally the informants or collaborators who were used by white researchers to gain access to communities to collect data and then leave (White and Tengan 2001). The damaging outcomes of the collision between the Western research paradigm and indigenous communities have been particularly evident in the field of research evaluation (Kawakami et al. 2007; LaFrance 2004). Most evaluation studies have been conducted by non-indigenous outsiders who "stand with their feet firmly planted in their own worldviews and have themselves failed to gain any true understanding of our ways, our knowledges, and our world" (Kawakami et al. 2007, p. 326), leading to over-researching, exploitation, deficiency models, misinterpretation of data, incongruent solutions, and disregard of cultural and spiritual protocols, ethics, and values. It is no surprise then that indigenous communities are largely incredibly wary of anything called "research," even if it is being done by one of their own.

Trauma inflicted on our people through research continues to bubble up today in the form of anger, despair, and suspicion. However, "historically rooted injustices can be allayed only when the people most negatively impacted by systems of power/knowledge realize control over the means to change those systems" (Goodyear-Kaʻōpua 2013, p. 10). Reclaiming the research process to answer our own questions for the benefit of our own communities through the development and application of our own theories and methodologies is a form of resistance and survival that aligns with Paulo Freire's (2011) "pedagogy of the oppressed." Because we have been historically oppressed in the system of research, we are the only ones who can transform the system and liberate ourselves (and our oppressors): The "oppressed must be among the developers of the pedagogy" (p. 54), and it "must be forged *with*, not *for*, the oppressed" (p. 48). In the end, "when indigenous peoples become the researchers and not merely the researched, the activity of research is transformed. Questions are framed differently, priorities are ranked differently, problems are defined differently, people participate on different terms" (Smith 1999, p. 193). This transformation is certainly taking place in the field of evaluation where indigenous people are becoming the evaluators and uniting behind the idea that "we have lived under the gaze of newcomers who have evaluated us within their own belief systems . . . [and] this gaze has come to represent a truth about us, a truth that is not of our own making. It is appropriate that the gaze be returned now and that we do our own gazing" (Kawakami et al. 2007, p. 329).

There are many success stories of native peoples who are working to flip this colonial paradigm and "return the gaze" in terms of research by taking control, shaping, and building their own research agendas and methodologies around their own indigenous epistemologies. They make up a collective, indigenous genealogy of resistance and survival through research that inspires, guides, and informs my work. I hope that my research will contribute to this paradigm shift through my use of mele as a waihona (repository) of Hawaiian epistemology, which provides the theoretical lens through which to view the 'ike or data I gathered during my evaluation of a successful Hawaiian place-based program.

Using Mele to Create Counter-Stories: A Critical Race Methodology
My hula genealogy was ultimately the reason I found myself coming back to the mele "A Maunakea 'o Kalani" when conducting my analysis and interpretation of the data I collected during my evaluation of the 2012 UHIP-IGOV place-based graduate exchange. In many ways it felt natural and familiar to rely on the words and images of this mele to help me make sense of the data. Reflecting back now, I know that was probably because I was unconsciously remembering, repeating, and reenacting the practices passed down to me through my many years in my hālau hula. I relate to the work of Keawe Lopes, Leilani Basham, and Kahikina de Silva (just to name a few) in how they all look to mele to structure the theoretical framework of their scholarship and to make sense of other data or the mele themselves. Lopes, Basham, de Silva, and I are all hula people, privileged to have learned our 'ōlelo makuahine (mother tongue) and to have been raised and mentored by our kumu hula. It is no surprise, then, that we all turn to mele written in 'ōlelo Hawai'i as the foundations of our research methodologies.

I am also influenced by the work of Chicana/o studies professors Daniel G. Solorzano and Tara J. Yosso (2002), who advocate for the application of critical race theory (CRT) in the field of education through a critical race methodology. By creating what they call "counter-stories from (a) the data gathered from the research process itself, (b) the existing literature on the topic(s), (c) our own professional experiences, and (d) our own personal experiences" (p. 34), we people of color can challenge majoritarian stories of privilege, push against and disrupt these dominant Western narratives, and simultaneously reveal our own histories and epistemologies. Solorzano and Yosso reference two concepts that they believe are essential to creating counter-stories: *theoretical sensitivity* and *cultural intuition*. According to Strauss and Corbin (as cited in Solorzano and Yosso 2002), the former refers to

> a personal quality of the researcher. It indicates an awareness of the subtleties of meaning in data. One can come to the research situation with varying degrees of sensitivity depending upon previous reading and experience with or relevant to the data. It can also be developed further during the research process. Theoretical sensitivity refers to the attribute of having insight, the ability to give meaning to data, the capacity to understand, and capability to separate the pertinent from that which isn't. (p. 33)

Cultural intuition adds "collective experience and community memory" (Solorzano and Yosso 2002, p. 33) to one's personal experience. From the Chicana context, Delago Bernal (as cited in Solorzano and Yosso 2002) explains,

> A Chicana researcher's cultural intuition is achieved and can be nurtured through our personal experiences (which are influenced by ancestral wisdom, community memory, and intuition), the literature on and about Chicanas, our professional experiences, and the analytical process we engage in when we are in a central position of our research and our analysis. Thus, cultural intuition is a complex process that is experiential, intuitive, historical, personal, collective, and dynamic. (pp. 33–34)

My approach to reframing and reclaiming Hawaiian place-based education through the evaluation of the UHIP-IGOV graduate exchange program primarily between Hawaiians, First Nations peoples, and settlers—which in 2012 took place in part on the islands of Kahoʻolawe and Molokaʻi—employed both theoretical sensitivity and cultural intuition. My past experience as a student in the 2011 UHIP-IGOV exchange—along with my background as an ʻōlapa and kumu hula in my hālau and the larger hula community, my personal connection with Kahoʻolawe throughout my life, my knowledge of the history of Kahoʻolawe within our larger genealogy of struggle for self-determination, and my familiarity with Queen Emma's mele tied to Maunakea—all developed my theoretical sensitivity and cultural intuition, thus facilitating my creation of a counter-story for Hawaiian place-based education. Even though I initially used the mele "A Maunakea 'o Kalani" as a tool to understand my evaluation data, the data eventually provided a new lens through which to view the mele as well. Through this process, I discovered the potential for my research to become a counter-story/narrative that decenters and deprivileges meta-narratives that permeate dominant, Western place-based discourse and that provides critical commentary to this phenomenon known as "Hawaiian place-based education."

I hope this discussion sheds some light on the strength and power of our native texts and their capacity to frame our scholarly work. We know that mele are sources of ancestral memory and Hawaiian epistemology that can help us engage with different beings and environments and make sense of different situations and information, so why not use them to engage with and make sense of data collected during our own research? As more and more of our people are engaging in the practice of research, there is "a call for Indigenous Peoples to live these teachings and stories in the diversity of their contemporary lives, because that act in and of itself is the precursor, propelling us into new social spaces based on justice and peace" (Simpson 2011, p. 148). This is a kuleana we must acknowledge and bear as indigenous researchers who were privileged to be exposed to and taught the knowledge and practices of our kumu and kūpuna.

I end this section with a short yet powerful story from the Alaska Native community that reminds us of the importance of developing and implementing our own theories and methodologies in order to make sense of our own situations as indigenous peoples. One of the Alaska Rural Systematic Initiative (AKRSI) co-directors told of an Alaska Native elder who pointed to a star in the heavens and said, "That star has my name." He shared this story at the 2003 National Indian Education Association conference and then "challenged his listeners to 'use your star system to teach your kids'" (Emekauwa and Williams 2004, p. 9). I think this challenge can be met in the field of educational research by developing our own theories and methodologies. It may be hard, but as Anzaldua[21] says, "if we have been gagged and disempowered by theories, we can also be loosened and empowered by theories" (as cited in Solorzano and Yosso 2002, p. 37). This is a kuleana we must acknowledge and bear as Kanaka researchers who are privileged to be exposed to and taught the knowledge and practices of our kumu and kūpuna.

Methods

As mentioned, I conducted an evaluation of the 2012 UHIP-IGOV place-based graduate exchange between the Indigenous Politics program at UHM (UHIP) and the Indigenous Governance program (IGOV) at the University of Victoria as a part of my dissertation research on Hawaiian place-based education. It was the evaluation data I collected during the exchange program that led me back to the mele and moʻolelo of Queen Emma, which in turn revealed the intimate relationship between my research and my many genealogies, thus informing the development of my research methodology. I was both a participant and an evaluator in the 2012 exchange, led by UHM professors Hōkūlani Aikau, Noelani Goodyear-Kaʻōpua, and Noenoe Silva and UVIC professors Taiaiake Alfred and Jeff Corntassel. The 2012 exchange was hosted by UHIP in Hawaiʻi and focused on contemporary Hawaiian efforts to restore kuleana to land and community both within and outside settler state structures. Students and faculty from both programs deepened their understandings of major political and social forces in Hawaiʻi over the past two centuries by learning about and traveling to Kahoʻolawe and Molokaʻi. These two Hawaiian islands were at the center of the Hawaiian renaissance and revitalization movements that began in the 1970s and will be forever connected by a history of activism and aloha ʻāina carried out primarily by Molokaʻi Hawaiians against the U.S. Navy's bombing of Kahoʻolawe, which lasted for more than fifty years, as well as by a relationship between people and place that continues to be nurtured by a new generation of Hawaiians who have accepted the kuleana to practice and cultivate aloha ʻāina consciousness on these islands and across Hawaiʻi.

In my evaluation of the 2012 UHIP-IGOV place-based graduate exchange I used both qualitative and quantitative methods that aligned with my epistemologically grounded methodology. The reflexive, mixed methods approach in the collection, analysis, interpretation, and reporting of data involves multiple sources, procedures, and instruments. Given my identity as a Kanaka educator and my positionality as an insider-outsider (Smith 1999)—a researcher and evaluator of curriculum and educational programming in the Hawaiian community who unapologetically privileges Hawaiian manaʻo (thoughts, beliefs, concerns, philosophies)—I naturally gravitate to responsive evaluation designs (Stake 2004) conceptualized and implemented through an indigenous worldview (Bare 2008; Halagao 2010; Halagao, Tintiangco-Cubales, and Cordova 2009, n.d.; Kaomea 2003; Kawakami et al. 2007; Lafrance 2004). I am also inspired by Hawaiian educational scholar Julie Kaomea's (2003, 2006) "theoretical framework and interpretive methods" that she characterizes as "intentionally eclectic, mingling, combining, and synthesizing theories and techniques from disparate disciplines and paradigms." Kaomea calls herself "an interpretative handy-man or *bricoleur*" (2003, p. 16), which comes from the bricolage approach of Kathleen S. Berry (2006). I see myself in a similar way—in essence, I have a toolbox full of various methods, theories, tools, and the like that I can draw from depending on what fits best and makes the most sense in a particular situation. I am flexible and attentive, mixing and matching methods and theoretical frameworks along the way, allowing the process to take me where it needs to go. While on the surface my methods may seem unrelated, they are all held together by my genealogical and epistemological research methodology.

After collecting formative and summative data from (1) talk-story sessions/interviews with the professors of the UHIP-IGOV exchange, (2) pre- and post-participant questionnaires I developed in partnership with the professors, (3) my field notes as a participant-observer in the 2012 exchange, and (4) reflections from my own experience as a student in the 2011 exchange in Victoria, BC, I analyzed and interpreted all of the data with Queen Emma as my guide. I used her mele, moʻolelo, and the rich pathway images embedded in them to help me identify patterns and relationships between the data and to understand their meaning and significance in terms of my working definition of "Hawaiian place-based education." My preliminary findings regarding the types of activities, perspectives, and outcomes that I believe should be present in any Hawaiian place-based curriculum or program are not a part of this chapter; however, they will be presented in my final dissertation by weaving lines from the mele "A Maunakea ʻo Kalani" together with the contemporary voices and experiences of the students, teachers, and community leaders who participated in the 2012 exchange. Through this process I have concluded that participants in successful Hawaiian place-based educational programs should be given the opportunity to recognize their kuleana and then define their different paths toward restoring and sustaining this kuleana long after the program is over.

I certainly was given that opportunity as a participant in the 2012 UHIP-IGOV place-based exchange. Our trip to Kahoʻolawe was a full-circle moment for me, which resulted in the affirmation and validation of my own kuleana. In the early 1990s, I traveled to Kahoʻolawe for the first time with my mother where we stayed with members of the Protect Kahoʻolawe ʻOhana (PKO) and her Ethnic Studies class on the Hakioawa side of the island for the opening of the Makahiki season. I returned in 2006 to the Honokanaiʻa side of the island with a small group of hula sisters to participate in the Kāholoikalani rain ceremony. By the time I returned to Hakioawa in 2012, it had been nearly twenty years since my first trip, but as soon as the boat stopped in front of the valley and the zodiac pulled alongside us, all the fuzzy images and childhood memories of that first trip came flooding back, more defined and vivid than ever. All the decisions and choices I had made during those intervening twenty years to take on the kuleana of learning my native language, practicing traditional hula, and studying the moʻolelo of my kūpuna set me on a path, unbeknownst to me, that would eventually lead me back to one of my mole, Kahoʻolawe. My path to fulfilling my kuleana is not finished, but it is good to know I am headed in the right direction. He ala nihinihi nō ia a hiki i ka mole!

Conclusion

Queen Emma's ala nihinihi to the summit of Maunakea brought her back not only to her physical mole—the gulch and pu'u named Kemole at the halfway point on her return journey—but also to her spiritual and emotional mole where she solidified her ancestral relationship and commitment to the extended family of her people and nation. As Kīhei de Silva writes, "What Emma learns at Maunakea's summit she must deliver to its mole or base" (2006, p. 5) because it is only through her application of what she learned at ka piko o Wākea that her kuleana to serve her people and nation could truly be realized. Like Queen Emma's journey, successful Hawaiian place-based programs should ultimately inspire and empower their participants to stay on their individual paths to kuleana so that they can ho'i hou i ka mole[22]—return to their mole with the knowledge and skills they have learned during their journey and apply them in their own communities for the betterment of their own people and places.

As I mentioned in the beginning of my chapter, in many ways, my first experience with Hawaiian place-based education was through my hālau hula. We are taught as 'ōlapa and kumu that researching the many-layered meanings of our mele and hula and then presenting them on the land for the purpose of honoring the place and remembering the people and events connected to that place are all part of what is required when you accept the kuleana to practice traditional hula. This kuleana to connect research and practice is one that I strive to uphold in my academic work as well. For this particular chapter, the cycle of research informing practice and practice informing research in terms of the mele "A Maunakea 'o Kalani" began for me in 2006. It was the initial research by Uncle Kīhei that informed our presentation of the mele and hula at Merrie Monarch that year; it was my continued chanting and dancing of this mele in ceremonies and cultural exchanges since then that inspired my use of this mele to interpret the data I present in my dissertation; and it was my use of the words of the mele to make sense of my evaluation research that eventually led me to the actual ala nihinihi of Queen Emma and the summit of Maunakea to 'ike maka iā Waiau. While writing this chapter, I got to a point when I knew I could no longer talk about "A Maunakea 'o Kalani" without having my own 'ike maka (firsthand, see-with-my-own-eyes) experience at ka piko o Wākea. It was as if Queen Emma and the mountain were calling me back, and I knew I had to go. Without literally traveling along Queen Emma's path myself, I had no kuleana to continue to talk about it metaphorically in terms of what it means for my research.

Coincidentally (or not), around the same time I had this revelation, my close friends from Hāmākua, Hawai'i, were planning a trip up Maunakea to offer ho'okupu at Waiau, which had shrunk to alarmingly low levels at the end of

2013. In a spur-of-the-moment decision, I caught a plane to Hilo Friday night and was in the back of an old four-wheel-drive pickup truck (Pi'ikuahiwi) early the next morning, making my way to the beginning of the old Mānā Road in the outskirts of Waimea. After a bumpy three-hour drive from Wahinekea to Pu'u Lilinoe without incident (there was no rainstorm to force us to take cover under a shelter of māmane branches, no thick fog to blind and confuse us, and no blown tires or transmissions that required makeshift repairs), we parked the truck along the side of the road and began our final ascent on foot to Waiau. This path was not easy or smooth; one may even refer to it as precarious. The air was thin and cold, making it hard for me to catch my breath and forcing me to keep my head down and take slow, deliberate steps along the rocky trail. When I reached the top of the hill, I looked up and saw with my own eyes the place I had read about, chanted about, danced about, and dreamed about for so long . . . *kēlā wai kamaha'o i ka piko o ke kuahiwi.*

We had entered the realm of Wākea. This was the site where Emma, more than a hundred years ago, immersed herself in the regenerative waters of Waiau, which strengthened her relationship with her ancestors and validated her seniority of rank to rule the nation. This is the site that inspired the writing of eight mele commemorating Emma's journey to ka piko o Wākea. And this is the site where I knelt at the water's edge and offered the first and last of those eight mele in honor of Queen Emma, as well as Wākea, Lilinoe, Poli'ahu, and all the other akua and kūpuna who have been there and still reside there. My chanting and dancing of mele written for that exact place about people who practiced their own rituals at that exact place "served the function of commemoration allowing present-day participants [like me and my friends] to recall an event, or ritually re-enact a narrative of the past" (Kikiloi 2012, p. 68). Waiau and Maunakea are

> not just random places of coincidence but rather ones where mana was known to be formed, built up, and concentrated. Through commemoration, that is the layering of important historical events on top of each other, the mana of these places, their historical events, and associated actors [are] doubled and glorified. It is through this cultural repetition between the past and present, ancestors and descendants, place upon place, that mana [is] continually established. (Kikiloi 2012, p. 25)

The mana of Waiau and the kūpuna who cleared the paths we now travel were all present that day in various forms, some visible and tangible right before our eyes and others only perceptible by our na'au. I can only hope our presence that day served to add to the collective mana of the place and the ongoing narrative of our people who continually travel the ala nihinihi to reclaim our rightful place in the history and genealogy of Maunakea; to reconnect with our akua, 'aumākua, and kūpuna who make Mauna a Wākea their home; and to reaffirm our kuleana to restore ea to the sacred mountain as well as our own kulāiwi across Hawai'i. The response from our kūpuna that day, which manifested in changes in the environment (hō'ailona) that I witnessed as I chanted and danced "A Maunakea 'o Kalani," was validation enough for me to know that I am doing what is pono and should feel confident to continue on with my research. Upon returning home to O'ahu, the impacts of this experience continued to resonate when I realized my direct family ties to the ahupua'a that surround and include Maunakea, further adding to my layered understanding of what drove me to return to ka piko o Wākea in the first place. It was not just Queen Emma and the divine ancestors of Maunakea that were calling me back, but also my own kūpuna. In order for me to fully employ my epistemologically grounded methodology, I needed to reestablish and strengthen my relationship to all my kūpuna by traveling to Mauna a Wākea and engaging in ceremonial practices involving pule and mele so that I could begin a dialogue with them about my research. By bridging the sacred space between my kūpuna and myself that day, my consciousness was raised and my confidence to continue was affirmed.

Because of my recurring trips to Kaho'olawe and my first journey to Waiau and Maunakea, I am beginning to envision my larger doctoral research as an attempt to literally and metaphorically restore and return to the once well-worn paths of our kūpuna. Many may now be overgrown and obscured due to neglect, but they are still here waiting to be traveled down once again. I am realizing that Hawaiian place-based education should provide opportunities for students and teachers to reclaim the ala nihinihi of our kūpuna that lead us back to our piko, so that we can 'ike maka and then return to our mole to apply the 'ike we have gained at the piko in our work to restore our presence on the land, our land-based practices, our right to self-determination, and our identity as Kānaka. As I continue to expand my research, I plan to look more closely at its purpose(s) in terms of Linda Tuhiwai Smith's (1999) twenty-five indigenous projects. As she writes, "The acts of reclaiming, reformulating, and reconstituting indigenous cultures and languages have required the mounting of an ambitious research programme, one that is very strategic in its purpose and activities and relentless in its pursuit of social justice. Within are a number of very distinct projects" (p. 142). The projects that resonate the most with me are those whose purposes are to reclaim, remember, reframe, restore, and, ultimately, return.

Wahi a kahiko, "E kolo ana nō ke ēwe i ke ēwe: The rootlet will creep toward the rootlets"—meaning "of the same origin, kinfolk will seek and love each other" (Pukui 1983, p. 39). As Hawaiians, we follow in the footsteps of our ancestors. We consciously and unconsciously return to the paths they have cleared for us, reenact their stories and rituals at significant sites along those paths, and pass on their lessons and values to future generations, who will eventually need these teachings in order to find those same paths once again and successfully navigate them on their way to recognizing and fulfilling their own kuleana.

NOTES

1. Poetry, histories, genealogies, wise sayings, place names.

2. I have chosen to spell Maunakea as one word in this chapter because that is how the name appears in "A Maunakea ʻo Kalani," the mele that first introduced me to the mauna and later became the inspiration for my research methodology.

3. Excerpt from Emma's January 20, 1881, diary entry (Bishop Museum Archives). Also cited by George S. Kanahele (1999) in his book *Emma, Hawaiʻi's Remarkable Queen* (p. 326).

4. William Seymour Lindsey, Emma's guide on her trip to Maunakea, told his story to his family who have kept it alive. Mary Kalani Kaʻapuni Phillips, one of his descendants, retold the moʻolelo to Larry Lindsey Kimura (also a descendant) in 1967; Bishop Museum Archives Audio Collection, 192.2.2, Side A.

5. The years 1881 and 1883 have both been given as possible dates for Emma's trip to Maunakea. De Silva rules out the 1883 date based on the birth of William Kahalelaumāmane Lindsey in 1882. He was the child of Emma's guide to Maunakea, William Seymour Lindsey, whose inoa Hawaiʻi was a gift from the queen that commemorated their time in Kahalelāʻau on their way up the mountain; there she was protected from the rain in a shelter Lindsey and her attendants made from māmane branches.

6. There are three known versions of "A Maunakea ʻo Kalani." The first is from the Mary Kawena Pukui Collection as taught to my kumu, Māpuana de Silva, by Patience Namaka Bacon on June 12, 1985. The other two are very similar and can be found in the HI.M.71:29 and HEN 3:248 collections in the Bishop Museum Archives, as well as in Marvin P. Nogelmeier's *He Lei no ʻEmalani* (2001), a compilation of chants for Queen Emma Kaleleonālani.

7. "A hiki a i ke Mole" is the handwritten line from the HI.M.71 version of the mele. It was edited to "A hiki a i ka mole" in Nogelmeier's *He Lei no ʻEmalani* (2001, p. 115).

8. I am still considering whether to continue using the term "place-based" in my final dissertation as a means of reframing and reclaiming it or whether to develop my own term based on my evaluation research. This is an emerging area of my research.

9. I am referencing the phrase "Nānā i waele ke ala, ma hope aku mākou, he opened up the path, we followed [respect the older sibling]," found in the *Hawaiian Dictionary* (Pukui and Elbert 1986, p. 375).

10. "According to the ancients" (translation by Pukui and Elbert 1986, p. 376).

11. A stiff coarse fiber from the outer husk of a coconut.

12. Here is the first verse of the mele that serves as the basis for Lopes's research methodology:

Ua noho au a kupa i kō alo	I sat until I've become accustomed to your presence
A kamaʻāina i kō leo	Until familiar to your dear voice
Ka hiʻona ka manaʻo lā i laila	The appearance of (your) thoughts are realized
I ʻaneʻi ka waihona a ke aloha	This is where the repository of love resides

13. My use of the word "traditional" here is intentional. I am aware of the problematic binaries that exist when using words such as "traditional" versus "modern." However, I do not use this word to mean the opposite of "modern," that which exists only in the past. Instead, I use it to suggest a tradition; that is, a lineage of hula people from whom I descend; a heritage by which the hula, oli, and mele have been passed down to me through my kumu; and a foundation on which I can stand today and compose new hula, oli, and mele that reflect the tradition from which I come. Being a practitioner of traditional hula does not leave me and my practices stuck in the past, but in fact allows me to truly be a lālā of my kumu—branching out into new contexts and spaces yet remaining always connected to my source that grounds and informs all of my decisions and actions.

14. This mele is from ʻAha Pūnana Leo's thirty-four-page, paperback book titled *Pai Ka Leo: A Collection of Original Hawaiian Songs for Children* (1989, pp. 6–7). No specific composers are named, but members of the Kōmike Hana Haʻawina are listed, such as Hōkūlani Cleeland, Kauanoe Kamanā, Larry L. Kimura, Kalena Silva, Noʻeau Warner, and William H. Wilson. There is also an accompanying cassette tape that includes all of the songs from the book. "Kuʻu Kumu" is sung by Haunani Apoliona on the cassette.

15. The Hawaiian archipelago.

16. "Graduation exercises, as for hula, lua fighting, and other ancient arts (probably related to niki, to tie, as the knowledge was bound to the student)" (Pukui and Elbert 1986, p. 372).

17. Where Uncle Kīhei and many other Kanaka researchers deviate from this approach are their positionalities as insiders to the body of knowledge and contexts they are researching about and are within. The literature on portraiture suggests that the portraitist or researcher is "the stranger, the newcomer, the interloper" (Lawrence-Lightfoot and Davis 1997, p. 50); therefore, he or she most commonly starts by "writing outside ins" (p. 62). This is not the case for many Kanaka researchers like Uncle Kīhei.

18. Also translated as a "place reserved for hula dancing" (Pukui and Elbert 1986, p. 301).

19. "Our songs are filled with lush [descriptions] of that thing aloha" (Pukui and Elbert 1986, p. 273); filled with prominent descriptions of the brave acts of our strong ancestors of the past; their famous deeds; their lives and their deaths. (The remainder is my translation.)

20. Composing mele is another expert and enlightened practice of the people of old, and they were famous for this skill . . . there are many types of mele and there is great value that can be found within mele written by our kūpuna. [Mele] were written about those of the heavens, the sky, the ocean, the land, the sun, the moon, the stars, and everything else. Mele were written with all the hidden treasures of the Hawaiian people

contained within, like our cultural practices and their deeper meanings. (This is my translation.)

21. Gloria Anzaldua was a scholar of Chicana cultural theory, feminist theory, and queer theory. This quote comes from her article titled "Haciendo caras, una entrada" in her edited volume, *Making face, making soul: Creative and critical perspectives by feminists of color* (San Francisco: Aunt Lute Books, 1990).

22. Pukui (1983, p. 109).

BIBLIOGRAPHY

'Aha Pūnana Leo (1989). *Pai ka leo: A collection of original Hawaiian songs for children*. Honolulu: Bess Press.

Atleo, E. R. (2004). *Tsawalk: A Nuu-chah-nulth worldview*. Vancouver: University of British Columbia Press.

Bare, J. (2008). Evaluation and the sacred bundle. *The Evaluation Exchange, 11*(2), 6–7.

Basham, L. (2007). I mau ke ea o ka 'āina i ka pono: He puke mele lāhui no ka lāhui Hawai'i. Unpublished PhD dissertation, University of Hawai'i, Mānoa.

———. (2008). Mele lāhui: The importance of pono in Hawaiian poetry. *Te Kaharoa, 1*, 152–164.

Beckwith, M. W., and K. Luomala (1972). *The Kumulipo: A Hawaiian creation chant*. Honolulu: University of Hawai'i Press.

Berry, K. S. (2006). Bricolage: Embracing relationality, multiplicity and complexity. In K. Tobin and J. Kincheloe (Eds.), *Doing educational research—A handbook* (pp. 87–115). The Netherlands: Sense Publishers.

Cajete, G. (2000). *Native science: Natural laws of interdependence*. Santa Fe, NM: Clear Light Publishers.

de Silva, K. (2006). *Merrie Monarch Hula Festival fact sheet*. Unpublished manuscript.

Edwards, S. (2013). Nā te mōhio ka mātau: Re-membering mātauranga Māori in localized practice. In S. Edwards and R. Hunia (Eds.), *Dialogues of mātauranga Māori: Re-membering* (pp. 42–62). Te Awamutu, NZ: Te Wānagang o Aotearoa.

Emekauwa, E., and D. T. Williams (Eds.). (January 2004). The star with my name: The Alaska rural systemic initiative and the impact of place-based education on native student achievement. *Rural Trust White Paper on Place-Based Education*. Retrieved from http://www.ruraledu.org/articles.php?id=2082.

Fornander, A., and T. G. Thrum (Eds.). (1999). *Fornander collection of Hawaiian antiquities and folk-lore: The Hawaiian account of the formation of their islands and origin of their race, with the traditions of their migrations, etc., as gathered from original sources*, Vols. 4 and 6. Honolulu: 'Ai Pōhaku Press.

Freire, P. (2011). *Pedagogy of the oppressed*. New York: Continuum International Publishing.

Goodyear-Ka'ōpua, N. (2013). *The seeds we planted*. Minneapolis: University of Minnesota Press.

Halagao, P. E. (2010). Liberating Filipino Americans through decolonizing curriculum. *Race Ethnicity and Education, 13*(4), 495–512.

Halagao, P., A. Tintiangco-Cubales, and J. Cordova (2009). Critical literature review of K–12 Filipino American curriculum. *AAPI Nexus: Asian Americans and Pacific Islanders policy, practice and community, 7*(10), 1–23.

———. (n.d.). A critical method to curriculum evaluation. Unpublished manuscript.

Johnson, R. K. (1981). *Kumulipo: Hawaiian hymn of creation,* Vol. I. Honolulu: Topgallant Publishing.

Kahaunaele, K. (2014). The welo and kuleana of mele integrity. In A. Yamashiro and N. Goodyear-Ka'ōpua (Eds.), *The value of Hawai'i 2: Ancestral roots, oceanic visions* (pp. 52–59). Honolulu: University of Hawai'i Press.

Kamakau, S. M. (21 Kēkēmapa 1867). Ka moolelo o nā Kamehameha. *Ka Nupepa Kuokoa,* p. 1.

———. (2–9 Ianuali 1869). Ka moolelo Hawaii. *Ka Nupepa Kuokoa.*

———. (7 Ianuali 1869–2 Pepeluali 1871). Ka moolelo Hawaii. *Ke Au Okoa.*

———. (1964). *Ka po'e kahiko, The people of old.* (M. K. Pukui, Trans.). Honolulu: Bishop Museum Press.

———. (1991). *Tales and traditions of the people of old: Nā mo'olelo o ka po'e kahiko.* Honolulu: Bishop Museum Press.

Kame'eleihiwa, L. (1992). *Native land and foreign desires.* Honolulu: Bishop Museum Press.

Kanahele, G. S. (1999). *Emma, Hawai'i's remarkable queen.* Honolulu: Queen Emma Foundation.

Kanahele, P. (2005). I am the land, and the land is me. *Hūlili: Multidisciplinary Research on Hawaiian Well-Being, 32*(2), 14–25.

Kaomea, J. (2003). Reading erasures and making the familiar strange: Defamiliarizing methods of research in formerly colonized and historically oppressed communities. *Educational Researcher, 32*(2), 14–25.

———. (2006). Nā wāhine mana: A postcolonial reading of classroom discourse on the imperial rescue of oppressed Hawaiian women. *Pedagogy, Culture & Society, 14*(3), 329–348.

Kauanui, J. K., and P. Wolfe (2012). Settler colonialism then and now: A conversation between J. Kēhaulani Kauanui and Patrick Wolfe. *Politica & Societa, 2,* 235–258.

Kawakami, A. J., K. Aton, F. Cram, M. K. Lai, and L. Porima (2007). Improving the practice of evaluation through indigenous values and methods: Decolonizing evaluation practice—Returning the gaze from Hawai'i and Aotearoa. *Hūlili: Multidisciplinary Research on Hawaiian Well-Being, 4*(1), 319–348.

Kikiloi, K. (2012). Kūkulu manamana: Ritual power and religious expansions in Hawai'i: The ethno-historical and archaeological study of Mokumanamana and Nihoa islands. Unpublished PhD dissertation, University of Hawai'i, Mānoa.

Kosasa, K. K. (2008). Sites of erasure: The representation of settler culture in Hawai'i. In C. Fujikane and J. Y. Okamura (Eds.), *Asian settler colonialism* (pp. 195–208). Honolulu: University of Hawai'i Press.

Kovack, M. (2005). Emerging from the margins, Indigenous methodologies. In L. Brown and S. Strega (Eds.), *Research as resistance: Critical indigenous, and anti-oppressive approaches* (pp. 19–36). Toronto: Canadian Scholars Press.

LaFrance, J. (Summer 2004). Culturally competent evaluation in Indian country. *New Directions for Evaluation, 102,* 39–50.

Lawrence-Lightfoot, S., and J. H. Davis (1997). *The art and science of portraiture.* San Francisco: Jossey-Bass.

Liliuokalani (1997). *The Kumulipo: An Hawaiian creation myth.* Kentfield, CA: Pueo Press.

Lopes, R. K. (2010). Ka waihona a ke aloha: Ka papahana ho'oheno mele: An interactive resource center for the promotion, preservation and perpetuation of mele and mele practitioners. Unpublished PhD dissertation, University of Hawai'i, Mānoa.

Louis, R. P. (2007). Can you hear us now? Voices from the margin: Using Indigenous methodologies in geographic research. *Geographical Research, 45*(2), 130–139.

Malo, D. (1987). *Hawaiian antiquities: Mo'olelo Hawai'i.* Honolulu: Folk Press.

Meyer, M. A. (2001). Our own liberation: Reflections on Hawaiian epistemology. *Contemporary Pacific, 13*(1), 124–148.

Nogelmeier, M. (2001). *He lei no 'Emalani.* Honolulu: Queen Emma Foundation and Bishop Museum Press.

O'Malley, A., and S. Tiakiwai (Eds.) (2010). *He rautaki āhuatanga whakaako, Innovative teaching and learning practices in Te Wānanga o Aotearoa settings.* Te Awamutu, NZ: Te Wānanga o Aotearoa.

Poepoe, J. M. (1906, Pepeluali 1). Ka moolelo Hawaii kahiko. *Ka Na'i Aupuni,* p. 1.

Pukui, M. K. (1983). *'Ōlelo no'eau: Hawaiian proverbs and poetical sayings.* Honolulu: Bishop Museum.

Pukui, M. K., and S. H. Elbert (1986). *Hawaiian dictionary.* Honolulu: University of Hawai'i Press.

Simpson, L. (2011). *Dancing on our turtle's back, stories of Nishnaabeg re-creation, resurgence and a new emergence.* Winnipeg, Manitoba: Arbeiter Ring Publishing.

Smith, L. T. (1999). *Decolonizing methodologies, research and Indigenous peoples.* Dunedin, NZ: University of Otago Press.

———. (2005). Building a research agenda for Indigenous epistemologies and education. *Anthropology & Education Quarterly, 36*(1), 93–95.

Solorzano, D. G., and T. J. Yosso (2002). Critical race methodology: Counter-storytelling as an analytical framework for education research. *Qualitative Inquiry, 8*(1), 23–44.

Stake, R. (2004). *Standards-based & responsive evaluation.* London: Sage.

White, G. M., and T. K. Tengan (2001). Disappearing worlds: Anthropology and cultural studies in Hawai'i and the Pacific. *Contemporary Pacific, 13*(2), 381–416.

Wolfe, P. (2006). Settler colonialism and the elimination of the native. *Journal of Genocide Research, 8*(4), 387–409.

Nā ʻIliʻili

Brandy Nālani McDougall

The young kahu was unloading one of his last boxes in the back office, when he saw a small fist rapping at one of the windows and heard a frantic young voice calling for him: "Kaaaahuuuuu! Kaaaahuuuu! Come help! We need help!"

The kahu rushed over to the window and opened it. "'Auē! He aha ka pilikia?"

"I saw Aunty Kamani dem bring one girl inside da house, but she looked really bad. I neva seen her before," exclaimed seven-year-old Kāʻeo Barrett, out of breath from running. "Aunty was screaming at me fo call 9-1-1 and I did, but den I came to get you, too, cuz I think the girl might—might—."

Kāʻeo's young eyes widened. "She might *die*, Kahu."

"Okay, Kāʻeo. It's going to be okay," said the young kahu, quickly turning to get his Bible from his wooden desk. "Don't be afraid. The doctors are coming to help and I'll run over there right now. Mahalo for coming to get me."

And with that, the young kahu ran toward the Kahulas' house, two houses away from his church on Kealalani Road. Even though he had only met Ed and Kamani last week, he believed he could provide some solace to them if the mysterious girl would die.

In his short time as a kahu, he had already led the funeral services for two men from Wailuku before he was transferred to the new little church in this village of Anamoʻo. One of the men had been in a car accident and required a closed casket. He did not know the ʻohana very well, but could sense that the funeral had allowed them some peace. But he had known the wife and daughter of the other man, Uncle Bully, as he was affectionately known. Uncle Bully, who was well into his eighties and a beloved kupuna in Wailuku, caught pneumonia after a heavy rain and then asked for the young kahu to see him. When he arrived, Uncle Bully sat up in his bed and asked him to schedule his funeral for the week after next and to pray for his wife and daughter that they would continue to live happy lives without him. Just two days later he was gone.

Shortly after Uncle Bully's funeral, some of the villagers in Anamoʻo asked that the young kahu be the pastor at its new church. Though he knew no one in Anamoʻo, and no one in Wailuku seemed to have even heard of the small village, he felt blessed to have been called back to a part of Maui where his great-grandmother was said to have lived.

He took off his shoes and opened the modest door to the Kahula house, and was immediately struck by a deafening sound. His ears started ringing, and he covered them as he walked inside. The whole house echoed with the percussive rhythm of high, guttural clicking from the largest infestation of moʻo he had ever seen or even heard of. The moʻo—some brown, some black, some green, and some a pale white—were of all sizes and were darting over the floor, running up and down the walls and across the table, filling every surface with their shiny fluid movement.

"Ed! Kamani! It's Kahu! Where are you?!" he called, unsure if he could even be heard above the pulsing noise.

"Kahu! We're in the bathroom!" yelled Ed, his voice in a panic.

Carefully, the kahu stepped over the moʻo toward whatever surface of the floor was partly visible beneath them in their dance; he walked toward the bathroom at the end of the hallway. The slender animals covered every surface, turning the dark hallway into a tunnel of pulsing darkness and primal sound. The smell of them was putrid, like something cooking and rotting at the same time. He gagged and coughed, staring straight ahead. He could hear Kamani screaming.

Down the hall and through the doorway to the bathroom, he saw the girl immersed in a tub filled with ice and water. She looked like she was four or five years old. Ed was holding her head above the water, and Kamani was covering her forehead and chest with ti leaves. Her body was convulsing. He noticed that her hair, hanging over the back of the tub, was wavy and reddish black, except for a long streak of white in the middle, starting at her crown and flowing like a wispy wailele.

The kahu was a few paces away; he would have to step on the moʻo to get to the girl who, he was almost certain, would give away her last hā within minutes. She would need his blessings to blanket her as she left this life.

"Komo. E komo aku hoʻi au ma loko. Please let me pass," he found himself saying out loud, "I am here to help. He kōkua o ke keiki au."

But the little writhing lizard bodies only piled themselves up higher in front of him, some even running over his feet and crawling up his legs. He could feel the slight weight and suction of their bodies as they moved over him. They were refusing to let him through.

He felt his blood begin pumping harder, going faster through his heart, which was now beating in time with the pulsing song of the moʻo. He let go of his Bible and clutched his chest in pain, feeling as though it would burst from within, wondering if this was what it felt like to have a heart attack. He dropped to his knees and then to the floor, and the thousands of little moving bodies began engulfing him. They writhed over him in unison, moving as though they were one claw clenching closed around him.

Breathing heavily against the pressure, he closed his eyes and began praying for his life, for all the good that he still hoped to do in Anamo'o. The claw of the mo'o bodies clenched harder as if to answer. Just then an old mele came to his mind. He managed to raspily cough out the beginning:

"Kololio ka makani o Waikapū ia
Malu ana i ke 'ao'ao Wailuku la"

The claw seemed to loosen enough for him to gasp in more air, and he continued the mele: "Na pili o kakae nā pua i mohala i ka pēlā, Kepaniwai a'o 'Iao . . ."

His mother's voice seemed to take over. It was she who had sung the mele for him as a child whenever he felt afraid.

The claw loosened even further, feeling almost like a cradle now, though he was still unable to feel his body. His eyes opened to the ceiling where he saw a large, dark mo'o form liltingly step past the light fixture above him. He could see its shiny black body heave with breath—its spine, rib cage, and legs rippling the way wind makes water move. Seeming to sense his gaze, the mo'o nui stopped and, though four feet ahead of him now, turned its right eye all the way back toward him.

The kahu lay there silent and unmoving, holding the mo'o nui's gaze for a second, before closing his eyes again.

In the darkness, he remembered how his mother would take him to gather 'ili'ili at the Wailuku riverbed as a child. She was so careful to inspect each one for its weight and smoothness before placing the 'ili'ili in her palms to feel how her hands bent around them, how she would feel holding them. If the pebbles felt good, she would then hold them between her fingers. She had to find four pebbles altogether, and not only did they individually have to feel right to her but they also had to feel right together. They had to make a certain deep and old sound when they clicked, and they had to move smoothly over each other.

His mother told him that the pebbles needed to want to be together, just as they needed to want to be with her. The whole process could take a few minutes, a few hours, or a few days, all depending on the 'ili'ili and his mother's sense of them.

When she found the ones she would use, she would always ask the ili'ili if they would allow her to take them home with her and use them in her hula. He used to love that part the best, because his mother told him to look for hō'ailona around them when she asked for permission.

Once he saw a low-lying rainbow appear out where the river used to meet the ocean before the drain grates came. Another time the wind blew a yellow hau blossom so it landed by his mother's feet. But most times a light rain would come, prickling their skin, and the distant click-clack sound of other ʻiliʻili, slick and wet with rain, moving down the riverbed, smoothing themselves against each other.

He loved to watch her hula ʻiliʻili, how she could look as strong and fluid as water, how the pebbles clicked delicately in her hands.

Seeing his mother do this, at school he would ask the rocks for permission before he used them for hopscotch. Every day, the kids would tease and taunt him. If he cried, the teacher would laugh at him too and tell him to not be so sensitive. After a while, he stopped talking to rocks. Instead, he began kicking the rocks in the playground like he saw the other kids do. He felt guilty at first, thinking that something bad might happen to him. But nothing happened, and soon he felt nothing. No shame, no guilt. Just rocks.

The next time his mother took him to the Wailuku river, he saw some boys from his class making their way down the riverbed. It had rained hard the night before, and there were still small pools of water here and there. The boys were grabbing ʻiliʻili and throwing them into the pools.

His mother yelled over to them to stop. The boys laughed defiantly at her, but started to walk farther up the riverbed away from them. He wished his mother would hurry so they could leave. His mother turned back to what she was doing, picked up an ʻiliʻili, and whispered to it. He saw the boys look back and laugh some more.

He was embarrassed by her, angry even. He stood up and started back up the hill without her, without looking for any hōʻailona. They went home in silence.

The next day, all the kids teased him. They said his mom was crazy because she talked to rocks. They laughed at him. Called him crazy too.

When he came home from school that day, he yelled at her as if she was the cause of all of his hurt: "Why do you have to be so *different*? Everyone laughs at us because of you!"

She didn't say anything as he yelled at her that day; she didn't even cry. She only looked at him, with a quiet stare, the pupils of her eyes like dark whirlpools of pity. And when he was finished and stopped crying, there was forgiveness in her eyes too, but they never again went to the river together to gather ʻiliʻili. And she was gone soon after that.

Amid the chorus of clicking moʻo tuk-tuk-tuks, their voices like thousands of ʻiliʻili moving around him, he had never felt more ashamed for yelling at his mother. He regretted that they never went to the river again. He should have honored his makuahine, the ʻāina, and his kūpuna as much as they were owed. A heavy stone settled in his throat.

He wasn't sure how long he was lying there, but when the kahu finally opened his eyes again and looked back up toward the ceiling, all he could see was the end of a massive black tail rounding the corner into the bathroom and then disappearing.

He realized that he could not hear Ed and Kamani anymore, only the incessant staccato of the mo'o's clicking song. But was it slower than it had been before?

He was finally able to stand up and brush the remaining mo'o off him. He could see Ed and Kamani in the bathroom at the end of the hallway again, still holding the little girl in the water. He walked toward them, still somewhat dazed. He could see that she had stopped convulsing, and her chest was rising and falling with her breath like a gentle tide.

The tuk-tuk-tuks of the little mo'o *were* slowing down; all of them were moving gingerly out of his way. Other little white, black, green, and brown bodies were falling from the walls, from the ceiling, letting go.

The kahu stood at the bathroom door's threshold, unsure if he should come in and not wanting to look up at the ceiling. "How is she?" he asked.

"'A'ole maopopo. I-I-I don't know what happened or what—well, what *they* did, but she seems okay now," answered Kamani. She held the back of her hand up to the child's forehead and cheek and began peeling the ti leaves from her face and chest. "Kahu, have you ever seen her before?"

The tuk-tuk-tuk slowed to a barely discernible rhythm, dying away.

"'A'ole," said the kahu, "but I'm sure her 'ohana is worried, wherever they are."

The mo'o song stopped its beating. There was now only silence and the exhausted breathing they all shared.

Ed lifted the child out of the water, and Kamani pulled off her wet clothes and wrapped a couple of towels around her.

"Eh, how did you two find her?" asked the kahu, trying to make sense of the situation.

"By da side of the road, when we were turning by da old sugar mill," answered Kamani. Her voice was barely audible. "She was just lying dere, shaking like she was being electrocuted or someting."

Ed picked her up and carried her to the pune'e in the living room. Mo'o corpses were piled all over the floor, on the table, on chairs. The kahu noticed that he stepped lightly, worried about grinding them under his bare feet. Still more carcasses covered the pune'e, where lay an old Hawaiian quilt, probably from Kamani's grandmother. The dying and dead mo'o seemed to have intentionally arranged themselves over the light blue handiwork. The kahu and Kamani lifted the quilt, and Ed placed the girl on the cool, clean sheet underneath. She slept.

"I never saw anyting like dat before," whispered Ed, shaking his head. The color was flushed out of his wet face. "She was so hot dat it hurt to hold her and all da shaking—I never even notice all dem coming into da house until dey were already inside."

"And when *she* went inside," asked the kahu, cautiously, "what happened, exactly?" He didn't know why he was so sure that the mo'o nui was a "she."

"You mean, da girl?" asked Ed, "Well, da shaking started to calm down a little bit, but—."

"No, I mean the really big"—the kahu hesitated for a moment—"one."

Kamani was sitting on the couch quietly crying. She looked up to meet the kahu's gaze. "What do you mean?"

Ed looked at him blankly, too.

The kahu didn't know how they could have missed the mo'o nui. She was so, so large, maybe four or five feet long, and her eyes, well, her eyes were like whirlpools of enveloping water, calm and knowing. The eyes were familiar.

As they waited for the ambulance, the air was still, but thick and heavy. Kamani went and brought back an old sheet from the garage. Kamani's right, the kahu thought: a plastic garbage bag grave wouldn't seem right given the circumstances. He bent down with her to pick up the soft corpses, which were still hot, from the floor and furniture. Her husband followed their lead. They placed each body gently into the sheet.

The kahu knew they were looking to him for guidance, some explanation. But those years of theological studies and the two funerals he had led on his own had not prepared him. He turned to Kamani and Ed and told them, "The mo'o should be planted, returned to the 'āina."

Outside, Ed dug a hole in the yard for the mass grave of mo'o bodies, and the kahu and Kamani held the bundled sheet reverently before laying it down to be buried.

A light rain began drumming softly against the galvanized steel roof of their garage. Tuk-tuk-tuk-click-click was the sound it made, keeping time as the kahu sang the old mele his mother used to sing to him as a child:

Komo ana i ka 'olu, o ke Kili'o'opu
Ka makani kaulana ia o ka 'āina
Me ka wai hu'ihu'i, wai a'o Eleile

Offering his leo, his hā, his aloha, his ha'aha'a, whatever was still left in him, he knelt so the mo'o could hear all the prayers of his heart, the 'ili'ili still in his throat.

Arriving at an ʻĀina Aloha Research Framework: What Is Our Kuleana as the Next Generation of ʻŌiwi Scholars?

Summer Puanani Maunakea

I would like to acknowledge and thank Drs. Davianna Pōmaikaʻi McGregor and Jonathan Kay Kamakawiwoʻole Osorio. I had the pleasure of interviewing these scholars as they helped me describe and construct what I understand to be research methodology rooted in ʻike kupuna—ancestral knowledge. Anyone who has learned from or been inspired by these kumu knows how important it is to put into action the knowledge that has been imparted to us. To the reader, please understand that I do not intend any disrespect by paraphrasing or selecting excerpts from the interviews conducted with these scholars. Rather, my manaʻo has been shaped and guided by the entirety of their narratives and comes from a place of deep respect. Also, please consider the English explanations that follow Hawaiian phrases as my clearest attempt to communicate enduring concepts that have been spoken and taught to me.[1] I share what follows in recognition of our kūpuna and their brilliance as they are reflected in the work of these scholars with the hope that they will resonate with all who conduct research within Hawaiian communities. Kumu Davianna and Kumu Jon, mahalo for all you have done to establish a place for us up-and-coming ʻŌiwi scholars. We are grateful to you for transforming academia and inspiring us all. Mahalo for helping me find my voice again.

A Journey Through Research and Academia

The leaders of contemporary Hawaiian scholarship whom we know from books and protests are the same Kānaka Maoli we call Kumu, Aunty, and Uncle. Influential scholars such as Drs. Osorio, McGregor, Lilikalā Kameʻeleihiwa, and Noʻeau Warner are among those whom I have learned from and look up to. Their work, among that of many other influential ʻŌiwi scholars, has changed the way we view research and has broadened what constitutes academic scholarship. Because of the resistance and persistence of these scholars, I and other ʻŌiwi have a place in academic scholarship at this university, the University of Hawaiʻi at Mānoa (UHM), that honors our ancestors. Because of their tenacity I will never waver on who I am as Kanaka Maoli. I am not alone; emerging ʻŌiwi scholars across a range of academic disciplines and institutions of higher education are thriving, driven by our kuleana to our 'ohana, our people, and our 'āina.

He ali'i ka 'āina, he kauwā ke kanaka
The land is chief, man is its servant

Ua lehulehu a manomano ka 'ikena a ka Hawai'i
Great and numerous is the knowledge of the Hawaiians

When I arrived at UHM, this 'ōlelo no'eau is what I believed to be true. Many of us 'Ōiwi come to the university rooted in our ancestral perspectives. The validity of 'ike kupuna in academia is no longer up for debate, as evident in the scholarship established in previous generations. What I am trying to learn now is how the western-academic-scientific methodologies and technologies taught across university disciplines can help us do what we know to be true and not question the value of 'ike kupuna that we are grounded in today.

This is where my struggle begins . . . and I have many questions. As the next generation of scholars, how do we fulfill the expectations of the leaders who have come before us? How do we take the learned methods and technologies that work for us and use them effectively as tools to solve our current problems? To move us toward answers to these questions, I share in this chapter how I arrived at a framework grounded in 'ike kupuna that guides the way I engage in research.

'Ike Kupuna as Academic Scholarship

Ma ka hana ka 'ike
Knowledge is gained through doing

Nē huli ka lima i luna, pōloli ka 'ōpū; Nē huli ka lima i lalo piha ka 'ōpū
When hands are turned up, the stomach is empty; When hands are turned down, the stomach is full

'O ke kahua ma mua, ma hope ke kūkulu
First the foundation, then the building

It is the 'āina that teaches us, and the oral traditions that document our relationship with the 'āina. The lessons our kūpuna learned and the interdependence they shared are alive in our 'āina today.[2] I am certain that the intricacies within 'ōlelo, mo'okū'auhau, mo'olelo, mele, lo'i, loko i'a, and heiau ground us in who we are as servants to this land and will manifest as the answers we need to thrive if indeed we look to these sources. In the context of research, this knowledge, experience, and aloha from 'āina will also provide the next generation of scholars with systematic frameworks to further liberate academic scholarship. My challenge has been to find the balance between growing in 'ike kupuna—standing firm on this foundation—and pulling in the tools necessary, wherever they may come from, to act in ways that move our people forward. I approached this challenge in the only way I felt pono to do so.

Methodology

Nānā i ke kumu
Look to the source

On March 6, 2014, I sought the guidance of Dr. Jonathan Osorio, professor at the Kamakakūokalani Center for Hawaiian Studies, and on April 16, 2014, I met with Dr. McGregor, professor of ethnic studies, with the intent of gaining insight into how they navigate research. I hoped to learn what continues to inspire their scholarship and the lessons they have learned in the process. Most of all, I hoped their mana'o could guide students like myself as we further construct our ideologies and approaches to inquiry. Excerpts from these interviews follow.

> Research is something young people should not be afraid of; it is not some kind of formal thing. You do not have to be taught to do it; you can learn by yourself. It helps if you have mentors and it helps if you have kumu who will give you some hints and show you a few things, but research is also personal. (Jonathan Osorio)

Indeed, the perspective on research methodology that I have been moving toward is personal, rooted in a place very special to me and familiar to many students at UHM: Ka Papa Lo'i 'O Kānewai, an ancient lo'i within the ahupua'a of Waikīkī, moku of Kona, mokupuni of O'ahu. The lo'i was restored in the 1980s by a group of Hui Aloha 'Āina Tuahine Hawaiian language club students—later known as Ho'okahe Wai Ho'oulu 'Āina—guided by kūpuna such as Harry Kunihi Mitchell of Ke'anae-Wailuanui, Maui. Ka Papa Lo'i 'O Kānewai is a sanctuary, a community-driven grassroots organization, and a department within the Hawai'inuiākea School of Hawaiian Knowledge at UHM that cares for endemic species of taro and offers college-level courses on traditional taro farming practices.

Ka Papa Lo'i 'O Kānewai has been my foundation for the last four years at UHM. The 'āina there continues to teach me mo'okū'auhau—that I descend from Hāloanakalaukapalili, that I am kaikaina to these islands and to the elements, and that I therefore have a kuleana to learn and serve. Ideas surface when I walk mauka to check the po'owai to ensure that the waters of Mānoa continue to flow through the land. The knowledge I gain comes from turning my hands down to work in the lo'i, learning from my kumu, and observing the keiki that come to mālama Kānewai each day. As I learn the levels of the 'auwai and how much water must flow in and out of the lo'i, I grow closer to understanding the complexities and beauty my kūpuna must have experienced. I am learning how this reciprocal relationship continues to construct new meaning in my life and helps me understand my role in academia.

Ho'okahe wai ho'oulu 'āina
Make the water flow, make the land flourish

Uncle Harry Kunihi Mitchell uttered the phrase "Ho'okahe wai ho'oulu 'āina" in the 1980s as the water began to flow once again throughout Kānewai. Until this day, three guiding principles are practiced at Ka Papa Lo'i 'O Kānewai and provide a means to organize the ideas presented in this chapter:

1. Mālama 'āina: to care for, protect, and maintain all that feeds—land, water, ocean, and all contained therein
2. Laulima: many hands working together toward a specific goal
3. Pu'uhonua: a safe place, a sanctuary for plants, animals, ecosystems, and all people in which to be, learn, work, and relax

As I worked one morning with fourth graders from a local school to clear the 'auwai, the voices of Drs. McGregor and Osorio flowed through my mind. I realized how mālama 'āina, laulima, and pu'uhonua not only guide our work at Kānewai but also coalesce and become a lens through which to understand the mana'o they shared with me. These three principles are intrinsically related to one another, and it is the value the community places on them that links the principles together. There is value in research done within Hawaiian communities that focuses on relationships and reaching collective understandings of the shared intent that affirms 'ike kupuna. That is the theory, the practice is aloha, and the approach is spiritual in every way—acting out of humility, talking story openly and honestly, and being led from the na'au. It is the integrity of the relationships I nurture that takes priority.

'Āina, 'ohana, kūpuna, teachers, community, academia, me—we are all related. Seeking to understand the interdependence of these relationships through the principled practice of aloha 'āina is 'āina aloha[3] and how the framework presented below was actualized. Therefore, the narrative presented here is a cyclical conversation comprised of Drs. Osorio and McGregor's interview

Mālama ʻĀina

Protection and advocacy for ʻāina

Relevant and initiated by the community

Kuleana of the researcher is recognized by the community

Community

Laulima

The role of the collective

Action-oriented and participatory methods

The weaving together of diverse sources of knowledge

Puʻuhonua

Protecting the intellectual rights of all knowledge sources

Remaining accountable to community

Presenting findings that are beneficial to the community

ʻĀina aloha research framework based on the principles established by Hoʻokahe Wai Hoʻoulu ʻĀina at Ka Papa Loʻi ʻO Kānewai, Waikīkī, Kona, Oʻahu.

excerpts and my perspectives on inquiry that aims to highlight how ʻŌiwi pursue research and carry kuleana.

The Relationship of Mālama ʻĀina and Research

I understand mālama ʻāina as the act of caring for and protecting all that feeds. In a research context I believe that inquiry done within Hawaiian communities and with a Hawaiian focus must produce outcomes that mālama ʻāina—that seek to protect and advocate for ʻŌiwi, our practices, and our resources.

> I am more interested in looking at where Hawaiʻi is going in the world and how we are being caught up in this global economy. What sort of sense we should have of this especially if we do become sovereign again, especially if our independence is earned again. Those are the kind of things that I am far more concerned about. I think while other people are doing research on what our nineteenth-century ancestors went through, I am interested in what the twenty-first-century Hawaiians are going through. That is what I write about,

that is what I look into, that is what I consider the most important things I can teach—how to pay attention to this, how to recognize what is going on, and how to advocate for older and traditional communities and values. (Jonathan Osorio)

The task of research has become somewhat easier because resources have been taken out of the deep archives and the basements of library microfilm and they are now more accessible to the community. Use it to inform and begin your process of research, but you still need to go into the community and speak with the community and work side by side with them. Feel the pain, understand both the best and the worst part of living in a place. How can our moʻolelo and the knowledge of our ancestors and the places where we live help us become more functional as families, better caretakers of the places where we live, more caring of our community, and compassionate leaders in our communities. It is not just getting the ʻike; it is also getting the ʻiʻo. And through this process becoming a compassionate person, really caring for our communities, and supporting them through their trials and tribulations. (Davianna McGregor)

Drs. Osorio and McGregor speak about action: advocacy for ʻāina, for our people in the present, and for our communities, the values held within, and how these enduring understandings contribute to our identity and path ahead. This continuum of ʻike kupuna and advocacy for the collective must drive inquiry because the contrary seeks to claim and appropriate ancestral knowledge, language, and practices and in the process produces hegemonic narratives that destroy the essence of our culture. This statement relates to a recent experience I had in a doctoral-level course. The class had read and discussed the professor's publication, which attributed the lower likelihood of Native Hawaiians to emerge as leaders in education to the Hawaiian value of "haʻahaʻa"— which the professor translated as "humility." The professor's interpretation and application of the value contradict what I know to be true about haʻahaʻa as exhibited by ʻŌiwi leaders. What can we learn from prevailing hegemonic narratives that continue to be taught across academic disciplines? Let us continue to identify, discuss, and critique them from multiple perspectives and discredit them completely.[4]

Research on "Hawaiiana" and writing on "Hawaiiana" in the twentieth century was basically not done for us. It was not done to save our culture. It was done to identify the culture that these people believed was disappearing. It was done to titillate, to educate, in order to stimulate people from America and from Europe and from other places about this place [Hawai'i]. It really had nothing to do with us except for we were the objects of the study. We were the "thing" being studied. What we are doing now is we are pulling all that stuff away and saying you have no authority to do this. The stuff that you are writing is not accurate, it is not truthful, it does not serve the kinds of purposes that education should serve, which are to empower and strengthen the people. It does not stop them from doing it, but we have this kind of advocacy, saying *what you are doing is not real. It fulfills some other kind of end, some other kind of objective.* But it does not fulfill any kind of end that matters to us. (Jonathan Osorio)

Before I begin any research project, I ask myself these two questions: What is my intent in conducting this project, and what are the goals of the community I am engaging in? If the answers to these two questions do not align, then these purposes and goals need to be addressed before I move forward. Dr. Osorio talks about the purpose of education being to empower and strengthen people. Research done with shared intention and respect within the community has the power to achieve that purpose.

Whether a project involves a formal research component or not, it should be initiated by the community because members of a community know what is important to them and what are the problems facing them, and they can visualize possible solutions. When communities address real problems, research has relevance to the struggles that Kānaka face.

There were many issues involving our members of the 'Ohana [Protect Kaho'olawe 'Ohana] on their home islands. It was apparent to me that the main threat in all of these rural communities was some form of development—the spaceport in Ka'ū, geothermal energy in Puna, tourism development in Hāna, the withdrawing of water from that whole Ko'olau coast of Maui to develop Kīhei, and plans for commercial tourism on Moloka'i. So everybody was facing their own kind of struggle and the 'Ohana was striving to support each of those efforts on each of those islands. (Davianna McGregor)

Kānaka know how to do research that is relevant for themselves. When I am advising graduate students that are writing theses or doing projects in their MAs, I tell them we are not here to teach you a particular kind of research. I am trying to teach people to understand and to recognize what it is that is most important to them as a student, as a Kanaka Maoli, as a member of a family. What is it that is most important to you, and how do you make the work that you are doing relevant to the things that are important to you? (Jonathan Osorio)

When I moved home in 2010 to pursue a master's degree in education, the research that seemed most relevant to me then was to find a solution to the health disparities affecting my 'ohana. Before moving home I was teaching kindergarten in Australia, and I wondered why their curriculum was full of lessons about their natural environment and hands-on learning about organic farming and healthy eating. I wondered why I did not learn these things about my home when I was growing up on O'ahu. I was saddened by the history of diet-related diseases prevalent in my 'ohana. I moved home with a desire to grow food for my family and understand the relationship among well-being, education, and 'āina. It took me twenty-four years to understand what was important to me as a Kanaka, a daughter, and a teacher, but when I found it, I knew what my kuleana would lead me to do.

For the researcher, the relationship between doing relevant research and having the kuleana to do it must be clear. I understand kuleana to be one's responsibility and one's privilege just as my kuleana in my 'ohana is to mālama my

Summer and her nephews, Koa and Jacob Maunakea, in their māla'ai at Waipahu, O'ahu. Photo by Jennifer Maunakea.

nephews and grow food for my family. I have a place in my 'ohana that is recognized by everyone, and I am beginning to understand my academic kuleana in research in the same way.

> The principal thing for me is that I have been fortunate to be invited into a community. The community really determines whom they want to work with. They will reject you or they will accept you. After the subsistence study in Moloka'i, I was involved again with Jon Matsuoka of the UHM School of Social Work and Luciano Minerbi of the UHM Department of Urban and Regional Planning on the social impact study for the proposed spaceport in Ka'ū. We worked with the members of the community who were most concerned about how the proposed industrialization would affect Ka'ū. They approached us to please get involved and to do the social impact study. So we worked with them to identify who were the people who should get invited to focus groups and who are the people we need to do more in-depth interviews with. (Davianna McGregor)

> There is a very, very different way of looking at knowledge if you are a Kanaka in terms of kapu, in terms of sacredness, in terms of where it comes, and in terms of your kuleana to it. If you do not have a kuleana to something, you should not be going there. If you have the kuleana it means being from a community in which you have a stake that everyone else recognizes; it is not something you can claim. One does not just get a kuleana; one is always given a kuleana. One is always handed it after some kind of training. So this is not about race, not about ethnicity; it does not have to be about koko. It has to be about, Does the community recognize you? If they do then you have a kuleana. (Jonathan Osorio)

The issue of kuleana is critical, particularly understanding that it is given, kuleana must continue to be earned, it is not claimed, and that it comes to be recognized by everyone involved. For me, fulfilling kuleana takes constant reflection on the words I speak in my researcher or evaluator role, as well as feedback from the community as to how I am completing the tasks asked of me.

The Relationship of Laulima and Research

I understand laulima to be the act of upholding my kuleana in a group and fulfilling that kuleana to the best of my ability to help the group succeed at the task at hand. I learned this principle at the age of eight when I started paddling canoe. My coach taught me that every seat has a responsibility. When I sit in seat one, I must set the pace and keep a steady rhythm for everyone to follow. If I sit in seat six, I am the steerswoman, and I must establish a good line, be aware of the elements, and encourage my team. If everyone fulfills his or her kuleana the wa'a will move smoothly. In the context of inquiry, the methods one chooses must value and work in harmony with all voices of the community of participants. Both scholars talked in terms of honoring every voice present in the research process and bringing together knowledge from diverse sources.

> Is there an indigenous methodology of research? No, I think there is an indigenous viewpoint, I think that Kānaka Maoli, like other native people, have a particular way of seeing the world. We have our own values, we have our own standpoint; we have our own perspectives on things and our own methodologies. The things we devise as ways of approaching research are varied and diverse. The thing that links us together is the sort of sense that *my Aunty's voice has value in this story, the land is speaking in this story, the rain is speaking in this story.* There are more things that are a part of this narrative that you are not going to find in a typical European, American kind of presentation. (Jonathan Osorio)

How do I explain the spiritual forces in my life and in nature and how they drive me to act? In terms of research methodology, how do I then articulate the unseen—but understood and revered—underpinnings of what we experience, such as the land speaking or the rains speaking? How do these forces affect the transcribing and sharing the stories of others? The community of participants must have full control over this process.

> I started to recognize that when you are researching peoples' lives you really have an obligation to include these subjects in the whole conversation about the research. You have no right to treat their stories as yours. (Jonathan Osorio)

As researchers, it is our kuleana to share the stories of participants in the way *they* want their stories to be shared. To do that and to truly advocate for others we must be able to open our minds, humble ourselves, and see things from other perspectives.

I see laulima as a way to approach inquiry as a team, with the community of participants setting in motion and guiding the entire process. Dr. McGregor, in partnership with scholars across academic disciplines, has constructed multimethod approaches involving community members in the protection of their practices and resources.

> The community approach that we use is actually called "participatory action research."[5] That is what the academy calls it, but it is very much community-based research—the idea being that it is participatory with the community, and it is action-oriented and geared toward a purpose. For the subsistence study on Molokaʻi we met with the community, and we decided to develop a multimethods approach that included an island-wide telephone survey, resource mapping, focus groups, and key informant interviews. We were very fortunate to have students from the community help conduct the survey, and we worked with the community to help develop a set of questions. We relied on people from the community to reach out and invite key hunters and key fishermen and women, limu gatherers, and farmers in each district to focus groups. We asked what were they concerned about. Because it was a policy-making process, we asked them what policies were needed to protect these resources.
>
> The importance is that the community invites you in or welcomes you. Then you work with the community and the families in the community to ask who are the long-time families living here that rely on these resources; and who would be willing to talk with us and which of those people would be good to do more in-depth interviews. (Davianna McGregor)

Laulima may also be approached as a way to gather knowledge from diverse resources and then cohesively weave them together to gain deeper understandings of people and place. When this is done, new knowledge is constructed and may be used as a tool for education and policy making for the broader community.

> Everyone who does an MA thesis in Hawaiian Studies or Hawaiian Language is basically doing this kind of research heavily informed by Hawaiian language newspapers. A good many people have looked back at the lives of individuals who were dealing with a new sort of American ideas but still were very much Kanaka Maoli. We have had people talking about Nāwahī, ʻŌpūkahaʻia, and chiefs like Lunalilo. We have students doing projects that really focus on particular land places—two ahupuaʻa in Hāmākua—creating a whole website for people who live and come from that community, to en-

able them to preserve that community from being overrun by new developments. We have somebody now working on a similar kind of project in Waiākea, Keaukaha, and Hilo. These kind of 'āina-based projects are slowly proliferating. When they do that, these projects tend to be this multimedia thing that goes onto a web—pictures, sound, and movie kinds of bites. They take newspaper articles that mention these places and bring them out and show them, transcribe them, and translate them—basically trying to get a sense of what that ahupua'a, what that wahi pana looked like 100 years ago, 200 years ago, and how it was shaped by each new human community. (Jonathan Osorio)

You document the spiritual connection with the 'āina through the mo'olelo and who were the deities who lived here and shaped the landscape. Oli and songs all document what our ancestors observed since it was an oral culture. What did our ancestors observe about these areas in their lifetime and passed down to us through the mele, the oli, the 'ōlelo no'eau, the names for all these places, the winds, and the rains? Then we proceed with the story of the people. Who and at what point were the chiefs associated with the place? Who were some of the families whose names were associated with the place? What can you find out about the chiefs of different eras? Now you have Kēhau Abad's work, which looks at a genealogy of the chiefs on each island put together from all the various genealogy sources, especially Fornander and Malo. So, looking at all those genealogies that were put together by the original Hawaiian scholars Malo, and Kamakau, 'Ī'ī, and Kepelino, is there anything in their writings about this place? As you move forward in time you look at the Māhele records and see what were the lands that were claimed and what were the testimonies that the kua'āina provided to get their claims. So that would reveal what resources were there. And then there is mapping. Looking at historical maps will identify place names and resources. So what do the maps tell us about the changes to the landscape in these areas? Look and see what is in the newspapers and what is in the Hawaiian ethnographic collection at the Bishop Museum about these places. (Davianna McGregor)

In her 2006 book, Dr. McGregor detailed her approach to reconstructing a history of a place using both historical documentation and a contemporary multi-methods approach done within the communities of Moloka'i, Maui, Puna,

Kā'u, and Kaho'olawe.[6] Through our conversations as well, I am beginning to see the relationship of laulima and research through the working together of people and diverse sources of knowledge.

The Relationship of Pu'uhonua and Research

The final component within the framework is pu'uhonua, which I have come to understand as a place of safety, whether it is a physical space or a metaphorical environment of safety that imbues a setting. As an educator, it is especially important to establish a safe classroom where all my students and their 'ohana feel comfortable coming to me as the teacher and trust that I have their children's best interests at heart. I view pu'uhonua as conducting research in a way that is safe and protects all involved. For the researcher it is being mindful and respectful of individuals' intellectual rights and honoring their wishes as to whether to keep their stories secret or to share them.

> There is a right way to get at any question that you deserve to ask. Part of the issue for Kānaka is that there are some questions that are not for us to ask. That is another thing, something that westerners do not believe. In fact, they find this kind of statement really frightening. There are things that people do not want to respond to, things that are secret, things that people feel are a family possession. And that sharing it even within the family, if it means that if that story gets out to everyone in the public, they are not going to share it. As Kānaka we need to be very mindful and completely respectful of that. (Jonathan Osorio)

> You really have to respect each community and their intellectual rights to their old ways and respect what they want to have shared. So I have seen people from outside be welcomed and do very good jobs. I think though, that it is important to train a new generation of Hawaiian researchers as a process of learning and giving back to the community. Then people may have more confidence in them and want to share more.
> The goal was to protect resources, not to expose them so that they become vulnerable, but to document them so that they would be protected. Our big concern in conducting surveys is only asking the number and kind of questions you need for the purpose for which you are doing the research. Keep focused. Otherwise, it is really just maha'oi and getting information you are not going to use and you do not really need. Simply focus your survey questions to the point. (Davianna McGregor)

I am learning that being accountable to a community starts with understanding myself first as servant and second as a researcher. Gaining this understanding requires me to constantly reflect and look within myself to ensure that my actions have integrity and are transparent to everyone involved.

> If you are an unknown Kanaka Maoli and you are trying to get people to give you kuleana, then you have to work with them and sometimes over a long period of time—you can't get impatient. You can't start thinking they should just accept me. Here is another thing: You can never think to yourself, I have earned their trust or I have arrived. You have to continue to live up to their trust. (Jonathan Osorio)

> I was in partnership with two non–Kanaka Maoli researchers who were committed to working with the Native Hawaiian community and empowering the community in this process. We were very conscious of being respectful of the Hawaiian values. How much can we inquire without being perceived as maha'oi, where is that boundary, always being very respectful, and assuring that if they do not want it shared then we would not share it. We allowed the community to read the draft report so if they felt it did not reflect their mana'o they had a chance to change it. I was always concerned to make sure that it represented their mana'o in the best way. Maybe not exactly word for word, but it flowed and it represented their thoughts. (Davianna McGregor)

Living up to the trust of each community one works with, and representing the mana'o of kūpuna especially, is a heavy kuleana I am still learning to carry. The researcher must remain accountable to the community throughout the inquiry process when presenting research findings and later as well. The process in which findings are shared as well as the findings themselves must be relevant, useful, and safe for the community of participants involved.

> Many times when we went to talk to people in the community they would say, "I've been concerned that researchers come get all this information and I do not know where it goes, I never see it, and then it just ends up on some shelf." So we were very committed to making sure that they saw what our findings and our conclusions were and that they had input in the recommendations that arose from the findings. We reserved money to duplicate the reports so we could give them copies. One of the main recommendations that came out of the

Moloka'i subsistence study was to establish a community-based subsistence fishing management area for the Mo'omomi Bay and adjacent Kawa'aloa Bay. For the report, we drafted a bill that was later revised and submitted as a bill in the legislature. The report did not just end up on a shelf.

When I did my book I integrated the research I did for my dissertation, which was ethnographic research and historical documentation, on those rural places. I drew upon the audio recording collection at the Bishop Museum. I was very fortunate because up until that time no one else had been allowed to access the audiotapes. It was important that those tapes could get out to the communities. So I worked with the librarian on Moloka'i to request that the tapes be placed in the library on Moloka'i so that students on Moloka'i would have access to them. That way they do not have to come all the way to the Bishop Museum to hear the tapes of the kūpuna from their community. (Davianna McGregor)

As I listened to my conversations with Drs. Osorio and McGregor and reviewed the transcripts, I started to see how the three principles—mālama 'āina, laulima, and pu'uhonua—collectively were present in every excerpt. This is the lens I am looking through now: a growing foundation of 'ike kupuna. We must take the enduring understandings of our ancestors into the next phase of 'Ōiwi scholarship.

Conclusion

The key concept that emerged from the time spent talking story with Drs. Osorio and McGregor was the relationship between research and mālama 'āina, laulima, and pu'uhonua. The wealth of this project came from ku'u 'āina aloha o Kānewai. When I did not know how to make sense of the brilliance shared with me by these scholars, when I stared at their transcripts for months and made no progress, it was cleaning the 'auwai with fourth-graders that inspired me and led me to this approach to research that I hope will resonate with each reader and learner.

It is clear to me that the purpose of inquiry within Hawaiian communities and Hawaiian-focused research should be rooted in one's kuleana to mālama 'āina—for the protection and advocacy of our places, for the resources needed to survive, and for the Hawaiian communities, their values, and knowledge sources to be involved in the research. Research outcomes must be beneficial for the community involved, and the scholarship produced must affirm and actively move 'Ōiwi knowledge systems forward. In terms of methodology, the community must guide and inform every aspect of the process, and researchers must humble themselves to truly understand the realities of those they are researching while being honest and open about the research intent. This creates a safe space for all involved in the process. As a researcher, one must first listen and then do everything possible to protect the community and its intellectual rights while advancing collective goals. The researcher must honor all the voices and stories shared and use them to benefit those who gave of their knowledge. Finally, those with kuleana should engage in research because we are the ones who know what we need for our language, culture, and people to survive. Young learners and scholars must not be fearful, because in the process of research and academia we are supported by our kūpuna and kumu who have come before us with guiding insights to help us move forward.

Uncle Calvin Hoe, kumu of Hakipu'u Learning Center in Ko'olaupoko, O'ahu, once told me, *"Nānā i ke kumu,"* which means to seek knowledge not only from teachers but also from within. I do not believe that research frameworks should be constructed merely by choosing Hawaiian words or phrases or recognizable symbols within our culture, figuring out a way for them to work, and running with them. I think the deep understandings that make our culture so beautiful and true are directed by one's na'au and are found within our 'āina where our kūpuna dwell. The answers to our questions about research, education, sovereignty, health, economics, and well-being can be found in an interdependent relationship with community, 'āina, and 'ike kupuna.

At the beginning of this chapter I raised two questions. As the next generation of scholars, how do we fulfill the expectations of the leaders who have come before us? How do we take the methods and technologies that work for us and use them effectively as tools to solve our current problems? The next generation of learners who arrive here at UHM will be grounded in 'āina and its teachings, will be educated, and will be hungry for more. We see this already in our keiki and 'ōpio. Will we be ready to feed them what they need? Will we be able to model some sort of union between 'ike kupuna and western-academic-scientific methodology without conflict? I would like to have more conversations about the kuleana of our generation in academia. Let us do it together and have impacts that will elevate our lāhui.

The time spent in conversation with Drs. Osorio and McGregor left me inspired and recharged in my academic journey at a time when I really doubted myself. I will conclude with their words of advice and encouragement for all of us as we move forward:

> If you find something that you are really passionate about, that is something you can't go to sleep at night until you figured out this one little thing, or you can't fold up your computer and leave your

office until you have figured out this one little thing, then you need to trust that passion and that's the thing that is going to drive you through. There will be no shortage of people who come and say to you, "That is so dead end kind of research." And the thing about it is, I just don't believe that to be true. I think you have to trust that your spirit knows what it was placed on the earth to do. When you find it you know it. You feel this is it because you really can't stop thinking about it; you really can't stop talking about it. When you find that kind of thing, you can't let anybody talk you out of following that path until it ends. And it doesn't mean it's going to end in a well-paying job. But if you're on the path you're supposed to be, other paths will open. This is something I have seen in my own life; I know that it's a true and a real thing. I don't think that it's something that any, that very many Haole teachers are going to tell you. Because I don't think they buy this sort of mysticism. But I think Kānaka in general understand this. They understand that's your 'aumakua, that's your kūpuna speaking to you, that's Akua speaking to you. You are being guided. So the hard part sometimes is trying to figure out what that thing is. Some people don't have any trouble, and some people it takes a long time. This is not necessarily something that comes to people right away. So yes, if it's your spirit, if it's for you, your spirit knows it and you should trust it. (Jonathan Osorio)

George Helm always said follow your na'au, but do your homework. You really have to do your homework and research. Start looking; become knowledgeable on your own before you reach out to ask for more information. Like I said, it is important to ask but first you need to do that groundwork—be it on the computer, or be it in the library, the archives, or the museum. Do the legwork; you need to read at least fifty sources before you can get a picture of the places and the life of the people there. Just going through all our original sources from our Hawaiian historians from the 1800s and those who came later in the newspapers. So do your groundwork, and then you have earned the right to go and ask the kūpuna for information. Then maybe they will share if they think you have done your homework. You have to also convince them to have confidence in you, that you will take care of the mana'o because it is precious and you do not want it to be misused. Go out and do it; hear the voices of the land and the voices of our kūpuna; let that inspire you. (Davianna McGregor)

NOTES

1. If English explanations for Hawaiian words within the text are needed, see M. K. Pukui and S. H. Elbert (1986), *Hawaiian Dictionary* (Rev. and Enl.) (Honolulu: University of Hawaii Press), or search www.wehewehe.org. Several of the ʻōlelo noʻeau can be found in M. K. Pukui (1993), *ʻŌlelo Noʻeau: Hawaiian Proverbs & Poetical Sayings* (Honolulu: Bishop Museum Press).

2. For additional discussion on the interrelation of ʻāina and Kānaka and its implications for education and well-being, see G. Cajete (1994), *Look to the Mountain: An Ecology of Indigenous Education* (Durango, CO: Kivaki Press); N. Goodyear-Kaʻopua (2013), *The Seeds We Planted: Portraits of a Native Hawaiian Charter School* (Minneapolis: University of Minnesota Press); K. Hoʻomanawanui (2008), "ʻIke ʻĀina: Native Hawaiian Culturally Based Indigenous Literacy," *Hūlili*, 5, 203–244; P. Kanahele (2005), "I Am This Land, and This Land Is Me," *Hūlili*, 2, 21–30; C. K. Naone (2008), *The Pilina of Kanaka and ʻĀina: Place, Language and Community as Sites of Reclamation for Indigenous Education: The Hawaiian Case* (Doctoral Dissertation), retrieved from http://scholarspace.manoa.hawaii .edu/handle/10125/20846; K. Oliveira (2014), *Ancestral Places: Understanding Kanaka Geographies* (Corvalis: Oregon State University Press); J. K. Osorio (Ed.) (2014), *I Ulu I Ka ʻĀina: Land* (Honolulu: Hawaiʻinuiākea School of Hawaiian Knowledge); and www .ecoliteracy.org.

3. Manulani Aluli Meyer says this about ʻāina aloha: "Aloha aina then becomes again the more ancient aina aloha in Hawaiʻi—an interdependence gained when we explore our essential relationships and respond accordingly, thus the energy and life-force found in *meaning as it relates to our universe. . . . It is the quality of our relationships that will help us evolve.*" See M. Meyer (2013), Holographic Epistemology: Native Common Sense, *China Media Research, 9*(2), 94–101, quote on p. 99. A way ʻŌiwi relate to the universe is through the Kumulipo. Lilikalā Kameʻeleihiwa states, "Hawaiian identity is, in fact, derived from the Kumulipo, the great cosmogonic genealogy. Its essential lesson is that every aspect of the Hawaiian conception of the world is related by birth, and as such, all parts of the Hawaiian world are one indivisible lineage." See L. Kameʻeleihiwa (1992), *Native Land and Foreign Desires: Pehea La E Pono Ai? How Shall We Live in Harmony?* (Honolulu: Bishop Museum Press), p. 2.

4. For discussion on research and cultural hegemony, see L. T. Smith (2012), *Decolonizing Methodologies: Research and Indigenous Peoples*, 2nd Edition, Rev. Edition (London: Zed Books). For discussion on the pressing importance of research and education designed by the Hawaiian community, for the benefit of the Hawaiian community, see K. Kahakalau (2004), "Indigenous Heuristic Action Research: Bridging Western and Indigenous Research Methodologies," *Hūlili*, 1, 19–34; and K. Hoʻomanawanui (2008), "ʻIke ʻĀina: Native Hawaiian Culturally Based Indigenous Literacy," *Hūlili*, 5, p. 237.

5. For community-based research and participatory action research (PAR) methods developed by Davianna McGregor, Jon Matsuoka, and Luciano Minerbi for the Molokaʻi subsistence study, see J. K. Matsuoka, D. P. McGregor, and L. Minerbi (1998), "Molokaʻi: A Study on Hawaiian Subsistence and Community Sustainability," in M. Hoff (Ed.), *Sustainable Community Development: Studies in Economic, Environmental, and Cultural Revitalization*, pp. 25–44 (Boca Raton, FL: CRC Press).

6. See D. P. McGregor (2006), *Nā Kuaʻāina: Living Hawaiian Culture* (Honolulu: University of Hawaiʻi Press).

Contributors

Brandi Jean Nālani Balutski is from Kahaluʻu, Oʻahu, Hawaiʻi. She is a research and assessment specialist for the University of Hawaiʻi at Mānoaʻs Hawaiʻinuiākea School of Hawaiian Knowledge and Native Hawaiian Student Services. In this role, she is responsible for designing and implementing critical original research on Native Hawaiian higher educational access and success. She has a bachelor's degree in business administration from Loyola Marymount University, a master's degree in Hawaiian studies from UH Mānoa, and is currently pursuing her PhD in Educational Administration.

Noelani Goodyear-Kaʻōpua is a Kanaka ʻŌiwi who was born and raised on Oʻahu, in the ahupuaʻa of Kalihi and Heʻeia. Her genealogy also connects her ʻohana to Hawaiʻi and Maui Islands, as well as southern China and the British Midlands. She is an associate professor of political science at the University of Hawaiʻi at Mānoa. She is the author of *The Seeds We Planted: Portraits of a Native Hawaiian Charter School* (University of Minnesota Press, 2013) and the co-editor of *A Nation Rising: Hawaiian Movements for Life, Land, and Sovereignty* (Duke University Press, 2014) and *The Value of Hawaiʻi, 2: Ancestral Roots, Oceanic Visions* (UH Press, 2014). Her academic work is part of a lifetime commitment to aloha ʻāina. Noelani is a co-founder of the Hālau Kū Māna public charter school and of MANA, a movement-building organization supporting Hawaiian independence. Her most treasured role is being a mom.

Haley Kailiehu, born and raised in Kukuipuka in the ahupuaʻa of Kahakuloa, Kaʻanapali, Maui, is kamaʻāina to the steep cliffs and rugged coastline of Makamakaʻole Valley. She is a descendant of generations of ʻŌiwi artists. Haley's art is shaped by the genealogy and ʻāina of which she was born. In 2009, she graduated from the University of Hawaiʻi at Mānoa with a bachelor of fine arts degree, with a focus in drawing and painting. In 2012, Haley earned a master's of education and teaching degree from the Hoʻokulāiwi Center for Native Hawaiian and Indigenous Education. Currently, Haley is pursuing a doctorate in education with a focus in curriculum studies. Her research is focused on community- and ʻāina-based art as a means of reclaiming ʻŌiwi spaces and places.

Kaiwipunikauikawēkiu Lipe, known to most as Punihei, is a native Hawaiian mother, wife, daughter, granddaughter, sister, and hula dancer. Her dissertation focused on how the University of Hawai'i at Mānoa can be transformed into a Hawaiian place of learning given that it is currently a predominantly non-Hawaiian institution. She is currently a faculty member in Hawai'inuiākea focusing on Native Hawaiian affairs. She holds a doctorate in educational administration from UH Mānoa (2014), a master's in counseling psychology from Chaminade University of Honolulu (2008), and a bachelor's in Hawaiian studies from UH Mānoa (2005).

R. Keawe Lopes Jr. is a native of Nānākuli. He currently resides in Pū'ahu'ula, Ko'olaupoko, O'ahu, with his wife, Tracie Ka'ōnohilani Farias, and three daughters Pi'ikea, Ka'ōnohi, and Hāweo. He is an assistant professor at the Kawaihuelani Center for Hawaiian Language and currently teaches Hawaiian language courses that include the study and practice of mele (Hawaiian poetic expression) in the enhancement of Hawaiian language acquisition. He is the director of Ka Waihona A Ke Aloha, an interactive resource center for the promotion, preservation, and perpetuation of mele and mele practitioners. He and his wife are the kumu hula of Ka Lā 'Ōnohi Mai o Ha'eha'e. He holds a doctorate in teacher education and curriculum studies (2010) and master's (1997) and bachelor's degrees in Hawaiian language (1995) from UH Mānoa.

Summer Puanani Maunakea is daughter of Hadassah Puahi Maunakea and James Kulanakila Maunakea Jr. and is from Waipahu, 'Ewa, O'ahu. Summer works as educational specialist at Ka Papa Lo'i 'O Kānewai within the Hawai'inuiākea School of Hawaiian Knowledge at the University of Hawai'i at Mānoa. Currently pursuing a doctorate in education, she is conducting research that seeks to advocate for mālama 'āina practitioner-educators and programs. Summer strives to awaken the critical need for all people of Hawai'i to reconnect to and act upon their kuleana to 'āina through huli ka lima i lalo—turning one's hands down into the land—to be healed, nourished, and led into a thriving future for 'Ōiwi.

Brandy Nālani McDougall is from Kula, Maui, and is the author of a poetry collection, *The Salt-Wind, Ka Makani Pa'akai* (2008); the co-founder of Ala Press and Kahuaomānoa Press; and the co-star of a poetry album, *Undercurrent* (2011). A recipient of the Richard Braddock Award (2012), she was also awarded a Mellon-Hawai'i Postdoctoral Fellowship and a Ford Foundation Postdoctoral Fellowship for 2013–2014 to complete her book on the practice of kaona. She is an assistant professor specializing in Indigenous studies in the Department of American Studies at UH Mānoa.

Katrina-Ann R. Kapā'anaokalāokeola Nākoa Oliveira is an associate professor of Hawaiian language and the director of Kawaihuelani Center for Hawaiian language at UH Mānoa, where she earned a doctorate in geography. Her research interests include Kanaka geographies, epistemologies, language-acquisition methodologies, experiential learning curricula, and environmental kinship. She is the author of *Ancestral Places: Understanding Kanaka Geographies*, published by Oregon State University Press in 2014.

Maya L. Kawailanaokeawaiki Saffery was born and raised in Ko'olaupoko, O'ahu, and is an ongoing student of the language and culture of her ancestors. With a bachelor's degree in Hawaiian language and a master's of education in teaching degree (MEdT) from UH Mānoa, she became the curriculum specialist for the Kawaihuelani Center for Hawaiian Language in 2005, where she is responsible for researching, developing, implementing, and evaluating graduate and undergraduate curricula for use within Kawaihuelani as well as in the broader community. The philosophy that guides her work is grounded in the kanaka-'āina relationship and its importance to our individual and collective healing and resurgence as a lāhui. Her work is also largely influenced and informed by her continued practice of traditional hula as a graduated 'ōlapa and kumu hula from Hālau Mōhala 'Ilima. Her overarching research interests include Hawaiian language and culture revitalization; culturally grounded, Hawaiian place-based/conscious, and experiential curriculum and program development; and traditional and contemporary living narratives for sacred and significant places of Hawai'i. Her current doctoral research in curriculum and instruction is focused on reclaiming and reframing "Hawaiian place-based education" by exploring what it means to apply the theory and practice of place-based education and the critical pedagogy of place in an indigenous context.

Mehana Blaich Vaughan grew up in the rural Halele'a district of the island of Kaua'i and is the mother of three kamali'i. She is an assistant professor in the Department of Natural Resources and Environmental Management, Sea Grant and Hui 'Āina Momona at UH Mānoa. Her research focuses on people's relationships with the places they care about, and she works to enhance community ability to mālama 'āina. For more than ten years, Mehana taught middle and high school and worked on developing place-based education programs with Kaua'i community groups. Mehana is grateful to her tūtū and all of her 'ohana, as well as the friends, students, and community members of Waipā, Hā'ena and Halele'a who contributed to the experiences described in her chapter.

Erin Kahunawaika'ala Wright is Kanaka 'Ōiwi Hawai'i (Native Hawaiian) from Kalihi, O'ahu, raised on the land that has fostered her mother's family for the last five generations. She serves as an assistant professor of educational administration at the College of Education at UH Mānoa. Her research interests stem from understanding Native Hawaiian student success in higher education, particularly on the intersections of culturally based higher education and identity development. She is a coeditor of *A Nation Rising: Hawaiian Movements for Life, Land and Sovereignty,* published by Duke University Press in 2014.

Hawai'inuiākea Series

The Hawai'inuiākea Series provides a multidisciplinary venue for the work of scholars and practitioners from the Hawaiian community, a platform for thinkers and doers who grapple with real-world queries, challenges, and strategies. Each volume features articles on a thematic topic from diverse fields such as economics, education, family resources, government, health, history, land and natural resources, psychology, religion, and sociology. Each volume includes kupuna reflections, current viewpoints, and original creative expression.

No. 1   *I Ulu I Ke Kumu*, Puakea Nogelmeier, editor, 2011.
No. 2   *I Ulu I Ka 'Āina*, Jonathan Osorio, editor, 2013.
No. 3   *'Ike Ulana Lau Hala*, Lia O'Neill M. A. Keawe, Marsha MacDowell, and C. Kurt Dewhurst, editors, 2014.

Proposals for volume themes may be submitted to:
Hawai'inuiākea School of Hawaiian Knowledge
Hawai'inuiākea Series
Office of the Dean
2450 Maile Way
Spalding 454
Honolulu, Hawaii 96822

http://manoa.hawaii.edu/hshk/